Defying the Odds

The 2016 Elections and American Politics

James W. Ceaser, Andrew E. Busch, and John J. Pitney Jr.

ROWMAN & LITTLEFIELD

Lanham • Boulder • New York • London

Published by Rowman & Littlefield
A wholly owned subsidary of The Rowman & Littlefield Publishing Group, Inc.
4501 Forbes Boulevard, Suite 200, Lanham, Maryland 20706
www.rowman.com

Unit A, Whitacre Mews, 26–34 Stannary Street, London SE11 4AB

British Library Cataloguing in Publication Information Available

Library of Congress Cataloging-in-Publication Data

Names: Ceaser, James W., author. | Busch, Andrew, author. | Pitney, John J.,
  Jr., 1955– author.
Title: Defying the odds : the 2016 elections and American politics / James W.
  Ceaser, Andrew E. Busch, and John J. Pitney Jr.
Description: Lanham, Maryland : Rowman & Littlefield, [2017] | Includes index.
Identifiers: LCCN 2017003382 (print) | LCCN 2017005702 (ebook) | ISBN
  9781442273467 (cloth : alk. paper) | ISBN 9781442273474 (pbk. : alk.
  paper) | ISBN 9781442273481 (electronic)
Subjects: LCSH: Presidents—United States—Election—2016. | Political
  culture—United States. | United States—Politics and government—2009–
Classification: LCC JK526 2016 .C43 2017 (print) | LCC JK526 2016 (ebook) |
  DDC 324.973/0932—dc23
LC record available at https://lccn.loc.gov/2017003382

♾ ™ The paper used in this publication meets the minimum requirements of American
National Standard for Information Sciences—Permanence of Paper for Printed Library
Materials, ANSI/NISO Z39.48–1992.
Printed in the United States of America

Defying the Odds

Contents

Preface

Bitterness and joy, outrage and satisfaction, shame and pride, escapes to safe spaces and displays of celebration—these were just a few of the conflicting reactions that greeted the election of Donald Trump on November 8, 2016. Feelings in the aftermath ran so high, dividing families and testing friendships, that finding anything that both sides could agree on seemed a near impossibility.

One point, however, lies beyond dispute: the selection of Donald Trump as the forty-fifth president of the United States was an event that defied all odds.

Start with those who know the business of odds making: When Trump descended the escalator from his $100 million penthouse in June 2015 to announce his candidacy, the world's premier political betting firm, Paddy Power, set his chances of becoming president at 100 to 1. As late as October 2016, he was listed as less than one in five. Paddy Power even began payoffs to preferred customers who bet for Hillary Clinton. In the end, the firm admitted to being "thumped by Trump," leaving it "with the biggest political payout in the company's history and some very, very expensive egg on our faces."[1]

Turn next to the political pundits, the experts in the study of campaigns: Analysts over the years have developed a catalog of critical assets that help explain success, but Donald Trump was deficient in almost all of them. Here is a partial list: (1) *A record of public service.* All previous presidents have either held elective office or served in a high administrative post. Donald Trump did neither. (2) *A well-organized and professional personal campaign organization.* Trump never had one—at least in comparison to his principal foes. He was woefully behind Jeb Bush and Ted Cruz in the nomination contest, and Mrs. Clinton in the final election campaign. (3) *Money.* True, Donald Trump had his personal wealth and spent some of it, though never as liberally as many expected. But he was outspent by rivals at the key points in the nomination campaign, and hugely so by Mrs. Clinton in the final election. (4) *Endorsements of important political leaders.* Trump had no more than a handful until near his nomination, and he struggled even afterward to round up support from many Republicans. (5) *Favorable media coverage.* Trump certainly managed to get his share of coverage (and then some), but the slant of articles from the major media sources, both television and print, was hostile. When it came to endorsements by newspapers, the number Trump received can practically be counted on one hand. (6) *Backing of public intellectuals and opinion makers.* There was scarcely a figure of major significance who backed Trump during the nomination contest. Many conservative writers refused to rally to him during the campaign.

These critical assets were often arraigned in 2016 not just to be unsupportive but specifically to oppose Donald Trump. Trump was a candidate with a target on his back. Many in the donor class of the Republican Party sought at a late point in the nomination campaign to block his path to becoming the party's standard bearer. Political figures in both parties singled him out as the one person uniquely unqualified to be president. And opponents in the Republican Party joined in a movement under the label of "Never Trump." The antagonism was unprecedented.

Pollsters, another important institutional player in presidential campaigns, also acted against him. The overwhelming view among analysts was that Hillary Clinton would be elected president. Greater prudence in their prognostications was no doubt warranted, as the average of the major polls showed that the race was frequently within or near the margin of polling error. Perhaps the analysts' overconfidence was conditioned by the fact that, after the conventions, Mrs. Clinton was never behind. Whatever the explanation, the effect was to create an expectation that Trump would go down to defeat. His victory therefore appeared as a stunning upset. It reminded people of Harry Truman's surprise victory over Governor Thomas Dewey in 1948, an event made famous by the photograph of a smiling Harry Truman holding up a newspaper with the headline "Dewey Defeats Truman." Something reminiscent of this event played out on the television networks on election eve. Anchors began coverage with an all-going-as-expected tone, but it began to fade as the actual voting results came in. The disbelief and shock were palpable.

If you happened to have fallen asleep at 8 p.m. in the East and awoke a few hours later, you might have thought yourself, in an accelerated version of Rip Van Winkle, in a different world. And perhaps you were.

TRUMP'S VICTORY

How was it that Donald Trump managed to defy these odds, improbably capturing the nomination of the Republican Party and then going on to win the presidency? There is obviously no single answer, and this book will set out the different reasons for his success at each stage. But there is one general explanation that stands out, and it is connected to the same set of reasons that lengthened the odds against Donald Trump. In a feat of political alchemy, Trump ran against the assets (or establishments) that normally contribute to success, and he turned these deficiencies into advantages. Stated differently, he was an outsider at a time when many Americans craved an outsider.

Look again at some of the items on the list of assets. Trump made the fact that he had not held elected office a primary virtue. The politicians, as he called them, did not know how to solve problems, and they were tainted by the need to solicit favors from others. In contrast, Trump offered himself as an entrepreneur who had built a great company. He showed that he could get things done. Trump also ran against the donor class and against Wall Street generally. Pledging to make his nomination campaign self-financing, he could be independent of the usual ties that bound candidates to the big interests. Trump was the people's billionaire, offering unashamedly what the average American wanted, a Trump steak or a night at a casino, or showing the kind of luxury people could only yearn for, like a personal airplane. Donald Trump ran against the media, courting their disdain in order to build up his own support, and he challenged many of the higher-ups in the party, claiming that the party needed to be shaken up. Finally, Donald Trump did not need a large professional personal organization, because he developed a direct relation to the people. He was the spokesperson of a popular movement.

There were others in the nomination races in 2016 who caught this spirit of outsiderism, whether by their personal situation (never having held office) or by their ideas (opposition to the media or to party elites), or both. There was Ben Carson, Carly Fiorina, and Ted Cruz. Yet Trump was more entertaining and thoroughgoing, and he proved by the end to be the most popular in the group. And in the final election campaign against Mrs. Clinton, he had full title to this outsider argument and ran on this theme until the last day.

This was the orientation or style, but what was the substance? Donald Trump in the final election reached out to "the forgotten," the blue-collar Americans who had not kept up with the gains made by those living on the coasts. Here was the pivotal group that Trump picked up in the upper Midwest and Pennsylvania, enough to push him over the top. Take, for example, counties right in the heart of Wisconsin—Juneau, Adams, and Marquette—which

Obama had carried in 2012, but which Trump captured this time; or in Michigan, Lake County in the west and Macomb County in the east, which Trump flipped; or in Michigan's "thumb" or in western Pennsylvania, where he upped the percentage of those who supported him. In places like this, microcosms of the rest of America, Trump found his margin of victory.

The reasons for the change were no doubt partly economic. This circumstance accounts for Trump's pledge to build a wall along the southern border and his promise to level the playing field in trade negotiations. People, he argued, would be protected from the ravages of unfair job competition and the danger of unjust exchange. But the cultural element was just as important. Many in this group had seen their views pushed aside or ignored, as if they could be forgotten in the changes taking place in American politics. They were, in words that Mrs. Clinton would come to regret, in the "basket of deplorables," the "racist, sexist, homophobic, xenophobic, Islamaphobic—you name it."[2] Trump would be their spokesman.

BY THE NUMBERS

Each national election is, of course, unique—that is one of the things that makes them so interesting. But there is still much that can be learned from comparing a president's election with those of his predecessors. Trump was elected by earning 56.9 percent of the Electoral College vote, ignoring here the faithless electors. Compared to the thirty preceding presidential contests since 1896—often counted as the beginning of modern presidential politics—Trump's self-proclaimed electoral-vote "landslide" is an exaggeration (see table P.1).[3] The size of presidential victories over the period have varied greatly, ranging from Franklin D. Roosevelt's massive win in 1936 to George W. Bush's squeaker in 2000, but Trump's victory falls on the lower end of this spectrum, ranking twenty-sixth out of thirty-one.

Many prefer to measure presidential elections by the nationally aggregated popular vote. Donald Trump fares similarly here, ranking twenty-eighth with 47.0 percent of the popular vote. Because of votes for third- and fourth-party candidates, many presidents have been chosen without receiving an outright majority of the ballots cast. The more notable point, however, is that Trump received fewer votes than Mrs. Clinton, placing him with George W. Bush in 2000 as the only presidents in the modern period to have won in this way. Both Mrs. Clinton and Donald Trump knew, of course, the system they were in, making it impossible afterward to proclaim that they were unjustly denied the presidency. But the question of whether this system will continue remains open.

Table P.1.   Electoral College, Popular Vote Rankings of Winning Candidates, 1896–2016

Rankings	Percent of Electoral College	Electoral Score	New President	Percent of Popular Vote	New President
1	98.49%	523–8	F. Roosevelt (1936)	61.05%	L. Johnson (1964)
2	97.21	525–13	R. Reagan (1984)	60.80	F. Roosevelt (1936)
3	96.83	520–17	R. Nixon (1972)	60.67	R. Nixon (1972)
4	90.89	489–49	R. Reagan (1980)	60.32	W. Harding (1920)
5	90.33	486–52	L. Johnson (1964)	58.77	R. Reagan (1984)
6	88.88	472–59	F. Roosevelt (1932)	58.21	H. Hoover (1928)
7	86.22	457–73	D. Eisenhower (1956)	57.41	F. Roosevelt (1932)
8	84.56	449–82	F. Roosevelt (1940)	57.37	D. Eisenhower (1956)
9	83.62	444–87	H. Hoover (1928)	56.42	T. Roosevelt (1904)
10	83.24	442–89	D. Eisenhower (1952)	55.18	D. Eisenhower (1952)
11	81.92	435–88–8	W. Wilson (1912)	54.74	F. Roosevelt (1940)
12	81.36	432–99	F. Roosevelt (1944)	54.04	C. Coolidge (1924)
13	79.33	426–111	H. W. Bush (1988)	53.39	F. Roosevelt (1944)
14	76.08	404–127	W. Harding (1920)	53.37	H. W. Bush (1988)
15	71.94	282–136–13	C. Coolidge (1924)	52.93	B. Obama (2008)
16	70.59	336–140	T. Roosevelt (1904)	51.64	W. McKinley (1900)
17	70.45	379–159	W. Clinton (1996)	51.57	W. Taft (1908)
18	68.77	370–168	W. Clinton (1992)	51.06	B. Obama (2012)
19	67.84	365–173	B. Obama (2008)	51.02	W. McKinley (1896)
20	66.46	321–162	W. Taft (1908)	50.75	R. Reagan (1980)
21	65.32	292–155	W. McKinley (1900)	50.73	W. Bush (2004)
22	61.71	332–206	B. Obama (2012)	50.08	J. Carter (1976)
23	60.63	271–176	W. McKinley (1896)	49.72	J. Kennedy (1960)
24	58.05	303–219	J. Kennedy (1960)	49.55	H. Truman (1948)
25	57.06	303–189–39	H. Truman (1948)	49.24	W. Wilson (1916)
26	**56.88**	**306–232**	**D. Trump (2016)**	49.23	W. Clinton (1996)
27	55.95	301–191–46	R. Nixon (1968)	47.87	W. Bush (2000)
28	55.31	297–240	J. Carter (1976)	**45.94**	**D. Trump (2016)**
29	53.26	286–251	W. Bush (2004)	43.42	R. Nixon (1968)
30	52.17	277–254	W. Wilson (1916)	43.01	W. Clinton (1992)
31	50.47	271–266	W. Bush (2000)	41.84	W. Wilson (1912)

In comparing elections, it is most helpful to focus on "like" cases in which the structural circumstances are the same. The most important category is that Trump was running in an election following at least two terms in which the same party has held office and is running without an incumbent. This situation, often referred to as the sitting president's "third term" election bid, has been a fairly common event in modern presidential politics, occurring ten times since 1896. The question in such elections is whether the sitting president can pass the baton to a successor, further confirming his vision for the country and cementing a legacy. Would-be successors often try to create some distance from the president, establishing themselves as their "own person," but they are inevitably viewed as connected to the incumbent. Hillary Clinton chose to tie herself as closely to the incumbent as anyone in this group, rarely breaking with President Obama and relying on him and the First Lady to campaign regularly on her behalf. For his part, Obama went to great lengths to seal this bond, suggesting that not voting for Clinton would be "a personal insult, an insult to my legacy."[4] Here was truly a case in which, at least during the campaign, both the candidate and the president treated the election as a "third term" bid.

A rule of thumb in American politics is that candidates seeking a "third term," like Hillary Clinton, fare poorly. They have prevailed in just three instances. The reason usually offered is that, after eight years of one-party rule, the public is inclined to seek change. By this view, history was working against another Democratic victory in 2016. Yet the matter is not, in the end, so clear. A look at table P.2 shows just how narrow the victories of the repudiating candidates can sometimes be. The category contains three of the closest elections in American history: Kennedy's win over Richard Nixon in

Table P.2. Electoral Performance after Two Terms of One-Party Control with No Incumbent Running

		INCUMBENT PRESIDENT'S PARTY LOSES			
Year	New President	Incumbent President	Winner Pop. Vote Share	New President Senate Seat Pick-Up	New President House Seat Pick-Up
1920	W. Harding	W. Wilson	60.32%	+10	+62
1952	D. Eisenhower	H. Truman	55.18%	+1	+22
1960	JFK	D. Eisenhower	49.72%	−1	−18
1968	R. Nixon	L. Johnson	43.42%	+7	+5
2000	W. Bush	W. Clinton	47.87%	−5	−3
2008	B. Obama	G. W. Bush	52.93%	+8	+24
2016	D. Trump	B. Obama	45.94%	−2	−7
		INCUMBENT PRESIDENT'S PARTY WINS			
Year	New President	Incumbent President	Winner Pop. Vote Share	New President Senate Seat Pick-Up (% change)	New President House Seat Pick-Up (% change)
1908	W. H. Taft	T. Roosevelt	51.57%	−1	−5
1928	H. Hoover	C. Coolidge	58.21%	+8	+32
1988	H. W. Bush	R. Reagan	53.37%	+0	−2

1960, George W. Bush's over Al Gore in 2000, and now Donald Trump's over Hillary Clinton. If there is a breeze blowing at the back of the change candidates, it is much milder than many assume.

Finally, there is the question of Donald Trump's relationship with Congress. He had an unusual reaction to other Republicans, having taken the nomination away from those who were much closer to them, and his positions were not fully in the mainstream. But after the election they were in it together, and Donald Trump had control over both houses of Congress. In fact, the Republican Party was at or near its high point, with fifty-two seats in the Senate and twenty-four in the House, as well as control of thirty-four governors, thirty-five state senates, and thirty-two state houses. Whether this remains the case is in the hands of this new leader.

NOTES

1. See http://www.dailymail.co.uk/news/article-3924156/Bookmakers-Paddy-Power-lose-4-5million-Donald-Trump-s-shock-win-paying-1million-punters-backed-Hillary-Clinton-election-over.html#ixzz4VBLkpFHj.

2. See http://www.zerohedge.com/news/2016-09-10/hillary-calls-half-trump-supporters-racist-sexist-homophobic-basket-deplorables.

3. While two of Donald Trump's electors ultimately voted "faithlessly" on December 19 in the states' Electoral College meetings, throughout this section we tally the electoral returns as if all electors followed their expected pledges. Five of Clinton's pledged electors also voted faithlessly, although the bulk of those votes were part of an effort to defeat or undermine Donald Trump, not to defect from Mrs. Clinton. According to Kyle Cheney of *Politico*, 2016 had the largest number of faithless votes ever cast in a single presidential election; the previous record set in 1808, when five Democratic-Republican electors voted against James Madison. See Kyle Cheney, "Electoral College Sees Record-Breaking Defections," *Politico*, December 19, 2016, http://www.politico.com/story/2016/12/electoral-college-electors-232836 (last accessed December 30, 2016).

4. See http://www.realclearpolitics.com/video/2016/09/17/obama_i_will_consider_it_an_insult_to_my_legacy_if_you_do_not_vote_want_to_give_me_a_good_send_off_go_vote.html.

Acknowledgments

We would like to acknowledge the research assistance of Nicholas Jacobs at the University of Virginia and Ellen Lempres at Claremont McKenna College. We would also like to thank our friends Lloyd Green, who provided valuable research advice, and Steven E. Schier, who read the manuscript under serious time pressures and offered many useful suggestions and insights, not least on the role of demotic rhetoric in Trump's ascent. We owe a debt to the staff at Rowman & Littlefield, especially Kate Powers and Patricia Stevenson, who supervised production, and the inestimable Jon Sisk, whose commitment to this project dates back to 1992. Finally, and not least, we thank our families for their patience, which has to be renewed quadrennially. In particular, we dedicate this work to Lisa, Mindy, and Blaire.

Chapter One

Twenty-Four Years Later

1992 and 2016

Election Day marked "the end of an Alice in Wonderland year in which American politics seemed to be turned upside down and inside out."[1] That description, which applies so well to the 2016 campaign, comes from the opening line of the first book in this series, *Upside Down and Inside Out: The 1992 Elections and American Politics*.

Think of the 2016 election as the Coen Brothers' version of the 1992 race. Joel and Ethan Coen have made wonderful films (*Barton Fink*, *Hail Caesar*) that take scraps of history and quilt them into radically new patterns. Like the earlier campaign, the 2016 contest included a Clinton (Hillary instead of Bill), a Bush (Jeb instead of George), and a fiery progressive outsider (Bernie Sanders instead of Jerry Brown). The winner was a Coen-esque mashup of three figures from 1992. Like Bill Clinton, Donald Trump had skirted Vietnam-era military service and enjoyed a louche personal life that enriched supermarket tabloids. Like independent candidate H. Ross Perot, he was a bombastic billionaire fond of trade protectionism and factless pronouncements. And like Pat Buchanan, who mounted a right-wing challenge to Bush in the 1992 GOP primaries, he indulged in nationalistic rhetoric that drew accusations of racism and anti-Semitism.

The 1992 campaign seemed odd and disruptive at the time. Previously, most of the political community would have thought the revelations about Bill Clinton's personal history to be politically fatal. However, not only did he prevail, but his victory also came after Republicans had won five of the six past presidential elections, a record that had led many to assume a GOP "lock" on the electoral college. President George H. W. Bush had seemed invincible right after the American success in the 1991 Persian Gulf War, but he ended up with the smallest share of the popular tally of any incumbent president since William Howard Taft in 1912. Perot broke another record dating back to the same election, drawing nearly 19 percent of the vote, the greatest for any non-major-party candidate since Theodore Roosevelt's Bull Moose campaign.

As *Upside Down and Inside Out* explained, however, the 1992 election was not as revolutionary as many commentators said. After the longest peacetime expansion in American history, the U.S. economy had just scraped through a recession. President Bush was sixty-eight years old and in shaky health. Many voters saw him as old and tired, especially in comparison with the forty-six-year-old dynamo from Arkansas. Perot proved that massive sums of money could break through the institutional barriers facing independent candidates—not a startling revelation.[2] His failure to win a single electoral vote also confirmed the conventional wisdom that the Electoral College works against independent candidates lacking a strong regional base. So although many details of the campaign seemed unusual, the basic storyline was not.

The election of 2016 really did live up to the title of the 1992 book. Hillary Clinton, of course, was the first woman to win a major-party nomination. Though historic, her nomination itself was hardly a shock, as it came decades after other major democracies had chosen female heads of government. What few foresaw was that she would face such a serious and well-funded challenge from Sanders, a self-described socialist who had never identified as a Democrat in any previous race for office. Trump was a far greater jolt. Based on recent trends in nomination politics, many pundits confidently predicted that such a controversial and inexperienced figure would fade quickly, and that GOP leaders would have the last word. Primary voters instead scorned party insiders, spurned candidates with distinguished resumes, and instead voted to hand the party's crown to a reality TV star. On the eve of the general election, nearly every national poll showed that Clinton would win. On the evening of November 8, as political activists and commentators saw state after state tip into the Trump column, their assumptions turned to ashes.

One could argue that the 2016 election, like its 1992 doppelganger, was more conventional than it seemed. When one party has held the White House for at least two terms, many voters start to think that it is time for a change. As President Obama's former secretary of state, and a two-term First Lady before that, Hillary Clinton had the disadvantage of personifying the status quo. Moreover, ethics controversies over her decades in public life had made many voters uneasy about her. The economy, often the biggest thumb on the election scales, was not an asset to the Democrats. Though the Great Recession had officially ended years earlier, growth had been slow, and many

Americans were still struggling. Accordingly, a strong majority told pollsters that the nation was on the wrong track.[3] When scholars cranked such considerations into their forecasting models, most found that the election would be close or that the GOP would win.[4] Similarly, the Electoral College map did not indicate a radical realignment. Most states voted as they did in 2012, with one key difference: Trump narrowly won several states where Romney had fallen short.[5] And finally, the national polls did get it right, since Clinton ended up with a statistically notable and legally meaningless plurality of the popular vote.

But claiming that the 2016 election followed certain established patterns is like saying *The Odyssey* was about a round-trip ship voyage—true in a narrow sense, but oblivious to essential parts of the story.[6] There had never been a candidate quite like Donald J. Trump. Every previous major-party nominee had either served in the military or held civilian public office. (Even businessman Wendell Willkie, who won the 1940 GOP nomination without political experience, had been an army officer during the First World War.) His positions on trade, immigration, and foreign policy were fundamentally different from those of other recent GOP candidates. Few elected officials endorsed him in the early stages of the campaign, and after he was the nominee, some leading Republicans took the extraordinary step of either withholding or withdrawing their public support. Gallup found that while 51 percent of registered voters thought that Clinton had the personality and leadership qualities a president should have, only 32 percent thought the same of Trump.[7] He finished the campaign as the most unpopular nominee since Gallup started polling on the question in 1956.[8] Even scholars whose models pointed to a Trump victory thought that his liabilities would cause him to underperform so much that he would lose the election.[9]

The outcome was a humbling reminder that the expectations of media commentators and the models of political scientists were rooted in a very small number of races. Between 1789 and 2016, there were only 58 presidential elections in all. For the first nine elections, there are no reliable records of the popular vote, so we have tallies for just 49. If we want to take public opinion into account, the number is much smaller, because scientific surveys started on the national level only during the 1930s. So with a starting point of 1936, when Gallup took its first presidential election poll, we have public opinion data on twenty-one elections. Many election forecasting models involve economic data that are unavailable for election years before 1948, leaving a grand total of eighteen. If we want to consider nomination politics, the number shrinks further. The current process, consisting mostly of primaries and caucuses, dates back only to 1972. On the GOP side, incumbent presidents did not face major intraparty challenges in 1972, 1984, and 2004, meaning that there have been *nine* real nomination fights. Bill Clinton (1996) and Barack Obama (2012) had uncontested renominations, so the Democratic total is *ten*. We should be wary of deriving "iron laws" from so few cases.

Moreover, generalizations and predictions in social science depend on background conditions that we may not even notice because they have been in place for so long but are still subject to change. Political scientist Yascha Mounk asks, "Do parties still retain the same influence over primary voters once public trust in politicians has plummeted to record lows? . . . And will wealthy liberal democracies continue to be stable when, for the first time since their founding, the living standards of average citizens have barely increased in a generation?"[10] One way to notice shifts in background conditions and understand the evolution of the political system is to compare two elections taking place many years apart. And by happy coincidence, the 1992 election offers a good point of departure.

INSIDE AND OUTSIDE

Outsiders played starring roles in the 1992 and 2016 campaigns, so, before delving deeper into either election, we should briefly review the history of outsiderism. In the eighteenth century, Scottish philosopher David Hume wrote that the great political division in Britain lay between the "court party" that backed the monarchy and the "country party" that purported to stand for the great mass of the people.[11] Ever since the early days of the American republic, a similar split between insiders and outsiders has repeatedly cropped up in American politics.[12] In a 1793 letter to James Madison, Thomas Jefferson laid out embryonic lines, pitting "fashionable circles" and "paper men" against "tradesmen, mechanics, farmers and every other possible description of our citizens."[13]

Outsiderism is all about "not being part of" the establishment, whether that establishment lies in Washington, Wall Street, Hollywood, Madison Avenue, or Harvard Yard. It is blurry and multifaceted, but through its many forms, it has always served as a receptacle of resentments. As the outsiders try to distill these angry feelings into political fuel, the insiders warn that the outsiders have a hidden agenda. In *Federalist* no. 1, Alexander Hamilton said that "of those men who have overturned the liberties of republics, the greatest number have begun their career by paying an obsequious court to the people; commencing demagogues, and ending tyrants."[14] It was already clear at the time that insiderism and outsiderism in America did not always line up with social origins. Hamilton, though famously described by Lin-Manuel Miranda as "the bastard orphan son of a whore and a Scotsman dropped in the middle of a forgotten spot," identified with the elites. Jefferson, who sided with the tillers of the soil, lived on a vast estate and had slaves to do the work for him. Hamilton was aware of the disconnect. "Demagogues are not always inconsiderable persons," he said at the Constitutional Convention. "Patricians were frequently demagogues."[15]

Other features of outsiderism have echoed throughout political history. One is the notion that the insiders have rigged the system. After the 1824 election produced a deadlocked vote in the Electoral College, the House of Representatives chose John Quincy Adams as president. Followers of losing candidate Andrew Jackson charged that outcome stemmed from a "corrupt bargain" between Adams and House speaker Henry Clay, who became secretary of state. Jackson, a rough Tennessean who championed the common man (though he was a wealthy slave-owner), turned antagonism against the aristocratic Adams into a victory in the next presidential election.

Outsiders frequently indulge in conspiracy theories and stoke prejudice against various ethnic and religious groups. The Jackson years coincided with the brief emergence of the Anti-Masonic Party, whose members believed that the Freemasons were an elite society that secretly controlled the government. The American (or "Know-Nothing") Party arose in opposition to the immigrants who came in large numbers during the 1840s and 1850s. The Know-Nothings suspected that the Irish Catholics owed their allegiance to the pope instead of the Constitution, and they contended that these newcomers brought crime, disease, poverty, and alcoholism.

During tough economic times, outsiders focus on the rich. The recession of the 1890s gave rise to a Nebraska outsider named William Jennings Bryan. In his famous speech at the 1896 Democratic convention, he said, "My friends, in this land of the free you need not fear that a tyrant will spring up from among the people. What we need is an Andrew Jackson to stand, as Jackson stood, against the encroachments of organized wealth." He finished with a famous allusion to the New Testament: "You shall not press down upon the brow of labor this crown of thorns, you shall not crucify mankind upon a cross of gold."[16]

During the Great Depression thirty-eight years later, Senator Huey Long of Louisiana also deployed Christian imagery against the plutocratic insiders: " 'Come to my feast,' He said to 125 million American people. But Morgan and Rockefeller and Mellon and Baruch have walked up and took 85 percent of the victuals off the table!"[17] In a radio address, Long elaborated on the powerful few: "They own the banks, they own the steel mills, they own the railroads, they own the bonds, they own the mortgages, they own the stores, and they have chained the country from one end to the other."[18] Long led a movement with a large conspiracy-minded element, including some who believed that Franklin Roosevelt was a Jew whose real name was Rosenfeld. The FDR birthers got enough attention that the president thought it necessary to publish a dignified response.[19] Beyond the eccentric fringe, Long spoke to millions who thought that the system had left them behind. His slogan—"Every Man a King"—appealed to their craving for respect and dignity. If not for his assassination in 1935, Long might have mounted a serious third-party challenge in 1936, a prospect that worried Roosevelt.

In 1968, former Alabama governor George Wallace carried several Southern states under the banner of the American Independent Party. A few years earlier, he had literally stood in the schoolhouse door as federal officials arrived to integrate the University of Alabama. Now he was running as a fighter for the little guy, attacking the "pseudo-intellectuals and the theoreticians and some professors and some newspaper editors and some judges and some preachers" who looked down on "the pipe-fitter, the communications worker, the fireman, the policeman, the barber, the white-collar worker."[20] Wallace boasted that he would run over demonstrators who tried to lie down in front of his car. Though he never did any such thing, his supporters cheered the threat. Columnist David Broder wrote, "When Wallace has finished his harangue, the emotion is closer to that of a lynch mob—a pack of angry, frustrated men and women, who see his cause, not just as a chance for victory but as a guarantee of vengeance against all who have affronted them for so long."[21]

With Democratic presidential contender Jesse Jackson in 1984, outsiderism took a different form. Whereas Wallace had stood for segregation, Jackson led a "Rainbow Coalition" of African Americans and other minority groups. His language, ironically, had a faint echo of Wallace: "My constituency is the desperate, the damned, the disinherited, the disrespected, and the despised."[22] As with so many outsider movements, the 1984 Jackson campaign had a whiff of prejudice and menace. Jackson confronted charges of anti-Semitism after a press report revealed that he had referred to Jews as "Hymie" and New York City as "Hymietown."[23] Louis Farrakhan, minister of the Nation of Islam and a key Jackson supporter, said that he would "'make an example' of the reporter who disclosed the comments, and at one point said, 'At this point, no physical harm.'"[24] (He did not follow through.)

Jackson ran again in 1988. His second campaign was more professional than his first, buffing off some of the rough edges. Among other things, he hired a campaign manager who happened to be Jewish. But like the earlier effort, his 1988 campaign was still in the outsider tradition, emphasizing positioning over positions, attitude over agenda. Journalist Elizabeth Drew wrote:

For a large portion of Jackson's supporters and would-be supporters, whether his proposals stand up to scrutiny is irrelevant. Their support for him is in a different category—as the leader of a movement. Jackson has become the vehicle for their discontent—with current policies, with the other candidates. He stands in bold, interesting contrast to some fairly dull candidates. He is the anti-politics candidate. Measuring his program is linear, rational, while most of the support for him is based on emotion.[25]

Substitute "Trump" for "Jackson," and that passage would fit nicely into an account of the 2016 campaign. It is also worth noting that Jackson got an endorsement from the socialist mayor of Burlington, Vermont—Bernie Sanders. In a speech for Jackson, Sanders said, "Tonight we are here to endorse the candidate who is saying loud that enough is enough, that it's time that this nation was returned to the real people of America, the vast majority of us, and that power no longer should rest solely with a handful of banks and corporations who presently dominate the economic and political life of this nation."[26]

By the time of the 1992 campaign, conditions were ripe for a spurt of outsiderism. The recession of 1990–1991 was not long or deep by historical standards, but it seemed harsh to many Americans because it hit right after a lengthy economic boom. And unemployment kept creeping up after the recession had officially ended, peaking at 7.8 percent in the summer of 1992. These developments followed the collapse of the savings and loan industry. The crisis had not only endangered the savings of millions of Americans but also revealed widespread corruption in the industry and the officials who were supposed to regulate it. A government bailout gave rise to charges that Washington cared less about struggling Americans than about the corporations that had hurt them. Meanwhile, scandals involving members of Congress had deepened the mood of cynicism. Despite a burst of good feeling following victory in the 1991 Gulf War, polls found satisfaction with the state of the nation dropping from 66 percent in February 1991 to 14 percent in June 1992. Trust in government plunged from 47 percent in March 1991 to 22 percent in October 1992.[27]

Anger at insiders naturally fell upon President George H. W. Bush, the kind of man whom the Federalists would have recognized as one of their own. Even apart from his status as the incumbent, nearly everything about him radiated old-fashioned insiderism. He was a rich Wall Street banker's son, a high church Episcopalian, a Yale graduate, and a veteran of the oil industry. Before winning the 1988 election, he had held government posts ranging from House member to CIA director to vice president. He was a profoundly decent man, but his WASP reserve could come across as cold indifference. By early 1992, it looked as if a Democrat could beat him. But which one?

The Democratic nomination contest saw a flameout of two Washington insiders: Senator Tom Harkin of Iowa and Senator Bob Kerrey of Nebraska. Paul Tsongas, a former senator from Massachusetts, tried to run as an outsider but was miscast for the role. His cerebral approach to policy focused on fiscal responsibility, and he said that proposals for a middle-class tax cut amounted to pandering. He soon found that the Democratic primary electorate did not consist of pitchfork-bearing accountants. Meanwhile, another contender for the Democratic outsider mantle was Jerry Brown, who had been a two-term governor of California, just like his father, and whose sister was serving as the state's treasurer. Despite these establishment credentials, he got a bit of traction by courting labor, opposing NAFTA, and attacking big money in politics.

The winner was Bill Clinton. His career was an epic tale of contradictions and ambiguities, so it makes sense that he was a hybrid of insider and outsider. On the one hand, he had never held office in Washington and was governor of Arkansas, a poor state far removed from the seats of political and economic power. On the other hand, his resume was deeply wired to the inside: Georgetown University, an internship with Senator J. William Fulbright, a Rhodes Scholarship, Yale Law School. He campaigned as a change agent who would put people first, even as he aggressively raised special-interest money and had personal financial dealings that would cause him years of political trouble. As early as the 1992 campaign, Jerry Brown was alleging conflicts of interest arising from Hillary Clinton's legal work in Little Rock. Brown's criticism foreshadowed attacks that both Bernie Sanders and Donald Trump would mount against her in 2016.

Within his own party, Bush faced an unexpectedly strong primary challenge from columnist Pat Buchanan. After growing up in Washington, D.C., earning degrees at Georgetown and Columbia, working as a White House aide in two Republican administrations, and logging many hours on the television talk-show circuit, Buchanan was yet another insider who took up outsiderism. Specifically, he became a spokesperson for a faction of conservatism that disdained internationalism and free trade, and even flirted with Holocaust denial. Bush's support for NAFTA and Israel outraged him. "He is yesterday and we are tomorrow," Buchanan said in his announcement speech. "He is a globalist and we are nationalists. He believes in some Pax Universalis; we believe in the Old Republic. He would put Americans' wealth and power at the service of some vague New World Order; we will put America first."[28] After the Los Angeles riots, he placed much of the blame for disorder on undocumented immigrants: "Foreigners are coming into this country illegally and helping to burn down one of the greatest cities in America." His solution will sound familiar to those who saw the 2016 campaign: "If I were President, I would have the (Army) Corps of Engineers build a double-barrier fence that would keep out 95% of the illegal traffic. I think it can be done."[29]

Buchanan also saw the budding desperation of the white working class. In his 1992 convention address, he said:

> There were the workers at the James River Paper Mill, in the frozen North Country of New Hampshire—hard, tough men, one of whom was silent, until I shook his hand. Then he looked up in my eyes and said, "Save our jobs!" There was the legal secretary at the Manchester airport on Christmas Day who told me she was going to vote for me, then broke down crying, saying, "I've lost my job, I don't have any money; they're going to take away my daughter. What am I going to do?"[30]

Similar concerns drove the candidacy of Ross Perot, who said that incompetence and corruption lay behind trade agreements that purportedly hurt U.S. interests. "[We] have made the strangest trade agreements in the world with our international competitors. They have picked our pockets. Why? They knew how to negotiate. The people we sent over didn't. And the people we sent over to negotiate know that, if they keep their noses clean, that in a short period of time they can be hired for $30,000 a month as a Japanese lobbyist."[31]

Buchanan and Perot seemed on track to become central figures in American politics. It was not to be. Buchanan upset Bob Dole in the 1996 New Hampshire primary, but never posed a serious threat to his nomination, and failed to get a speaking role at the party convention. In fall of that year, Perot ran as the Reform Party candidate but his share of the popular vote was less than half of his 1992 level, and he quit politics. When Buchanan took up the Reform Party label in 2000, he got less than 1 percent of the popular vote, and his only major influence on the campaign was accidental: Democrats claimed that faulty ballot design caused hundreds of Gore supporters in Palm Beach County to vote for Buchanan by mistake, tipping Florida and the presidency to George W. Bush.

Fast-forward to 2016. Like their predecessors in the world of outsiders, Bernie Sanders and Donald Trump said American workers were suffering because of the perfidy of special interests and their enablers in the government. In particular, Trump was the culmination of more than two centuries of outsiderism: a silver-spoon populist (widely seen as a demagogue) who warned of rigged political processes, dangerous foreigners, slick lobbyists, greedy rich people, and snooty intellectual elites. He trafficked in insults and unfounded conspiracy theories, and some of his followers responded with a nasty zeal that crossed the line into bullying and violence.

He also took his party in a different ideological direction.

LEFT, RIGHT, AND THE GRID

The inside-outside spectrum represents just one dimension of American politics. Another is the traditional dimension of party-and-issue-position, ranging from left to right. As the 1992 book explained, it is possible to put these axes together in a grid that locates major figures on the American political landscape. (See table 1.1.)

As subsequent chapters will explain in much more detail, this grid helps us see the relationships of presidential candidates and congressional leaders. Sanders and Trump were both outsiders, but the former's issue stands placed him well to the left. For a while early in the campaign, Cruz had a good relationship with fellow outsider Trump, but his own ideology was distinctly more conservative. House Democratic leader Nancy Pelosi held off on an endorsement until the end of the primary campaign, and the grid illustrates the cross-pressures that she faced. On the one hand, she and many of her backbenchers were sympathetic to Sanders's issue positions, but, like Clinton, she was also a wealthy insider who had raised millions from business and financial interests. (Also like Clinton, she was a *legacy* insider: both her father and her brother had served as mayor of Baltimore.)

Any discussion of the left-right dimension requires some context. As issues evolve, so does the ideological spectrum. From the mid-nineteenth

Table 1.1.

	Left	*Center*	*Right*
Outside	Bernie Sanders	Donald Trump	Ted Cruz Rand Paul Ben Carson Mike Huckabee Tea Party
Middle (Inside-Outside)		Jim Webb Chris Christie	Marco Rubio
Inside	Nancy Pelosi	Mitch McConnell John Kasich Jeb Bush	
	Hillary Clinton		Paul Ryan

century until the Second World War era, conservative Republicans believed in protectionism, while liberal Democrats championed free trade. By late twentieth century, they had switched sides. In his 1979 announcement of candidacy, Ronald Reagan proposed what eventually became the North American Free Trade Agreement (NAFTA). In the 1990s, Bill Clinton solidified his standing as a moderate by endorsing NAFTA over the objections of most congressional Democrats. He secured its passage by building a coalition of the minority of Democrats who favored free trade, along with the overwhelming majority of Republicans. His partner in this effort was House minority whip Newt Gingrich. Twenty-four years later, the partisan and ideological lines seemed to be on the verge of another change, with Trump joining Sanders in criticizing NAFTA and opposing a Pacific trade agreement.

Sometimes, the country settles certain issues, thereby moving the ideological goalposts. In the 1950s and 1960s, for instance, there was a great debate over basic civil rights laws. *National Review* opposed federal legislation in this field, and in 1957 ran an editorial "Why the South Must Prevail."[32] By 2016, conservatives were routinely quoting Martin Luther King, and they knew that questioning the 1964 Civil Rights Act was beyond the pale in national politics. (While preparing for his ill-fated 2016 presidential race, Senator Rand Paul awkwardly walked back his earlier comments on the law.[33]) Equally dramatic was the transformation of the politics of marriage. In 1992, Bill Clinton opposed legal recognition of same-sex marriage, and, in 1996, he reluctantly signed the Defense of Marriage Act. As late as 2004, conservative Republicans hoped to score gains on the marriage issue, and President Bush endorsed a constitutional amendment to define marriage exclusively as the union of a man and woman. By 2016, public opinion had undergone a radical transformation in favor of same-sex marriage and the Supreme Court had ruled that the Fourteenth Amendment's Due Process Clause guarantees the right to marry a member of the same sex.[34] In the presidential campaign, Republican candidates seldom mentioned the issue.

And then there was the dog that did not bark: affirmative action. In the 1990s it was still a live issue, and even in Democratic-trending California, voters passed a 1996 ballot measure banning racial preferences. In the following years, however, discussions of affirmative action nearly vanished from campaign rhetoric. In 2016, the Supreme Court voted 4–3 to approve the consideration of race in ensuring a diverse student body.[35] The decision occurred in the middle of the presidential race, and it might have come out as a 4–4 tie if Justice Scalia had not recently died. In spite of these potentially electric circumstances, GOP candidates said little about it, and the issue did not even come up in debates.

On a couple of occasions, reporters did ask Trump about affirmative action. His brief responses revealed something both about the extent to which the issue had gone to rest and about his approach to policy in general. Late in 2015, Scalia was still alive and he suggested in oral argument that affirmative action programs might place some African American students in overly demanding programs. "I don't like what he said," Trump said when a reporter asked him about the comment. "No, I don't like what he said. I heard him, I was like, 'Let me read it again' because I actually saw it in print, and I'm going—I read a lot of stuff—and I'm going, 'Whoa!' "[36] On *Meet the Press*, he said, "Well, you know, you have to also go free market. You have to go capability. You have to do a lot of things. But I'm fine with affirmative action. We've lived with it for a long time. And I lived with it for a long time. And I've had great relationships with lots of people. So I'm fine with it."[37]

Trump's attitude on this issue, as on most others, was essentially pragmatic, which is why our grid does not place him on either the left or the right. Political commentators often use *pragmatic* interchangeably with words such as *practical* or *prudent*. It means something different. Pragmatism is a school of thought that shuns abstract theories and ultimate truths in favor of "what works."[38] Trump often made clear that he was a "what works" kind of guy, and if he had ever read William James, he would have smiled at the way he posed pragmatism's usual question: "What, in short, is the truth's cash-value in experiential terms?" In the case of affirmative action, Trump's position turned on convenience and familiarity rather than any deep thought about equal rights. He usually dismissed high ideals by reducing them to crude material terms. Consider, for instance, America's foundational proposition that all men are created equal. "The world is not fair," Trump said in a 2006 video. "You know they come with this statement 'all men are created equal.' Well, it sounds beautiful, and it was written by some very wonderful people and brilliant people, but it's not true because all people and all men [laughter] aren't created [equal] . . . you have to be born and blessed with something up here [pointing to his head]. On the assumption you are, you can become very rich."[39] Similarly, Trump did not think of "American exceptionalism" as a way of thinking about the nation's role as a beacon for equality and liberty. As he said in 2015, it was all about the Benjamins.

> I want to take everything back from the world that we've given them. We've given them so much. On top of taking it back, I don't want to say, "We're exceptional, we're more exceptional." Because essentially we're saying, "We're more outstanding than you. By the way, you've been eating our lunch for the last 20 years, but we're more exceptional than you." I don't like the term. I never liked it.[40]

Trump's disdain for these ideas put him at odds with a major strain of conservative thought that revered the Declaration.[41] It surely set him apart from conservatives who loved to quote Reagan's rhetoric of a "shining city on a hill" and who faulted President Obama for seeming to belittle American exceptionalism. Trump just did not care very much for conservative ideology. In May 2016, he said, "This is called the Republican Party. It's not called the Conservative Party."[42] Trump pollster Tony Fabrizio told a post-election conference, "One of the problems is many people tried to look at the Donald Trump phenomenon through the ideological lenses which had defined previous Republican presidential nominating contests. Donald Trump is post ideological. His movement transcends ideology."[43]

His movement did appeal to "alt-right" activists who believed in an American nationalism rooted in "blood and soil." Unlike Pat Buchanan, however, who had raised this theme in his 1992 campaign, Trump did not draw from any consistent philosophy. In 2012, he had taken a totally different tack when he criticized Mitt Romney on immigration: "He had a crazy policy of self-deportation which was maniacal. It sounded as bad as it was, and he lost all of the Latino vote. He lost the Asian vote. He lost everybody who is inspired to come into this country." Trump said that the GOP needed a comprehensive policy "to take care of this incredible problem that we have with respect to immigration, with respect to people wanting to be wonderful productive citizens of this country."[44] A few years later, he could see that a hardline immigration policy would win him some support—so, in true pragmatic fashion, he reversed himself.

Until 2016, politicians and journalists typically assumed that the GOP electorate cared mostly about the Reaganite agenda of limiting the power of the federal government. According to conservative writer Yuval Levin, Trump demonstrated to GOP politicians that "the people they claimed to represent were not quite who they imagined they were." He elaborates: "Trump showed that much of the base of the party was driven far more by resentment of elitist arrogance, by a rejection of globalism, and by economic and cultural insecurity than by a commitment to conservative economic or political principles."[45] Buchanan had appealed to such sentiments, too, but why did they carry so much more force in 2016 than they had in 1992? The answer lies in some very large changes in American society.

COMING APART

In a prescient 1992 article, Nicholas Lemann noted that the Clintons were the first products of the meritocracy to reach the White House. FDR, JFK, and George H. W. Bush were all intelligent, but they entered the Ivy League when it still catered to rich students instead of smart ones. Truman did not go to college, and Johnson, Nixon and Reagan went to obscure local schools. Eisenhower and Carter got into military academies on merit, wrote Lemann, "but for them college was the doorway only into a narrow elite, the officer corps, not the common run of leadership positions." He went on:

> Bill Clinton and Hillary Clinton will be the first occupants of the White House who truly meet the big break test: the day that fat letter from an elite college (Georgetown and Wellesley, respectively) arrived in their middle class, middle-of-the-country mailboxes was the day the trajectory of their lives changed dramatically. The Clintons met and courted on the campus of the elite Yale Law School; as the sociologist E. Digby Baltzell has observed, for meritocrats the dean of admissions functions as a de facto marriage broker.[46]

The trends that brought the Clintons together had been under way for some time. In 1947, the year that Hillary Clinton was born, only 5.4 percent of Americans over the age of twenty-five had four years of college or more.[47] In 1970, the year of the Clintons' storied first meeting at the Yale Law Library, that figure was up to 16.4 percent. The ranks of higher education had swollen because of the GI Bill of Rights, the growth of state university systems, and the expansion of financial aid. At the kind of high-ranking institutions that the Clintons had attended, standardized testing had helped create an efficient "sorting machine," spotting smart youths and bringing them to campus.[48] Higher education stayed busy during and after the Clinton administration. Between 1992 and 2015, the share of college-educated adults rose from 23.6 percent to 35.6 percent.

It makes sense that a better-educated America would become a more prosperous America, and certain topline statistics seem to bear out this assumption. In the third quarter of 1992, real gross domestic product per capita (2009 dollars) was $36,184. In the third quarter of 2016, the figure stood at $51,473—up 42 percent.[49] In October 1992, unemployment was 6.9 percent. Twenty-four years later, it was down to 4.7 percent.[50] On Election Day 1992, the Dow Jones Industrial Average closed at 3,252.48.[51] On Election Day 2016, it finished at 18,332.74—a 464 percent increase. These improvements came about even with the tech-bubble recession of 2001, the Great Recession of 2007–2009, and the sluggish growth of the Obama years.

Economic life did get a great deal better—for college graduates. For people whose schooling stopped short of a bachelor's degree, the picture was darker. From 1990 to 2015, the top sector for employment growth was educational services (105 percent), while manufacturing employment fell by 30 percent.[52] In the early 1990s, the median worker over age twenty-five with a bachelor's degree (but no higher degree) made 40 percent more than a worker with just a high school diploma. By 2015, that difference was 70 percent.[53] Moreover, people with college degrees were more likely to have jobs in the first place, gaining from both lower unemployment rates (2.6 versus 5.4 percent in 2015) and higher rates of labor force participation (74 versus 57 percent in 2015).[54]

Families headed by college graduates had higher median wealth in 2013 than in 1989, while families headed by those with less education saw no improvement.[55] This gap stemmed from income trends, as well as the distribution of benefits from the soaring stock market. A 2013 Pew poll found that 77 percent of college graduates had money in stocks, either directly or through retirement plans. For those with some college but no degree, the figure was 45 percent. Among those with only a high school diploma or less, only 24 percent owned stock.[56]

Notwithstanding anecdotes about cab-driving philosophy majors, Americans with degrees generally did so well because the economy placed increasing value on the kinds of skills that colleges teach. Technology was a key reason. The Internet had existed since 1969 but was still not in wide use as Clinton took office: in 1992, there was a grand total of ten websites.[57] In the years to follow, the rapid growth of the Internet profoundly affected economics and society, creating entirely new job categories (e.g., webmaster) and providing great new opportunities for people whose jobs involved such activities as coding, writing, research, and graphic design. For those in blue-collar occupations, the change was not as positive.[58] Driving a delivery truck was pretty much the same in 2016 as it was decades before, but now the drivers were accountable to black boxes that tracked their every move. (That is why the people in brown uniforms run so fast and look so tense.) Since automation had put some blue-collar workers out of a job completely, these drivers might have considered themselves lucky—except that self-driving trucks were looming as a near-term threat to their employment.[59]

Blue-collar workers saw danger from other quarters as well. One was economic globalization, along with the trade agreements that greased its way. Although NAFTA had a modestly beneficial impact on the economy overall, it did cost thousands of jobs in manufacturing and agriculture.[60] To auto workers who saw their plants move south of the border, it was no comfort to learn that other Americans could now buy Mexican and Canadian goods more cheaply.

People were also crossing borders. The 1990 census found 19.8 million foreign-born residents, accounting for 7.9 percent of the population. By the 2010 census, the raw number had doubled to 40 million, and the population share was up to 12.9 percent.[61] When Pat Buchanan railed against undocumented immigrants in 1992, they numbered somewhere between 4 and 6 million. When Donald Trump did the same in 2016, there were more than 11 million.[62] (That level had dropped from a 2007 peak of more than 12 million, thanks to the Great Recession and deportations.) Whether correctly or incorrectly, many native-born white working people were seeing an economic threat from immigrants, especially the undocumented. According to a 2016 survey by the Public Religion Research Institute and the Brookings Institute, a plurality of white college-educated Americans thought that undocumented immigrants do more good than harm by providing low-cost labor, but 71 percent of white working-class Americans—those with neither a four-year college degree nor a salaried job—said that the undocumented hurt the U.S. economy by depressing wages.[63] These were, in essence, two perspectives on one point.

The gap between college America and non-college America went beyond economic issues. It literally extended from birth to death.

In 2009, only 8 percent of college-educated white women were unwed when they gave birth, compared with 34 percent of white women with some college, and *51 percent* of those with no more than a high school diploma.[64] A 2015 survey found that 88 percent of children with least one college-graduate parent were living in a two-parent household, compared with 59 percent of those whose parents had only a high school diploma and 54 percent of those whose parents did not finish high school.[65]

There was a rise in the mortality of middle-aged (forty-five to sixty-four) non-Hispanic whites between 1999 and 2013. (African Americans and Hispanics saw mortality rates fall.) This change stemmed mostly from drug and alcohol poisonings, suicide, and chronic liver diseases and cirrhosis. Mortality for those with a high school diploma or less increased by 134 per 100,000. Those with some college saw little change while with a bachelor's degree or more saw death rates fall by 57 per 100,000.[66] There was a similar pattern among younger people. The death rate for whites between the ages of twenty-five and thirty-four rose between 1990 and 2014. For those with a college degree, the increase was a modest 4 percent. For those without a high school education, it was 23 percent.[67]

In other words, non-college families were less stable than college families, and they disproportionately suffered from substance abuse and other pathologies that showed up in death statistics. Accordingly, working-class whites had a more negative view of American society than other groups. The Public Religion Research Institute found that 62 percent of African Americans and 57 percent of Hispanics said that American society had changed for the better since the 1950s. The figure was similar among college-educated whites: 56 percent. But among working-class whites, 65 percent said that things were now worse.[68] Sociologist Andrew J. Cherlin writes that these differences reflected starkly different reference points:

[African Americans] may look back to a time when discrimination deprived their parents of equal opportunities. Many Hispanics may look back to the lower standard of living their parents experienced in their countries of origin. Whites are likely to compare themselves to a reference group that leads them to feel worse off. Blacks and Hispanics compare themselves to reference groups that may make them feel better off.

In the fourth quarter of 2015, the median weekly earnings of white men aged 25 to 54 were $950, well above the same figure for black men ($703) and Hispanic men ($701). But for some whites—perhaps the ones who account for the increasing death rate—that may be beside the point. Their main reference group is their parents' generation, and by that standard they have little to look forward to and a lot to lament.[69]

Between 2007 and 2016, whites between the ages of twenty-five and fifty-four lost about 6.5 million more jobs more than they gained. Hispanics in the same age group gained some 3 million jobs net, Asians 1.5 million and African Americans 1 million.[70] Although such figures do not prove employment bias against whites, the trend fueled a sense of resentment. The Public Religion Research Institute found that about two-thirds of working-class whites agreed that the discrimination faced by whites is as big a problem as the discrimination faced by non-whites. Only about 43 percent of white college-educated Americans took this view.[71] On this issue, as on many others, members of the latter group were adopting socially liberal positions that often put them on the same side as African Americans and Hispanics.

College America was becoming a class apart. Its members had their own tastes, preferences, and neighborhoods. And its children were marrying one another.[72] (For instance, the Clintons' daughter wed a fellow Stanford graduate whose parents had both served in the House of Representatives.) College-educated parents passed along good genes, provided their children with cultural opportunities, paid for test-prep classes, and used their connections to open the doors for internships and jobs. Darren Walker, the president of the Ford Foundation, writes of friends who ask for his help in getting internships for their children. "I understand what they're doing; this is part of being a parent. Still, it's a reminder that America's current internship system, in which contacts and money matter more than talent, contributes to an economy in which access and opportunity go to the people who already have the most of both."[73]

Lauren A. Rivera explains that college America reproduces its own advantages in subtler ways. "Upper- and upper-middle-class parents are more likely to know that enrolling their children in structured leisure activities pays off in selective college admissions and beyond than are working- and lower-middle-class families."[74] Admissions officers and corporate recruiters prefer applicants who have taken part in elite sports such as squash, which poor kids do not play—or even know about. When bright students from blue-collar families do get into good schools, they are still not on a level playing field. They often assume that grades are the only key to success, so they tend to spend less time on extracurricular activities than their peers from affluent, educated backgrounds. Rivera writes, "Ironically, working class students' focus on academics (rather than social or extracurricular activities) while in school constrains, not expands, the types of jobs and incomes available to them when they graduate."[75] Even if guidance counselors clue them in about getting the "right" extracurricular credentials, they stay a step behind. "This is because simply knowing this rule of the hiring game in insufficient for passing résumé screens. Students need to have evidence of participation, and real material constraints (e.g., joining fees, equipment costs, time away from paid work, and forgone wages) limit their involvement."[76]

So to the extent that blue-collar Americans thought that the system was rigged in favor of college America, they were not entirely wrong. They also had reason to think that college America looked down on them. Charles Murray writes:

> Try using "redneck" in a conversation with your highly educated friends and see if it triggers any of the nervousness that accompanies other ethnic slurs. Refer to "flyover country" and consider the implications when no one asks, "What does that mean?" Or I can send you to chat with a friend in Washington, D.C., who bought a weekend place in West Virginia. He will tell you about the contempt for his new neighbors that he has encountered in the elite precincts of the nation's capital.[77]

Joan C. Williams, a law professor from a working-class background, observes that blue-collar Americans resent professionals but not the wealthy. "Why the difference? For one thing, most blue-collar workers have little direct contact with the rich outside of *Lifestyles of the Rich and Famous*. But professionals order them around every day."[78]

Such attitudes help explain a puzzle. The Democratic Party has long been the natural home for organized labor, so why did so many blue-collar workers turn toward the GOP? One answer is that unions are increasingly the domain of the professional class that they dislike. At the start of 2016, the Bureau of Labor Statistics reported that barely over one in ten wage and salary workers belonged to a union, but just under half of union members worked for the government.[79] On the union rolls, white-collar workers outnumbered blue-collar workers. For instance, 6.1 union members worked in management, professional, and related occupations while just 2.4 million worked in production, transportation, and material moving occupations. In other words, a union member was much more likely to be a teacher than a teamster.

Non-college whites felt isolated, and in a direct geographical sense. In recent years, the people most likely to move for better opportunities were the highly educated, who clustered in places such as Silicon Valley, New York, Boston, and Seattle.[80] The counties encompassing such areas accounted for much of the growth in new businesses after the Great Recession. Government spending enabled lobbyists and contractors to flourish: five of the nation's ten wealthiest counties were suburbs of Washington, D.C.[81] Meanwhile, small rural counties shrank and faltered. In the recovery of the early 1990s, they had accounted for a third of the net increase in new businesses. From 2010 through 2014, they lost more businesses than they generated.[82]

The physical and psychological separation of college America and non-college America left a mark on politics. As college America got more liberal and geographically concentrated, certain areas became overwhelmingly Democratic. The resulting inefficient distribution of the Democratic vote had major implications for the electoral vote and House elections, as we shall discuss in later chapters. More broadly, the separation meant that members of the elite could be blind to problems afflicting people who were out of sight and out of mind. Take crime, for instance. In 2016, people without college degrees were telling pollsters that crime was on the rise, whereas college graduates said that it was not.[83] Pundits dismissed worries about crime concerns as inaccurate and possibly racist, but FBI data later confirmed that the number of murders increased nearly 11 percent between 2014 and 2015, and overall violent crime rose by nearly 4 percent.[84] Perhaps the people who lived in more vulnerable places could see things that were invisible to those who dwelled in gated communities and high-security apartment buildings.

The social and economic forces driving the two Americas apart had been brewing for a long time. But why did they have such impact in 2016, and not ten years earlier? One reason was the Great Recession, which slammed working-class communities, and whose effects lingered long after its official conclusion. In 2016, Pat Buchanan looked back at his 1992 race and told journalist Jeff Greenfield, "Those issues started maturing. Now we've lost 55,000 factories. . . . When those consequences came rolling in, all of a sudden you've got an angry country. We were out there warning what was coming."[85]

Another reason was President Obama. Some of his supporters said that opposition was really a reaction to his heritage, or, as he put it diplomatically, "my unique demographic."[86] Racial prejudice surely played some part, but something else was also at work. President Obama, whose parents met at the University of Hawaii, was a product of college America—and its elite wing at that. His father went on to graduate study in economics at Harvard, and his mother earned a PhD in anthropology. Obama himself attended an exclusive prep school in Honolulu and got his bachelor's degree at Columbia and his law degree at Harvard, where he headed the law review. As of 2014, two-thirds of his cabinet appointees had attended an Ivy League institution.[87]

Many in non-college America had a hard time believing that he was on their side. During the 2008 campaign, he told a group of rich contributors, "And it's not surprising then they get bitter, they cling to guns or religion or antipathy to people who aren't like them or anti-immigrant sentiment or anti-trade sentiment as a way to explain their frustrations."[88] His supporters said that his policies benefited working people, but non-college America had a different view. Immigration, trade, and crime were all sore points—and so was health care. The Affordable Care Act did have some positive effects through the creation of the exchanges and the expansion of Medicaid. But those on employer-provided coverage saw their deductibles rise and their choices shrink. The president's often-repeated promise that "if you like your plan, you can keep it" became a bitter joke. Six years after a 2008 campaign pledge to fix health care for veterans, journalists uncovered that waiting lists were so long that some veterans died before they could get medical treatment. The president again vowed action and again fell short. A year after the Veterans Administration scandal broke, progress was halting at best.[89]

As for the president's determination to curb lobbyist power, interest group representatives continued to ply their trade.[90] Liberal author Thomas Frank observed unhappily that the nation got a lesson in how that trade works: "Like simple class solidarity between the Ivy Leaguers who advise the president and the Ivy Leaguers who sell derivative securities to unsuspecting foreigners. As that inspiring young president filled his administration with Wall Street personnel, we learned that the revolving door still works, even if the people passing through it aren't registered lobbyists."[91]

Those things were still in the future in 2008, when a combination of a bad economy and an unpopular war all but guaranteed Obama's victory, and even many of the "bitter clingers" voted for him. Two years later, the outsider reaction was already forming, and Republicans took control of the House. Obama narrowly won reelection in 2012. He had the advantage of incumbency, and the economy had improved just enough to make him electable. Moreover, the Republicans nominated Mitt Romney, a governor's son who had grown up in wealth, earned two professional degrees at Harvard, and made a fortune in private equity. For all his virtues, it is hard to think of anyone less suited for leading a revolt against insiders. Two years later, Republicans won control of the Senate, bulked up their majority in the House, and scored historic gains in governorships and state legislatures. White working-class voters were a major source of GOP support.[92]

Then came the 2016 election, with its surprising showings by Sanders and Trump. Although both had elite educations (Sanders at the University of Chicago, Trump at the Wharton School), neither sounded like it. They grew up only fifteen miles apart, and both retained their distinctly non-elite outer-borough accents. In different ways, and with different emphases, both men spoke to the anxieties and resentments that recent decades had produced. And the previous twenty-four years had given them new means of reaching their audience and bypassing existing political structures.

OVER RED AND BLUE

In its account of the 1992 campaign, *Upside Down and Inside Out* described two broad categories of mass media. One was the older collection of big units: the broadcast networks, wire services, major newspapers and magazines. The defining characteristic of this category was gatekeeping, the process by which editors, producers, and other media figures decided what parts of the candidates' messages could reach the public. The other category consisted of alternative means by which political figures could communicate with voters more or less directly, including talk radio and cable television. Ross Perot took full advantage of the second category, reaching millions via speeches on C-SPAN and softball interviews on Larry King's CNN program. Clinton spoke to younger voters via appearances on *Arsenio Hall* and MTV.[93]

Upside Down and Inside Out caught a snapshot of the second category in its embryonic form, and correctly noted that it had not yet become dominant. "[The] 'mediated' channel of news and interpretation . . . still commands most of the attention, and the media tribunes remain at the center of media power."[94] By 2016, that center had shifted. As more and more Americans got their news online, print newspaper circulation plunged and newsrooms emptied out. Between 1992 and 2016, employment in the newspaper industry fell by more than half.[95] Newsmagazines shrank and either went digital or barely lingered in little-seen print editions. The evening news broadcasts of the big three networks continued to attract millions of viewers, but since 1980, they had lost more than half of their audience.[96]

Television viewers simply enjoyed many more choices. In the early 1990s, the average household received about thirty-six channels.[97] By 2016, that number had passed two hundred.[98] As the old media tribunes lost their dominance, political figures now had more opportunities to reach national audiences, with a special focus on their partisans. Republicans and conservatives now had Fox News, just as liberals and Democrats had MSNBC, neither of which existed in 1992.

This media environment was especially hospitable to celebrities with roots in the entertainment world. It would not be accurate to say that 1992 started the merger of entertainment and politics. During the 1968 campaign, for instance, Richard Nixon had a cameo on *Laugh-In*, and a dozen years later, former movie star Ronald Reagan became president. But the 1992 race did take the process a big step forward. In 1992, Tabitha Soren covered the campaign for the still-hip MTV network. In 2016, she reflected, "And I feel just a tiny bit sorry—not for what we did, but for what we enabled. In trying to interest young people in politics, MTV News inadvertently helped create a model for turning politics into entertainment."[99] Also in 1992, MTV premiered *The Real World*, which did much to establish the terms of reality television shows. At the time, no one saw that genre as a route to political prominence.

Enter Donald J. Trump. In the 1980s and 1990s, he became nationally prominent for both his business dealings and his extramarital affairs. He also flirted with politics, even making a brief run at the Reform Party presidential nomination in 2000. But it was reality television that made him America's fantasy boss. On *The Apprentice* and *The Celebrity Apprentice*, he introduced himself to millions as a tough, shrewd businessman that supplicants looked to for guidance and approval. Some no doubt saw him as the kind of take-charge man who could lead the country. Academics and political commentators were not paying much attention, however. If they were watching television at all, they were tuning in to the highbrow fare that the expanding cable menu had made available. They also overlooked his many appearances on niche networks such as the Golf Channel. Below the intelligentsia's radar, cable television was giving this billionaire the kind of positive name identification that money could not buy.

The 1992 book did not mention the Internet as part of the media picture: as mentioned earlier, few Americans had Internet access. Within a few years, cyberspace grew fast and became part of national politics.[100] In 1996, Bob Dole made a bit of political history by offering the first mention of a campaign website during a presidential debate—although he got the URL wrong.[101] With dramatic improvements in technology, the first decade of the twenty-first century saw the rise of social media and the migration of news from print publications to online sources. In a 2016 poll, most respondents expressed a preference for getting their news from a screen, whether it was a television, smartphone, or tablet.[102]

There was a website, Facebook group, or Twitter feed for just about every conceivable shade of political opinion. Once a campaign or cause reached a critical mass, it could now bypass the old media gatekeepers completely. With so many alternative perspectives—sometimes alternative realities— Americans continued to lose faith in the legacy media. By 2016, just 32 percent said that they had a great deal or a fair amount of trust that the media would "report the news fully, accurately and fairly"—the lowest point in Gallup polling history.[103]

In decades past, key magazines and newspapers shaped the political agenda and set the contours of ideological debate. With the rise of the Internet, they lost much of this power to outsiders. The case of the *National Review* illustrates the point. Starting in the 1950s, it did much to define American conservatism in the second half of the twentieth century. It policed the movement's outer boundaries, effectively excommunicating the likes of Ayn Rand, the John Birch Society, and the Liberty Lobby. In 1991, it ran a special issue concluding that Pat Buchanan was guilty of anti-Semitism.[104] Although the magazine did not stop Buchanan, it helped put a low ceiling on his support. Twenty-five years later, *National Review* (first online, then in print) ran a symposium against Trump.[105] It had far less effect because conservatives had a vast array of alternative sources of information, including Breitbart.com and Trump's own tweets. Longtime Republican operative Ron Kaufman told Jeff Greenfield, "If Buchanan had had social media he might have done a lot better. Back then in '92, people wouldn't have been hearing about it every 15 minutes. There was no Breitbart, no Politico."[106]

On the other side of the political spectrum, meanwhile, Internet publications such as the *Huffington Post* and *Daily Kos* supplanted old print journals such as the *New Republic*. During the campaign, an "alt-left" became evident, though it was not quite as notorious as the alt-right. After publishing a post-election critique of the Sanders campaign, historian Gil Troy wrote that he "received hundreds of obscenity-laden tweets, emails and Facebook posts condemning me, my looks, my suits, my intelligence, my professional judgment, my integrity, my motives, my religion. Some of these messages threatened violence and even mentioned my office address, trying to intimidate me."[107]

The media landscape of the twenty-first century had turned into a battlefield, with liberals and conservatives occupying different territories. Surveys found little common ground in the news sources that they consulted and trusted. When discussing politics online, they were likely with like-minded people.[108] This environment fed the growth of "fake news," deliberately falsified or distorted online stories that go viral within political communities of the left and right. One survey found that nearly 90 percent of Clinton and Trump supporters believed in conspiracies involving the other candidate, even without any real evidence.[109]

The Internet was a medium for campaign money as well as news and (mis)information. If you wanted to give money to a candidate in 1992, you usually had to write a check. The solicitation would come by postal mail (or, if you were a high roller, a phone call), and you would put pen to paper and place the check into postal mail. By 2016, many contributions came by credit card or even text. (Only partly tongue in cheek, campaign fundraisers spoke of "drunk donation.") Howard Dean in 2004 and Barack Obama in 2008 had already demonstrated that a progressive candidate could raise huge sums online. These precedents, along with technological advances that allowed candidates more easily to identify and solicit contributions in cyberspace, provided an electronic opening to an outsider such as Sanders.

An influential 2008 work of political science argued that party insiders were the major force in picking candidates. They had campaign organizations and access to fundraising networks. Perhaps most of all, they had the power of political persuasion: the ability to give cues to partisan voters.[110] The book was a well-researched and thoughtful analysis of political trends up to its time. But times were changing. Between the early 1990s and the run-up to the 2016 election, Americans grew more skeptical of political parties. Republicans in particular had increasingly unfavorable opinions of their own party.[111] The GOP's self-loathing may have reflected broad discontent with social conditions and the party's apparent inability to do anything about it. It may also have stemmed from the new media's conservative voices. Reflecting on the power of Fox News, right-wing websites, and radio hosts such as Rush Limbaugh and Michael Savage, Oliver Darcy and Pamela Engel wrote that "the conservative media industrial complex" locked GOP officeholders and party officials away from their own base by telling their audience not to trust politicians. The party establishment dared not criticize those who held the electronic keys to their voters. "The power the conservative press held allowed its members to decide who was accepted by the base and who wasn't. True conservatives could be painted as unprincipled moderates, and, as in the case of Trump, unprincipled moderates could be painted as exactly what the base wanted."[112]

As for organization and resources, GOP leaders were at a loss to stop a reality TV star with seemingly unlimited wealth and almost universal name recognition. In the other party, one candidate's monopoly of big-money contributors turned out not to be a barrier to an opponent who could build a big war chest by getting millions of people to send him $27 apiece on the Internet. In 2016, the new communications environment collided with the economic and social dislocation of the white working class and the long tradition of outsiderism in American politics to create a potent stew and a result that few experts saw coming. The political world was ready to turn upside down and inside out, again.

NOTES

1. James Ceaser and Andrew Busch, *Upside Down and Inside Out: The 1992 Elections and American Politics* (Lanham, MD: Rowman & Littlefield, 1993), 1.

2. Steven J. Rosenstone, Roy L. Behr, and Edward H. Lazarus, *Third Parties in America*, 2nd ed. (Princeton, NJ: Princeton University Press, 1996), ch. 9.

3. RealClearPolitics, "Direction of Country," November 13, 2016, http://www.real clearpolitics.com/epolls/other/direction_of_country-902.html.

4. James E. Campbell, "Forecasting the 2016 American National Elections: Introduction," *PS: Political Science and Politics* 46 (October 2016): 649–54.

5. Todd Eberly, "Trump Won, but Nothing Re-aligned," The Free Stater Blog, November 12, 2016, http://freestaterblog.blogspot.com/2016/11/trump-won-but-nothing -raligned.html.

6. The Homeric analogy lay behind the title of our book *Epic Journey: The 2008 Elections and American Politics*.

7. Frank Newport, "Clinton Holds Clear Edge on Having Presidential Qualities," Gallup, November 1, 2016, http://www.gallup.com/poll/196952/clinton-holds-clear-edge -having-presidential-qualities.aspx.

8. Lydia Saad, "Trump and Clinton Finish with Historically Poor Images," Gallup, November 8, 2016, http://www.gallup.com/poll/197231/trump-clinton-finish-historically -poor-images.aspx.

9. John Sides, "Five Key Lessons from Donald Trump's Surprising Victory," *Washington Post*, November 9, 2016, https://www.washingtonpost.com/news/monkey-cage/wp/ 2016/11/09/five-key-lessons-from-donald-trumps-surprising-victory.

10. Yascha Mounk, "How Political Science Gets Politics Wrong," *Chronicle of Higher Education*, October 30, 2016, http://www.chronicle.com/article/How-Political-Science -Gets/238175.

11. David Hume, *Essays Moral, Political, Literary*, edited and with a Foreword, Notes, and Glossary by Eugene F. Miller, with an appendix of variant readings from the 1889 edition by T. H. Green and T. H. Grose, revised edition (Indianapolis: Liberty Fund 1987), http://oll.libertyfund.org/titles/hume-essays-moral-political-literary-lf-ed.

12. This discussion tracks with chapter 1 of *Upside Down and Inside Out*.

13. Letter from Thomas Jefferson to James Madison, May 13, 1793, http://founders .archives.gov/documents/Jefferson/01-26-02-0021.

14. Publius (Alexander Hamilton), *Federalist* 1, http://avalon.law.yale.edu/18th _century/fed01.asp.

15. Alexander Hamilton, notes in the Federal Convention of 1787, June 6, 1787, http://web.archive.org/web/20160630002508/http://avalon.law.yale.edu/18th_century/ const05.asp.

16. William Jennings Bryan, "A Cross of Gold," address to Democratic national convention, Chicago, July 8, 1896, http://www.let.rug.nl/usa/documents/1876-1900/william -jennings-bryan-cross-of-gold-speech-july-8-1896.php.

17. Huey P. Long, address in Washington, DC, December 11, 1934, http://speakola .com/political/huey-long-share-our-wealth-1934.

18. Huey P. Long, radio address, February 24, 1934, http://www.senate.gov/artandhistory/history/resources/pdf/EveryManKing.pdf.

19. In a letter to the *Detroit Jewish Chronicle*, he briefly described his Dutch ancestors. "In the dim distant past they may have been Jews or Catholics or Protestants. What I am more interested in is whether they were good citizens and believers in God. I hope they were both." Franklin D. Roosevelt, "Letter on the President's Ancestors," March 7, 1935, http://www.presidency.ucsb.edu/ws/?pid = 15016.

20. George Wallace, address at Madison Square Garden, New York, October 24, 1968, http://www-personal.umd.umich.edu/~ppennock/doc-Wallace.htm.

21. David S. Broder, "Wallace Campaign Tactics Described," *Spokesman-Review*, August 21, 1968, https://news.google.com/newspapers?nid = 1314&dat = 19680821& id = tDtWAAAAIBAJ&sjid = dekDAAAAIBAJ&pg = 5292,1787167&hl = en.

22. Jesse Jackson, address to the Democratic National Convention, San Francisco, July 18, 1984, http://www.americanrhetoric.com/speeches/jessejackson1984dnc.htm.

23. Rick Atkinson and Milton Coleman, "Peace with American Jews Eludes Jackson," *Washington Post*, February 13, 1984, A1.

24. Frank J. Prial, "Black Journalists Critical of Muslim," *New York Times*, April 6, 1984, http://www.nytimes.com/1984/04/06/us/black-journalists-critical-of-muslim.html.

25. Elizabeth Drew, *Election Journal: Political Events of 1987–1988* (New York: William Morrow, 1989), 155–56.

26. Tim Murphy, "This Is the Campaign That Explains Bernie Sanders," *Mother Jones*, December 17, 2015, http://www.motherjones.com/politics/2015/12/bernie-sanders-jesse-jackson-campaign.

27. Pew Research Center, "Distrust, Discontent, Anger and Partisan Rancor," April 18, 2010, http://www.people-press.org/files/legacy-pdf/606.pdf.

28. Patrick J. Buchanan, "A Crossroads in Our Country's History," New Hampshire State Legislative Office Building, December 10, 1991, http://www.4president.org/speeches/buchanan1992announcement.htm.

29. Ronald Brownstein, "Buchanan Links L.A. Riot to Immigration Problems," *Los Angeles Times*, May 14, 1992, http://articles.latimes.com/1992-05-14/local/me-3227_1_illegal-immigrants.

30. Patrick J. Buchanan, Republican Convention speech, August 17, 1992, http://buchanan.org/blog/1992-republican-national-convention-speech-148.

31. Jim Mann, "Harsh Views on Japan May Help Fuel Perot Campaign," *Los Angeles Times*, June 11, 1992, http://articles.latimes.com/1992-06-11/news/mn-353_1_trade-talks.

32. Carl T. Bogus, *Buckley: William F. Buckley, Jr. and the Rise of American Conservatism* (New York: Bloomsbury Press, 2011), ch. 3; "Why the South Must Prevail," *National Review*, August 24, 1957, https://adamgomez.files.wordpress.com/2012/03/whythesouthmustprevail-1957.pdf.

33. Glenn Kessler, "Rand Paul's Rewriting of His Own Remarks on the Civil Rights Act," *Washington Post*, April 11, 2013, https://www.washingtonpost.com/blogs/fact-checker/post/rand-pauls-rewriting-of-his-own-remarks-on-the-civil-rights-act/2013/04/10/5b8d91c4-a235-11e2-82bc-511538ae90a4_blog.html.

34. Justin McCarthy, "Americans' Support for Gay Marriage Remains High, at 61%," Gallup, May 19, 2016, http://www.gallup.com/poll/191645/americans-support-gay-marriage-remains-high.aspx; *Obergefell v. Hodges*, 576 US _____ (2015), https://www.supremecourt.gov/opinions/14pdf/14-556_3204.pdf.

35. *Fisher v. University of Texas*, 579 U.S. ____ (2016), https://www.supremecourt
.gov/opinions/15pdf/14-981_4g15.pdf.

36. Eugene Scott, "Trump Hits Scalia Over Comments on Black Students," CNN,
December 13, 2015, http://www.cnn.com/2015/12/13/politics/donald-trump-antonin
-scalia-affirmative-action.

37. Chris Cillizza, "Donald Trump on 'Meet the Press,' Annotated," *Washington Post*,
August 17, 2015, https://www.washingtonpost.com/news/the-fix/wp/2015/08/17/donald
-trump-on-meet-the-press-annotated/?utm_term = .af57eff6a2d6.

38. Charles R. Kesler, *I am the Change: Barack Obama and the Crisis of Liberalism*
(New York: Broadside Books, 2012), xiv.

39. John J. Pitney Jr., "Trump on the Declaration: 'It's Not True,'" *Epic Journey*,
September 22, 2016, http://www.epicjourney2008.com/2016/09/trump-v-declaration-of
-independence.html.

40. Greg Sargent, "Trump's Revealing Quote about 'American Exceptionalism,'"
Washington Post, June 7, 2016, https://www.washingtonpost.com/blogs/plum-line/wp/
2016/06/07/donald-trumps-revealing-quote-about-american-exceptionalism/.

41. See, for instance, Harry V. Jaffa, *American Conservatism and the American
Founding* (Durham, NC: North Carolina Academic Press, 1984).

42. Veronica Stracqualursi, "The Note: Trump Takes on GOP Establishment," ABC
News, May 9, 2016, http://abcnews.go.com/Politics/note-trump-takes-gop-establishment/
story?id = 38977148.

43. James Hohmann, "Trump's Pollster Says He Ran a 'Post-Ideological' Campaign,"
Washington Post, December 5, 2016, https://www.washingtonpost.com/news/powerpost/
paloma/daily-202/2016/12/05/daily-202-trump-s-pollster-says-he-ran-a-post-ideological
-campaign/5844d166e9b69b7e58e45f2a/?utm_term = .4ed145a6545f.

44. Ronald Kessler, "Donald Trump: Mean-Spirited GOP Won't Win Elections,"
NewsMax, November 26, 2012, http://www.newsmax.com/Newsfront/Donald-Trump
-Ronald-Kessler/2012/11/26/id/465363.

45. Yuval Levin, "The New Republican Coalition," *National Review*, November 17,
2016, http://www.nationalreview.com/article/442238/republican-party-after-trump-new
-coalition-will-be-more-populist-nationalist.

46. Nicholas Lemann, "The Smart Club Comes to the White House," *New York Times*,
November 29, 1992, http://www.nytimes.com/1992/11/29/opinion/the-smart-club-comes
-to-the-white-house.html.

47. Data on educational attainment come from U.S. Census Bureau, "Percent of People 25 Years and Over Who Have Completed High School or College, by Race, Hispanic
Origin and Sex: Selected Years 1940 to 2015," March 2016, https://www.census.gov/hhes/
socdemo/education/data/cps/historical/tabA-2.xlsx.

48. Charles Murray, *Coming Apart: The State of White America, 1960–2010* (New
York: Crown Forum, 2012), 52–61.

49. U.S. Bureau of Economic Analysis, Real Gross Domestic Product Per Capita
[A939RX0Q048SBEA], retrieved from FRED, Federal Reserve Bank of St. Louis,
November 21, 2016, https://fred.stlouisfed.org/series/A939RX0Q048SBEA.

50. U.S. Bureau of Labor Statistics, Labor Force Statistics from the Current Population Survey, series LNU04000000, November 21, 2016, http://data.bls.gov/pdq/Survey
OutputServlet.

51. Securities and Exchange Commission, Dow Jones Industrial Average, https://www.sec.gov/Archives/edgar/data/357298/000035729801500016/dowjones.html.

52. Pew Research Center, "The State of American Jobs," October 6, 2016, http://www.pewsocialtrends.org/2016/10/06/the-state-of-american-jobs.

53. U.S. Council of Economic Advisers, "The Economic Record of the Obama Administration: Investing in Higher Education," September 2016, https://www.white house.gov/sites/default/files/page/files/20160929_record_higher_education_cea.pdf.

54. U.S. Council of Economic Advisers, "Investing in Higher Education: Benefits, Challenges, and the State of Student Debt," July 2016, https://www.whitehouse.gov/sites/default/files/page/files/20160718_cea_student_debt.pdf.

55. U.S. Congressional Budget Office, "Trends in Family Wealth, 1989 to 2013," August 2016, https://www.cbo.gov/sites/default/files/114th-congress-2015-2016/reports/51846-Family_Wealth.pdf.

56. Alec Tyson, "Economic Recovery Favors the More-Affluent Who Own Stocks," Pew Research Center, May 13, 2013, http://www.pewresearch.org/fact-tank/2013/05/31/stocks-and-the-recovery-majority-of-americans-not-invested-in-the-market.

57. Internet Live Stats, Total Number of Websites, November 25, 2016, http://www.internetlivestats.com/total-number-of-websites.

58. Murray, *Coming Apart*, 43–44.

59. Natalie Kitroeff, "Robots Could Replace 1.7 Million American Truckers in the Next Decade," *Los Angeles Times*, September 25, 2016, http://www.latimes.com/projects/la-fi-automated-trucks-labor-20160924/.

60. Christopher J. O'Leary, Randall W. Eberts, and Brian M. Pittelko, "Effects of NAFTA on US Employment and Policy Responses," OECD Trade Policy Working Papers, No. 131 (2012), http://dx.doi.org/10.1787/5k9ffbqlvk0r-en.

61. U.S. Census Bureau, "America's Foreign Born in the Last 50 Years," July 4, 2016, https://www.census.gov/schools/resources/visualizations/foreign-born.html.

62. Jeffrey S. Passel and D'Vera Cohn, "Overall Number of U.S. Unauthorized Immigrants Holds Steady Since 2009," Pew Research Center, September 20, 2016, http://www.pewhispanic.org/2016/09/20/overall-number-of-u-s-unauthorized-immigrants-holds-steady-since-2009.

63. Robert P. Jones et al., "How Immigration and Concerns About Cultural Changes Are Shaping the 2016 Election: Findings from the 2016 PRRI/Brookings Immigration Survey," Public Religion Research Institute, June 23, 2016, http://www.prri.org/wp-content/uploads/2016/06/PRRI-Brookings-2016-Immigration-survey-report.pdf.

64. Jason DeParle and Sabrina Tavernise, "For Women Under 30, Most Births Occur Outside Marriage," *New York Times*, February 17, 2013, http://www.nytimes.com/2012/02/18/us/for-women-under-30-most-births-occur-outside-marriage.html.

65. Pew Research Center, "Parenting in America," December 17, 2015, http://www.pewsocialtrends.org/files/2015/12/2015-12-17_parenting-in-america_FINAL.pdf.

66. Anne Case and Angus Deaton, "Rising Morbidity and Mortality in Midlife Among White Non-Hispanic Americans in the 21st Century," *Proceedings of the National Academy of Sciences*, 112, no. 49 (December 8, 2015), http://www.pnas.org/content/112/49/15078.full.pdf.

67. Gina Kolata and Sarah Cohen, "Drug Overdoses Propel Rise in Mortality Rates of Young Whites," *New York Times*, January 16, 2016, http://www.nytimes.com/2016/01/17/science/drug-overdoses-propel-rise-in-mortality-rates-of-young-whites.html.

68. Robert P. Jones, Daniel Cox, Betsy Cooper, and Rachel Lienesch, "The Divide Over America's Future: 1950 or 2050? Findings from the 2016 American Values Survey," Public Religion Research Institute, October 25, 2016, http://www.prri.org/wp-content/uploads/2016/10/PRRI-2016-American-Values-Survey.pdf.

69. Andrew J. Cherlin, "Why Are White Death Rates Rising?" *New York Times*, February 22, 2016, http://www.nytimes.com/2016/02/22/opinion/why-are-white-death-rates-rising.html.

70. Eduardo Porter, "Where Were Trump's Votes? Where the Jobs Weren't," *New York Times*, December 13, 2006, http://www.nytimes.com/2016/12/13/business/economy/jobs-economy-voters.html.

71. Jones, "How Immigration and Concerns About Cultural Changes Are Shaping the 2016 Election."

72. Murray, *Coming Apart*, 61–68.

73. Darren Walker, "Internships Are Not a Privilege," *New York Times*, July 5, 2016, http://www.nytimes.com/2016/07/05/opinion/breaking-a-cycle-that-allows-privilege-to-go-to-privileged.html.

74. Lauren A. Rivera, *Pedigree: How Elite Students Get Elite Jobs* (Princeton, NJ: Princeton University Press, 2015), 99.

75. Ibid.

76. Ibid.

77. Charles Murray, "Trump's America," *Wall Street Journal*, February 12, 2016, http://www.wsj.com/articles/donald-trumps-america-1455290458.

78. Joan C. Williams, "What So Many People Don't Get About the U.S. Working Class," *Harvard Business Review*, November 10, 2016, https://hbr.org/2016/11/what-so-many-people-dont-get-about-the-u-s-working-class.

79. U.S. Bureau of Labor Statistics, Union Affiliation of Employed Wage and Salary Workers by Occupation and Industry, January 28, 2016, http://www.bls.gov/news.release/union2.t03.htm.

80. Alec MacGillis, "Go Midwest, Young Hipster," *New York Times Magazine*, October 22, 2016, http://www.nytimes.com/2016/10/23/opinion/campaign-stops/go-midwest-young-hipster.html.

81. Four were in northern Virginia: Falls Church City, Loudon County, Fairfax County, Arlington County. One was in Maryland: Howard County. See U.S. Census Bureau, "Median Household Income: Counties in the United States," December 9, 2015, http://www.census.gov/did/www/saipe/data/highlights/files/releasesummary_county2014.xls.

82. Economic Innovation Group, "The New Map of Economic Growth and Recovery," May 2016, http://eig.org/wp-content/uploads/2016/05/recoverygrowthreport.pdf.

83. Alyssa Davis, "In U.S., Concern about Crime Climbs to 15-Year High," Gallup, April 6, 2016, http://www.gallup.com/poll/190475/americans-concern-crime-climbs-year-high.aspx.

84. U.S. Federal Bureau of Investigation, Crime in the United States: Violent Crime, September 26, 2016, https://ucr.fbi.gov/crime-in-the-u.s/2015/crime-in-the-u.s.-2015/offenses-known-to-law-enforcement/violent-crime.

85. Jeff Greenfield, "Trump Is Pat Buchanan with Better Timing," *Politico*, September/October 2016, http://www.politico.com/magazine/story/2016/09/donald-trump-pat-buchanan-republican-america-first-nativist-214221.

86. Jessica Taylor, "Obama Says Trump 'Exploiting' Anger, Fear Among 'Blue-Collar Men,'" National Public Radio, December 21, 2015, http://www.npr.org/2015/12/21/460281546/watch-obama-says-trump-exploiting-anger-fear-among-blue-collar-men.

87. Patrick J. Egan, "Ashton Carter and the Astoundingly Elite Educational Credentials of Obama's Cabinet Appointees," *Washington Post*, December 5, 2014, https://www.washingtonpost.com/news/monkey-cage/wp/2014/12/05/ashton-carter-and-the-astoundingly-elite-educational-credentials-of-obamas-cabinet-appointees/.

88. Mayhill Fowler, "Obama: No Surprise That Hard-Pressed Pennsylvanians Turn Bitter," *Huffington Post*, May 25, 2011, http://www.huffingtonpost.com/mayhill-fowler/obama-no-surprise-that-ha_b_9 6188.html.

89. Michael D. Shear and Dave Philipps, "Progress Is Slow at V.A. Hospitals in Wake of Crisis," *New York Times*, March 13, 2015, http://www.nytimes.com/2015/03/14/us/obama-va-hospital-phoenix.html.

90. Lee Fang, "Where Have All the Lobbyists Gone?" *The Nation*, February 19, 2014, https://www.thenation.com/article/shadow-lobbying-complex/. For a list, see "Obama Officials Who Have Spun through the Revolving Door," n.d., https://www.opensecrets.org/obama/rev.php.

91. Thomas Frank, "The Life of the Parties," Tomdispatch, June 30, 2016, http://www.tomdispatch.com/blog/176159.

92. Robert P. Jones, Daniel Cox, Juhem Navarro-Rivera, "What Motivated Voters During the 2014 Midterm Elections?" Public Religion Research Institute, November 11, 2014, http://www.prri.org/research/survey-2014-post-election-american-values-survey-what-motivated-voters-during-the-midterm-elections/.

93. Ceaser and Busch, *Upside Down and Inside Out*, 115. See also Gwen Ifill, "Clinton Goes Eye to Eye with MTV Generation," *New York Times*, June 17, 1992, http://www.nytimes.com/1992/06/17/us/the-1992-campaign-youth-vote-clinton-goes-eye-to-eye-with-mtv-generation.html.

94. Ceaser and Busch, *Upside Down and Inside Out*, 115.

95. U.S. Bureau of Labor Statistics, "Employment Trends in Newspaper Publishing and Other Media, 1990–2016," June 2, 2016, http://www.bls.gov/opub/ted/2016/employment-trends-in-newspaper-publishing-and-other-media-1990–2016.htm.

96. Emily Guskin, Mark Jurkowitz, and Amy Mitchell, "Network News: A Year of Change and Challenge at NBC," State of the Media, March 18, 2013, http://www.stateofthemedia.org/2013/network-news-a-year-of-change-and-challenge-at-nbc.

97. Dolf Zillmann, Jennings Bryant, and Aletha C. Huston, eds., *Media, Children and the Family: Social Scientific, Psychodynamic, and Clinical Perspectives* (Hillsdale, NJ: Erlbaum, 1994), 28.

98. The Nielsen Total Audience Report, Q2: 2016, September 26, 2016, http://www.nielsen.com/us/en/insights/reports/2016/the-nielsen-total-audience-report-q2–2016.html.

99. Tabitha Soren, "Hillary Clinton and the Ghosts of MTV," *New York Times*, August 21, 2016, http://www.nytimes.com/2016/08/21/opinion/campaign-stops/hillary-clinton-and-the-ghosts-of-mtv.html.

100. For an early analysis of the political Internet, see John J. Pitney Jr., "Tangled Web," *Reason*, April 1996, http://reason.com/archives/1996/04/01/tangled-web.

101. Cornelia Grumman, "Dole Error Hurts Web Site Plug," *Chicago Tribune*, October 8, 1996, http://articles.chicagotribune.com/1996-10-08/news/9610080226_1_bob-dole-dole-spokeswoman-dole-fruit.

102. Amy Mitchell, Jeffrey Gottfried, Michael Barthel, and Elisa Shearer, "The Modern News Consumer," Pew Research Center, July 7, 2016, http://www.journalism.org/2016/07/07/the-modern-news-consumer.

103. Art Swift, "Americans' Trust in Mass Media Sinks to New Low," Gallup, September 14, 2016, http://www.gallup.com/poll/195542/americans-trust-mass-media-sinks-new-low.aspx.

104. The issue became the basis for a book by William F. Buckley Jr., which Nathan Glazer discussed in "The Enmity Within," *New York Times*, September 27, 1992, https://www.nytimes.com/books/00/07/16/specials/buckley-anti.html.

105. "Against Trump," *National Review*, January 21, 2016, http://www.nationalreview.com/article/430137/donald-trump-conservative-movement-menace.

106. Greenfield, "Trump Is Pat Buchanan With Better Timing."

107. Gil Troy, "The Bernie Sanders–Fueled Alt-Left Viciously Attacked Me," *Time*, December 7, 2016, http://time.com/4593753/bernie-sanders-alt-left/.

108. Amy Mitchell, Jeffrey Gottfried, Jocelyn Kiley, and Katerina Eva Matsa, "Political Polarization & Media Habits," Pew Research Center, October 21, 2014, http://www.journalism.org/2014/10/21/political-polarization-media-habits.

109. Dan Cassino, "Fairleigh Dickinson Poll Shows 90 Percent of Trump and Clinton Supporters Believe in Conspiracies That Smear the Candidate They Oppose," Fairleigh Dickinson University, October 11, 2016, http://view2.fdu.edu/publicmind/2016/161011.

110. Marty Cohen, David Karol, Hans Noel, and John Zaller, *The Party Decides: Presidential Nominations Before and After Reform* (Chicago: University of Chicago Press, 2008), 5.

111. Pew Research Center, "GOP's Favorability Rating Edges Lower," April 28, 2016, http://www.people-press.org/2016/04/28/gops-favorability-rating-edges-lower.

112. Oliver Darcy and Pamela Engel, "The GOP Must Do Something About the Conservative Media Industrial Complex If It Wants to Survive," *Business Insider*, October 24, 2016, http://www.businessinsider.com/trump-conservative-media-hannity-limbaugh-drudge-2016-10.

Chapter Two

From Little Rock to Chappaqua

The Democratic Nomination Contest

In 1992, the Democratic Party nominated forty-five-year-old Bill Clinton of Little Rock, Arkansas. In 2016, it nominated sixty-eight-year-old Hillary Clinton of Chappaqua, New York. The nominees were different in important ways, and so was the party that they led. Before we examine her road to the nomination, we need to take a brief look at his.

BUBBA'S LOST WORLD

As *Upside Down and Inside Out* explained, Bill Clinton was the most conservative Democratic nominee since Jimmy Carter in 1976. His nomination was a triumph for the Democratic Leadership Council (DLC), a group founded by political operative Al From to encourage the party to adopt moderate positions. DLC members eyed Clinton as a possible champion in the 1988 nomination contest, but he opted out of the race. The nomination instead went to Governor Michael Dukakis of Massachusetts. Although the campaign of George H. W. Bush would paint him as a hardcore liberal, he tried to run as a non-ideological technocrat, emphasizing his record of getting poor people into gainful employment. "In many ways," wrote DLC's Al From, "he was the candidate of a party that had begun but not completed a transition. Dukakis sent the message that, unlike Mondale, he was not an interest-group liberal, but he never really told the voters who he was."[1] Bush's victory was a sobering moment for Democrats. No incumbent vice president had won a presidential election since Martin Van Buren. Only a year before, in the wake of the 1987 stock market crash and the Iran-Contra scandal, Bush had looked like a goner. If Democrats could not beat such a vulnerable candidate, many of them reasoned, they must be doing something wrong.

Concern about electability provided an opening for Bill Clinton, who had a record of winning moderate and conservative voters as governor of Arkansas. Despite his education at Georgetown, Oxford, and Yale, he had a cultural affinity for his fellow Southerners—hence his nickname of "Bubba." In 1989, he accepted From's offer to chair the DLC, which provided him with a travel budget and enhanced visibility.[2] Clinton ran for the 1992 nomination, benefiting from his position in the middle of the inside-outside axis. He lacked the insider liabilities of Washington-based candidates; yet his "outsiderism" was temperate enough for political leaders and campaign contributors.[3] The nomination calendar was another asset. "Super Tuesday" was the label coined in 1984 for a day on which multiple states, including several in the South, held primaries. In 1992, Super Tuesday worked as DLC had planned. Clinton had a base of lower-income working-class whites and got enough African American support to sweep the South.[4]

Clinton belonged to the "New South" generation of Democratic politicians who combined moderate-to-conservative positions on most issues with support for civil rights. In Arkansas, he had always enjoyed a strong relationship with African American voters, which gave him some flexibility. During the campaign, he criticized rap artist Sister Souljah, who made comments in an interview that appeared to endorse the killing of white people. (She said that Clinton had taken her words out of context.) When Jesse Jackson took exception, Clinton said that he would "not back down on what I said."[5] The episode strained his relationship with black leaders but did not break it. On the other hand, it reassured moderate white voters that he was not a captive of identity politics.

Disregarding the conventional wisdom that a running mate should provide regional and ideological balance, Clinton picked Al Gore, a fellow DLC politician who came from an adjoining state. And like Clinton, the 44-year-old Gore was a baby boomer. By choosing him, Clinton was sending a message that the Democratic Party was setting its 1980s ways aside, opening its doors to Southerners and moderates, and embracing youth. Soon after the convention, a TV spot drove the point home:

> They are a new generation of Democrats, Bill Clinton and Al Gore, and they don't think the way the old Democratic Party did. They've called for an end to welfare as we know it, so welfare can be a second chance, not a way of life. They've sent a strong signal to criminals by supporting the death penalty. And they've rejected the old tax and spend politics. Clinton's balanced 12 budgets and they've proposed a new plan investing in people, detailing $140 billion in spending cuts they'd make right now.[6]

It is common to dismiss campaign ads as fluff, but in important ways, this message did foreshadow Clinton-Gore policies. "End welfare as we know it" was a term of art, vague enough to encompass anything from modest reform to abolition. In the end, Clinton signed legislation that replaced the old federal welfare program with one that imposed work requirements and limited how long recipients could receive benefits. Congressional Democrats split over the issue, but the bill passed with overwhelming GOP support.[7]

Crime had long been a vulnerable point for Democrats. From the 1960s to the mid-1990s, the United States suffered historically high levels of crime.[8] (In 1992, the rate of reported violent crime was *more than four times higher* than it had been in 1962.[9]) Fear of crime had helped the Nixon and Wallace campaigns of 1968, and twenty years later, the Bush campaign used the issue against Dukakis by accusing him of letting murderers out on furlough. Clinton was determined not to be the crime issue's next victim. As president, he signed a far-reaching crime bill that funded thousands of police officers, expanded the federal death penalty, banned certain firearms, and mandated life sentences for many repeat offenders.

On economic issues, he did open his party to GOP attacks by pushing for a tax increase in 1993. But by his second term, the tax hike had combined with spending restraint and economic growth to produce budget surpluses. He worked with the GOP to pass NAFTA and even held secret talks with Gingrich on Social Security reform.[10] But before the talks could produce a legislative proposal, the Lewinsky scandal broke open. It would preoccupy Washington for months, and it ruined any chance for bipartisan cooperation on further domestic reform.

Clinton survived the scandal because Americans believed that his offense—lying about sexual misconduct—did not rise to the level of impeachment. But they did not think that the Clinton household was entirely clean.[11] Throughout his administration, there had been stories about questionable ethics, some centering on Hillary Clinton. During his governorship of Arkansas, for example, she had gotten a sweetheart deal in cattle futures through a lawyer for Tyson Foods, a key interest group in the state. "It's one of those things somebody gets put into a good thing," one legal expert told *Newsweek*. "It's harmless, but it doesn't look wonderful, does it?"[12] Such incidents took their toll. Even before the couple left the White House, "Clinton fatigue" was showing up in surveys.

In foreign policy, he signed legislation committing the nation to the removal of Saddam Hussein and the establishment of democracy in Iraq.[13] After Saddam stopped cooperating with nuclear inspectors in 1998, Clinton ordered air strikes. "If Saddam defies the world and we fail to respond, we will face a far greater threat in the future," he said. "Saddam will strike again at his neighbors. He will make war on his own people. And mark my words, he will develop weapons of mass destruction."[14]

Despite his troubles, Clinton ended his tenure with a good approval rating.[15] So suppose a time traveler had gone back to January 1, 1992, and told political commentators that the winner of that year's election would eventually boast of a balanced budget, welfare reform, tough crime legislation, and NAFTA. Moreover, the winner would also try to reform Social Security and oust Saddam Hussein. Most who heard the time traveler would have said, "Whoa, Bush is going to win this thing after all!" In many ways, Clinton overcame the legacy of Democratic defeats by preempting Republican issues. During the 1990s, commentators held that Clintonism would be the way of the Democratic future.

The Clintons themselves would continue to be major figures in the Democratic Party throughout the first 16 years of the next century. But Clintonism —or at least the version that America saw between 1992 and 2000—would go into decline. In fact, it would prove to be a burden for the Clinton who now carried the torch.

BACK AND TO THE LEFT

Health care was one issue on which Clinton's needle-threading failed badly. Many Democratic thinkers wanted to follow the Canadian example and move the United States toward a single-payer system. Clinton spurned that approach, instead opting for a system of mandates and subsidies, drawing on a proposal that Richard Nixon had offered nearly twenty years before. As head of the president's health care task force, Hillary Clinton supervised the drafting of the plan in 1993. As a brilliant policy maven, she understood the details, but practically no one else did. Clintoncare's complexity and cost proved to be drawbacks, and it died before reaching a vote on the floor of either chamber. Together with the 1993 tax hike, the health care plan wounded the Democrats on the domestic front.

Republicans were overdue for a victory. Population shifts had created many potentially winnable seats in the South and West, but the party had been unable to exploit the opportunity. It is very difficult for a party to gain downballot ground while holding the presidency, and Republicans had been in the White House between 1980 and 1992.[16] Now, with Democrats in control of the political branches in Washington, along with most governorships and state legislatures, Republicans could go on the offensive. Another political asset was the Voting Rights Act. By encouraging the creation of majority-minority districts, the law had the side effect of making the surrounding districts whiter and thus more Republican.[17]

In 1994, the GOP swept to majorities in both chambers of Congress for the first time since 1952, and it scored gains in statehouses as well. In the House, very conservative Republicans replaced fairly conservative white Democrats from Southern and border states. With fewer conservatives in Democratic ranks, the party's center of gravity started to shift leftward, and many congressional Democrats took a dim view of Clinton's bargains with the GOP majority. In 1996, they noticed that Clinton won a comfortable reelection while they languished in the minority. They concluded that Clintonism was good for Clinton, but not for the Democratic Party. When they rallied to his side during the impeachment controversy, their motivation was less about support for the president than anger at the Republicans.[18]

The 2000 Democratic nominee was Al Gore, who had grown more liberal since his DLC days. In the fall, he lost every state of the Old Confederacy— the first time such a thing had ever happened to a Democratic nominee from the South. The party did fight the GOP to a draw in the Senate, and its most prominent victor was Hillary Rodham Clinton. After Senator Daniel Patrick Moynihan of New York announced his retirement, she ran for his seat even though she had never lived in the state. The Clintons bought a large house in Chappaqua, an upper-class community in Westchester County, and she commenced a "listening tour." Republicans had high hopes for their candidate, Representative Rick Lazio, but she easily dispatched him.

The Clintons' move to New York State would reshape their political lives. Whereas she had once been First Lady of a conservative Southern state, she was now a U.S. senator representing a liberal Northern state. During the next eight years, she built a liberal voting record that would have been toxic in Little Rock but was popular in Manhattan.[19] The job also tightened her ties to the financial community. Several days after the attacks of September 11, 2001, the New York Stock Exchange held a ceremonial reopening, and she was on the dais. Meanwhile, Bill Clinton had headquartered the Clinton Foundation in the city, where he raised money from rich people.

Her most fateful decision in the Senate was her 2002 vote to approve the invasion of Iraq. Explaining her position, she recalled presidential action that she had seen up close: "When Saddam blocked the inspection process, the inspectors left. As a result, President Clinton, with the British and others, ordered an intensive four-day air assault," she said. "In 1998, the United States also changed its underlying policy toward Iraq from containment to regime change."[20] Soon, the American presence in Iraq would take a bad turn, and she would regret that vote.

In 2004, she decided not to run against Bush. The nomination instead went, as it had in 1988, to a Massachusetts liberal. John Kerry had been in the Senate since 1984, and before that, he had briefly served as lieutenant governor under Michael Dukakis. Trying to re-create the old Democratic coalition, Kerry chose a running mate from South Carolina, Senator John Edwards. The choice did not work. As they had four years earlier, Democrats failed to carry a single Southern state. At the national level, Kerry lost the electoral and popular vote by small margins, and after the election, Democrats concluded that Bush and the Republicans had outclassed them in organization and technology.[21]

The left regrouped. Wealthy liberals formed the Democracy Alliance, a network designed to coordinate contributions to progressive groups. Middle-class liberals found one another through an ever-expanding set of Internet sites such as MoveOn.org. Reporter Matt Bai observed, "What MoveOn had done, along with popular leftist blogs like Daily Kos and MyDD, was to establish a virtual clubhouse for like-minded liberals clustered in hostile places."[22] This clubhouse took on a militant air. "The conservatives have declared war on liberalism, and we have been treating it like we can appeal to people on the basis of reason," said Markos Moulitsas Zuniga (a.k.a. "Kos," founder of the eponymous website). "We need to be down and dirty and absolutely tear them apart." He explained the site's purpose: "I look at this as [training] armies. It's training our troops how to fight rhetorically."[23]

In 2004 former Vermont governor Howard Dean had tried to mobilize liberals online. Although he raised a surprising amount of money, he was an inept candidate. Looking ahead to 2008, liberals were looking for a new standard-bearer, and Hillary Clinton would have a hard time convincing them that she was that candidate. When Bill Clinton spoke to Democracy Alliance donors in 2006, one member challenged him on Hillary Clinton's Iraq vote. His answer betrayed his anger and frustration: "You're just wrong. Everything you just said is totally wrong. Wrong, wrong, wrong. . . . Only in this party do we eat our own. You can go on misrepresenting and bashing our people, but I am sick and tired of it."[24]

After Democrats won House and Senate majorities in the 2006 midterm election, presidential candidates came forward with high hopes about regaining the White House. Clinton was the early favorite, but there was also buzz about John Edwards. The third candidate, Senator Barack Obama of Illinois, seemed to be a long shot. He was a freshman senator who had achieved national prominence only because Kerry had chosen him to keynote the 2004 Democratic convention. In *Epic Journey*, we told how Obama went from an improbability to a contender, and then to the forty-fourth president. We need not retell that story here. What matters for present purposes is that his tenure represented an important chapter in the transformation of the Democratic Party.

Time magazine, on the cover of its 2008 post-election edition, superimposed Barack Obama's head onto a photo of Franklin Roosevelt. A general assumption was that Obama, like FDR, would usher in an age of Democratic dominance. Columnist Harold Meyerson said that Obama's victory "inspires that sense of awe that comes when we realize we are in the presence of a momentous historical transformation." The American political future, he continued, "belongs to Barack Obama's Democrats."[25]

Not quite. His signature health care reform legislation proved to be unpopular, and although the economy eventually crawled out of the Great Recession, progress was slow. In the 2010 midterm election, Republicans won back the House, and just as important, scored gains in state legislatures just in time for the decennial redistricting. Obama did get a second term in 2012—with an asterisk. As we explained in *After Hope and Change*, he made history by winning reelection while losing vote share. Previous incumbents had either increased their electoral strength from their first election (e.g., Reagan in 1984, Clinton in 1996, G. W. Bush in 2004) or lost their bid for another four years (Carter in 1980, G. H. W. Bush in 1992). Obama broke this pattern, squeaking through but in a weaker position than before. Two years after that, Republicans won the Senate and strengthened their hold on the House and the legislatures.

President Obama failed to achieve the general electoral realignment that many had expected after 2008, but his time in office coincided with an ideological realignment within his own party. Liberals or progressives were now in the lead. At least in part, this result was a matter of subtraction. Among officeholders, advocates of rival positions—"New Democrats," "blue dogs," pro-lifers—had largely disappeared through either retirement or defeat at the polls. A symbolically significant turning point came in 2011, when the Democratic Leadership Council ran out of money and closed its doors. Many progressive Democrats were still angry at DLC's efforts to compromise with Republicans during the Clinton and Bush years. "One of the things that's happening right now in Democratic politics is that progressives are winning the battle for the party," said Darcy Burner, president of a liberal group called the Progressive Congress. "The corporate-focused DLC type of politics isn't working inside the Democratic party."[26]

Political scientists will long debate whether the increasingly leftward tilt of Democratic politicians was a cause or a consequence of an ideological shift among Democratic voters. There is little doubt, however, that such a shift did occur. In 2000, Bill Clinton's last year in office, 44 percent of Democrats told Gallup that they identified as moderates, compared with 29 percent as liberals, and 25 percent as conservatives. By 2015, moderates were down to 35 percent and conservatives to 17 percent. Liberals had become the dominant group, with 45 percent.[27]

One might argue that the meanings of "liberal" and "conservative" are fuzzy to many voters, but the Pew Research Center found a similar pattern by looking at responses to questions about political values. Both parties have become more ideologically consistent, Democrats moving to the left and Republicans moving to the right, with less common ground in between. In 1994, 64 percent of Republicans were to the right of the median Democrat. Twenty years later, that figure was 92 percent. In 2014, 94 percent of Democrats were to the left of the median Republican, up from 70 percent in 1994.[28]

The demographic composition of the party had changed. Between 1992 and 2016, the percentage of Democrats and Democratic-leaning independents under age 30 ticked up from 18 percent to 20 percent. Meanwhile, the figure for the GOP dropped from 21 percent to 13 percent, meaning that younger Democrats would have proportionately more sway in their party than their Republican counterparts. Not surprisingly, African Americans, Hispanics, and college graduates added up to a much larger share of the Democratic Party in 2016 than they had in 1992. As mentioned before, Bill Clinton's first nomination campaign depended on a core of working-class whites. It was a smart strategy at the time, since whites without a college degree made up 59 percent of Democrats and Democratic-leaning independents. By 2016, however, this category had shrunk to 32 percent.[29]

It is hard to overstate the significance of that last figure. Working-class whites in both the North and the South had been a mainstay of the Democratic Party at least since FDR. Now the party was more a coalition of people of color and college-educated whites. Furthermore, the latter group was becoming even better educated: greater numbers of college graduates were going on to graduate or professional school, and people with such education

Table 2.1. Democratic Demographics, 1992 and 2016

	1992	2016
White	76	57
Hispanic	06	12
African American	17	21
Under age 30	18	20
College graduates	21	37
Non-college white	59	32

Source: Carroll Doherty et al., "The Parties on the Eve of the 2016 Election: Two Coalitions, Moving Further Apart," Pew Research Center, September 13, 2016, http://www.people-press.org/2016/09/13/1-the-changing-composition-of-the-political-parties/.

were leaning more heavily Democratic. In 1992, people with postgraduate education were evenly split, with 47 percent identifying or leaning Democratic, and 46 percent Republican. In 2014, Democrats had a 56–36 percent lead.[30] This group was quite progressive. Pew found that 54 percent of people with postgraduate experience had consistently or mostly liberal values, compared with 44 percent of those with a bachelor's degree only, 38 percent of those with some college, and 26 percent of those with a high school diploma or less.[31]

The numbers would vary from state to state, of course, but the national data pointed in a clear direction: the Democrats were a party of ethnic diversity and political liberalism, especially on social issues. Writing on the eve of Obama's reelection, liberal columnist Joe Klein offered words of caution:

> The Democrats have a serious problem. It is a problem that stems from the party's greatest strength: its long-term support for inclusion and equal rights for all, its support of racial integration and equal rights for women and homosexuals and its humane stand on immigration reform. Those heroic positions, which I celebrate, cost the Democrats more than a few elections in the past. And they caused an understandable, if misguided, overreaction within the party—a drift toward identity politics, toward special pleading. Inclusion became exclusive. The Democratic National Committee officially recognizes 14 caucuses or "communities," most having to do with race, gender, sexual orientation or ethnicity.[32]

In 2016, candidates would face rigorous tests of loyalty to this orthodoxy. When it came to the Democratic presidential nomination, no Bubbas need apply.

THE BENCH

Each party's bench of potential presidential candidates has usually consisted of people who have served as governor, senator, or House member. The Democrats had a problem here, because the Obama years had left them in their weakest downballot position since the 1920s.[33] As the presidential campaign got under way in 2015, they held thirteen fewer Senate seats, sixty-nine fewer House seats, and eleven fewer governorships than they had when he took office.[34] As we shall see in the chapter on congressional and state elections, this weakness fed on itself, as it hobbled the party in recruitment and redistricting.

Among the biggest states, Republicans held the governorships of Texas, Florida, Ohio, Illinois, Michigan, Georgia, and North Carolina. Democrat Tom Wolf was governor of Pennsylvania, but he had just won his first term in 2014 and was unknown elsewhere. One of the Democratic Party's remaining big-state governors was literally a name from the past. In 1975, Jerry Brown of California had been the nation's youngest governor at the age of thirty-six. After losing a 1982 Senate race, he made a run for the presidency (his third) in 1992. He later reentered office as the mayor of Oakland and attorney general of California. He regained the governorship in 2010 and easily won reelection four years later. (In 1990, state voters had put a two-term limit on the governor, but it was not retroactive.) In 2015, forty years after starting his first term, he was the nation's oldest governor at age seventy-seven. There was some whimsical talk of his making a run, but Brown never took it seriously. The California political community saw him as a wise and prudent elder statesman—a stark difference from his 1970s "Governor Moonbeam" persona—while people east of the Sierra Madre Mountains had lost interest in him decades ago. He seldom got a glance from a national press corps that had lavished attention on his immediate predecessor, Arnold Schwarzenegger.

On the other side of the country was Governor Andrew Cuomo of New York. His father, Mario Cuomo, served three terms as governor and seriously considered a 1992 run but bailed out just hours before the filing deadline of the New Hampshire primary. Twenty-four years later, the younger Cuomo could not even contemplate a race as long as Hillary Clinton remained the favorite daughter of the state's Democrats. In any case, the pervasive sleaze of New York government would have been a stumbling block for him. The leaders of both chambers of the state legislature had left office after felony convictions. In 2016, several members of Cuomo's inner circle would face indictment on federal corruption charges.[35]

In the past, congressional leaders had been serious presidential contenders. Lyndon Johnson (1960) and Bob Dole (1996) were Senate majority leaders. In 1988, Democrat Richard Gephardt and Republican Jack Kemp were both chairs of their party caucuses in the House. In the run-up to the 2016 election, Capitol Hill did not look like the mother of presidents. The top three Democrats in the House—Nancy Pelosi, Steny Hoyer, and James Clyburn—were all deep into their seventies. Of the three, only Pelosi had made any impression on the national public, and it was a bad one.[36] On the Senate side, minority leader Harry Reid of Nevada was retiring. Not only was he another septuagenarian, but a household accident had also blinded his right eye. The other top Senate Democrats, Charles Schumer of New York and Richard Durbin of Illinois, were also in their seventies, and they were largely unknown outside Washington and their home states.

Beyond the leadership circle, Elizabeth Warren of Massachusetts drew interest from liberals. She was a fiery orator with credentials as a Harvard law professor and a consumer financial advocate in the Obama administration. She never got in the race, however, focusing instead on her Senate duties.

Since Richard Nixon's race in 1960, the vice presidency has often had the preferred spot on the bench. Joseph Biden, President Obama's vice president, did have a history of presidential ambition. His bid for the 1988 nomination ended after revelations that he had misstated his academic credentials and plagiarized a speech by the British Labour Party leader. He ran again in 2008 but withdrew after getting only 1 percent of the vote in the Iowa caucuses. Despite his poor showing, Democrats liked him, and President Obama picked him as a running mate because his sunny personality and appeal to working-class voters could help the Democratic ticket.

Biden thought about a 2016 run, but the untimely death of his son Beau devastated him. He grieved for months, unready to enter the race. In October 2015, he announced that it was too late to start a campaign, and that he would not run at all. Many Democrats later wondered whether he could have won the nomination and beaten Trump. We will never know, but there are reasonable arguments on both sides. On the one hand, he had decades of experience, deep knowledge of the issues, and reasonably strong favorability ratings with the public.[37] On the other hand, he looked like a terrific candidate only as long as he was not running. In the early days of his ill-fated 2008 nomination race, he boasted of his state's diversity: "You cannot go to a 7-Eleven or a Dunkin' Donuts unless you have a slight Indian accent. I'm not joking."[38] Once he was on the ticket, his gaffes annoyed Obama, who reportedly said, "How many times is Biden going to say something stupid?"[39] The gregarious Biden's tactile displays of affection sometimes resulted in embarrassing photographs.[40] "Joe is his own worst enemy," former representative Barney Frank (D-MA) said. "He's a very bright guy, very good values. But he just—he can't keep his mouth shut or his hands to himself."[41]

Without Biden in the race, it appeared that there was only one likely nominee.

HRC

For years, the cliché was that Democrats fall in love and Republicans fall in line. While the Democrats had a chaotic primary fight, the thinking went, the GOP would usually turn to the candidate who was "next in line," a runner-up from a previous contest. This description fit Ronald Reagan, George H. W. Bush, Bob Dole, John McCain, and Mitt Romney. In 2016, Republicans blew up the "next in the GOP line" theory by blowing off their 2008 and 2012 runners-up, Mike Huckabee and Rick Santorum. This time, the next-in-line theory applied better to the Democratic side.

Despite her loss to Obama in 2008, Hillary Clinton had come close. At the time that Obama clinched the nomination, Clinton had won a plurality of pledged delegates chosen in primaries.[42] Obama edged her out in the overall tally by winning more caucus delegates and superdelegates. She had made a strategic blunder by assuming that high-profile primary victories would create an unstoppable political momentum. The data-driven Obama campaign had correctly focused on fundraising and delegate arithmetic. She would remember this lesson.

In 2008, she had little time to mourn her defeat, because Obama chose her to be secretary of state. In one sense, the job was a traditional stepping stone to the White House. Thomas Jefferson, James Madison, James Monroe, John Quincy Adams, Martin Van Buren, and James Buchanan had all held the post before becoming president. True, no secretary of state had gone on to the White House since the Civil War, but the office would provide her with a chance to become a player on the world stage and gain high-level administrative experience. The meritocrat from Wellesley College and Yale Law School would gain unquestionable credentials as the "best-qualified" candidate.

By accepting the offer, she tethered her fate to Obama's. If he succeeded in foreign policy, she would share the credit. If he failed, she failed. It initially seemed like a great wager, because within two years, Obama had won the Nobel Peace Prize and ended the American combat mission in Iraq. Over time, the record got murkier. The war in Afghanistan did not really stop, and notwithstanding a drawdown, some U.S. troops would stay there through the last days of his administration. After a much-publicized "reset," relations with Russia remained difficult and eventually worsened. Civil war in Syria and the rise of ISIS roiled the Middle East. A 2012 terror attack on a diplomatic facility in Benghazi, Libya, led to the deaths of four Americans, including Ambassador J. Christopher Stevens. Mitt Romney tried to use the attack against Obama, without success. For Clinton, the Benghazi issue would have a surprising and distressing durability.

By the end of her State Department tenure in 2013, Hillary Clinton had come a long way from Little Rock. In the earlier days, the Clintons were a "two for one blue plate special," a pair of policy wonks who specialized in domestic issues. Now she was the lead Clinton and a foreign policy expert. Back then, they were not too far removed from ordinary life. Arkansas has long underpaid its governors, and even with her legal income, the Clintons were not living in luxury. Since his presidency, however, both had made millions through book sales and high speaking fees. They had befriended economic leaders throughout America and the world, and they had used these connections to fund the Clinton Foundation. Along the way, she grew vulnerable to the charge that she was living in an elite "bubble." When a journalist asked about her riches, she said that she and Bill Clinton had left the White House "dead broke"—a claim that drew scolding from fact-checkers and derisive laughter across the political spectrum.[43] She also acknowledged that she had not driven a car since 1996.[44] It was a small detail, and it was understandable in light of the couple's Secret Service protection. But it was one more thing that undermined her claim that she was in touch with struggling American families.

Another change was so obvious that it was easy to overlook: the sheer passage of time. In the 1992 campaign, the Clintons had run on their youth and energy, and their theme music was "Don't Stop Thinking about Tomorrow." As Hillary Clinton prepared for a 2016 campaign, she was a grandmother in her late sixties. She had earned her wrinkles, but, notwithstanding innuendos from the Trump campaign, there were no serious questions about her health. Other, more vexing problems would stem from the march of the decades. Things that the Clintons had said and done in the 1990s would stick to them, and these things had not aged well.

Her initial support for the Iraq War was, in part, an outgrowth of Bill Clinton's policies in the 1990s. Raising the specter of weapons of mass destruction, he had launched air attacks against Iraq. During the 2008 primary campaign, Obama effectively exploited her pro-war vote. Liberal Democrats had not forgotten about it, and they got another reminder of the issue when Obama sent thousands of American troops back to Iraq, this time to fight ISIS.

Bill Clinton had responded to the high crime rates of the early 1990s by signing a tough crime bill. In 1996, Hillary Clinton defended the bill by highlighting its anti-gang provisions: "They are often the kinds of kids that are called super-predators—no conscience, no empathy. We can talk about why they ended up that way, but first, we have to bring them to heel."[45] Twenty-four years later, many African Americans worried about over-incarceration. In 2016, Black Lives Matter objected to the legacy of the crime bill, as well as the use of terms such as "super-predators." Protesters from the group tried to disrupt one of Bill Clinton's campaign speeches for his wife, and he responded by talking over them loudly. He soon voiced regret for what he had done. "I know those young people yesterday were just trying to get good television," he said. "But that doesn't mean that I was most effective in answering it."[46] Compare that incident with his "Sister Souljah moment" in 1992, when he gained ground by sticking to his criticism of the rapper's inflammatory language. By this time, the issue context had changed, and, just as important, the Democratic electorate had changed.

The scandals stuck, too. In 2015, journalist Jonathan Chait recalled the "Clinton fatigue" of the 1990s: "After an exuberant election swept a young new Democratic president into power in 1992 after a long period of Republican rule, and a somewhat joyless reelection trudge four years later, by the seventh year of the Clinton administration ennui had set in among the base." He noted polling data that Americans had tired of the Clintons' ethics problems. In the years following her tenure at the State Department, there were new stories about foreign donations to the Clinton Foundation and her questionable use of a private email server for official business. Chait continued: "Those narratives feed into long-standing ethical concerns dating from the Clinton administration and the Clinton post-presidency, during which the former president profited immensely from relationships with figures who had a clear interest in currying favor, then or in the future, with his wife."[47]

With the Clintons, the past was never dead. It wasn't even past.

BERNIE

Vermont's Senator Bernie Sanders was five years older than Hillary Clinton, and he looked every day of it. Not only was he an old man from a small state, but he also embraced a label that would have been a lethal epithet a couple of decades earlier. In his book *Our Revolution*, he described his political education at the University of Chicago's library. "It was there that I was first exposed to *The Nation, Monthly Review, The Progressive* magazine, and other progressive publications."[48] There he joined the Young People's Socialist League, and from then on, he always identified himself as a democratic socialist.

If the passage of time was a problem for Clinton, it was an asset for Bernie Sanders. For more than a century, social scientists had been asking why socialism had never taken root in the United States. They had various answers, but one was the anti-communism that heated up after the Second World War. Our foe called itself the Union of Soviet Socialist Republics, so it was natural to assume a link between socialism and communism. The Soviet Union closed for business on Christmas Day 1991, but memories of Soviet communism were still fresh in 1992, and Republican operatives tried to make an issue of Bill Clinton's student trip to Moscow. By 2016, the Cold War was a memory that younger voters did not share. For much of the electorate, socialism had lost its taint and the Great Recession had raised doubts about capitalism. In one survey, 57 percent of Democratic primary voters said that socialism has a "positive impact on society."[49] Granted, the sponsor of this survey was a right-leaning group, but other surveys aligned with the finding. An Iowa poll found that 43 percent of Iowa caucus goers would use the term "socialist" to describe themselves.[50] A Harvard Institute of Politics poll of eighteen- to twenty-nine-year-olds found that 33 percent supported socialism and 42 percent supported capitalism—a plurality, but a narrow one by American standards.[51] "The word 'capitalism' doesn't mean what it used to," said a Harvard senior who had helped conduct the poll, referring to the 2008 global crisis from which the economy had not fully recovered.[52]

Sanders had always been an outsider as well as a socialist. In 1968, he moved to Vermont, bringing his thick Brooklyn accent with him. He worked a variety of jobs, including reporter for several Vermont newspapers, for which he did "man in the street" interviews. "I found that the views of ordinary people, for better or worse, did not necessarily jibe with those of the establishment," he recalled in his book. "I was surprised by the kind of support that George Wallace was generating."[53] In 1972, he ran in a special election for the Senate as the candidate of the small, left-wing Liberty Union Party. He got 2 percent in that election and 1 percent as the party's gubernatorial candidate several months later. After a couple of other losing third-party races statewide, he ran as an independent for mayor of Burlington in 1981. With a margin of just ten votes, he gained some national publicity by becoming the only socialist mayor in the United States. Despite opposition from Republican and Democratic politicians alike, he built a creditable record in city government. He also made attention-getting trips to the Soviet Union, Cuba, and Marxist-controlled Nicaragua.

In 1990, following eight years as mayor and unsuccessful races for governor and Congress, he won a U.S. House seat as an independent. Days after arriving on Capitol Hill, he cast his first important vote, in opposition to the Gulf War. Eleven years later, he voted against the Iraq War, a stand that would serve him well during the nomination contest against Hillary Clinton. He served in the House until 2006, when he won the first of his two terms in the United States Senate. Though he caucused with Democrats in both chambers, he always made a point of running as an independent. By traditional standards, his independent status should have hindered any race for a major-party presidential nomination. But as five-time party switcher Donald Trump showed on the Republican side, voters in the 2016 cycle did not care about the party loyalty of the people who sought to lead their parties.[54] If anything, they saw this distance from the parties as an asset.

On December 10, 2010, Sanders dramatized his independence and captured the imagination of liberals. In opposition to a tax deal between President Obama and Republican congressional leaders, Sanders gave a floor speech that lasted eight and a half hours, the longest in seven years. "The rich get richer," he said. "The middle class shrinks. Not enough, not enough.

The very rich seem to want more and more and more, and they are prepared to dismantle the existing political and social order in order to get it."[55] The speech drew so many viewers that it briefly crashed the Senate video server. It lit up Twitter, spiked the number of pageviews on his Senate website, and immediately doubled his number of Facebook friends. In 2011, Nation Books published the text as a book titled *The Speech*.[56] The old man was a multimedia hit.

Sanders did not challenge President Obama's reelection in 2012. As attention turned to the 2016 race, however, he disliked what he saw. "Did I believe that the same old establishment politics and establishment economics, as represented by Hillary Clinton, could effectively address these crises? No, I didn't." When it was clear that Elizabeth Warren would not run, he asked himself another question: "Was there a better potential progressive candidate out there than me? Probably not."[57]

THE ALSO-RANS

A couple of Democrats might have answered "Me, me!" to Sanders's rhetorical question. Lincoln Chafee of Rhode Island was the son of Republican Senator John Chafee, and upon the elder Chafee's death in 1999, the state's GOP governor appointed him to the seat. He won a full term as a Republican, only to lose a reelection bid in 2006. In 2008, he ran for governor as an independent, and eventually became a Democrat. He had a degree of independence from the party system, but his unusual policy positions (e.g., advocacy of the metric system) and flaky persona—more P. G. Wodehouse than Saul Alinsky—never caught on.

Martin O'Malley, with a liberal record as mayor of Baltimore and governor of Maryland, initially seemed like a more plausible candidate. As he termed out of the governorship in 2014, however, state voters soured on his record and chose a Republican successor. His record in Baltimore was another problem. The classic television series *The Wire*, set in Baltimore, featured a mayor based on O'Malley—and the portrayal was harsh.[58] Nobody who connected the fictional Tommy Carcetti to the actual Martin O'Malley would want to vote for such a shifty and manipulative political insider. In the spring of 2015, reality sealed his political fate when Baltimore broke out in riots that laid bare the city's social and governmental dysfunction.

Jim Webb, who had served one term in the Senate from Virginia, was an intriguing candidate. At a time when the political class was short on military experience, Webb was a graduate of the Naval Academy and a decorated Marine Corps veteran of the Vietnam War. (Webb had a featured place in

CLINTON VERSUS SANDERS

Hillary Clinton had entered the 2008 nomination race as the odds-on favorite. Her loss was searing but educational, and as she looked ahead to 2016, she set about to do several things differently. "In 2008 they didn't understand the delegate fight anywhere near the way that the Obama team did," one Democratic consultant told journalist Chris Cillizza. "This time [campaign manager] Robby [Mook] and team knew exactly what they needed to do to get the delegates they needed."[62]

First, she would not forget the caucus states. Assuming that primaries were the main event of 2008, the Clinton campaign failed to put enough money and labor into the caucuses, which ended up providing Obama with an edge. Indeed, as Clinton campaign chair John Podesta wrote in a leaked email, some in the Clinton camp still believed years later that "the Obama forces flooded the caucuses with ineligible voters."[63] Her campaign would spend considerable time and resources on the caucus states, which she started visiting as soon as she was in the race.

Second, she would work the superdelegates. The Democratic Party provided a certain number of convention seats (712 of 4,763 in 2016) to elected officials and other party figures who were free to exercise their own judgment, at least in principle. In 2008, Obama wooed the superdelegates more skillfully than Clinton, even persuading some Clinton supporters (e.g., Representative John Lewis of Georgia) to switch sides. This time, Clinton got to the superdelegates early, and by the fall of 2015, an AP survey found that she had support from 359 of them.[64]

Third, she would relentlessly court the African American vote, which accounted for a large share of the Democratic primary electorate. Clinton started the 2008 campaign with a big advantage over Obama among African Americans.[65] After Obama won Iowa, however, they suddenly moved in his direction. In the 2016 race, knowing that Obama had unique stature among African Americans, she took every opportunity to embrace his legacy. Because of the 1990s Clinton record on crime, she had a difficult relationship with the Black Lives Matter movement, and in summer 2015 she faced a backlash for saying that "all lives matter." She quickly adjusted her rhetoric: "Yes, black lives matter," she said in South Carolina. "We all have a responsibility to face these hard truths about race and justice honestly and directly."[66] Success in holding African American support would have a specific payoff in the delegate count, because it was the decisive element in several Southern primaries. "There's so much focus on Iowa and New Hampshire, but Secretary Clinton and her team know that the South will deliver a huge number of delegates that will essentially seal the nomination for her," said DuBose Porter, the Georgia Democratic Party chair and a Clinton supporter.[67]

Robert Timberg's *The Nightingale's Song*, a best-selling book about prominent Naval Academy graduates.) He went on to write several novels, as well
as a nonfiction book about the Scots-Irish in America. As a Republican, he
served in the Reagan administration as an assistant secretary of defense and
secretary of the Navy. He later broke with the GOP over both the Gulf War
and the Iraq War, and in 2006 ran as a Democrat against incumbent Senator
George Allen of Virginia. He won, and Democrats immediately picked the
antiwar war hero to deliver their official response to President Bush's 2007
State of the Union.

After voluntarily leaving the Senate in 2012, he began eying the White
House. Although liberals liked his dovish stance on foreign policy, his conservative positions on gun control, immigration, and the environment were
repulsive to them. A writer for *Mother Jones* put it this way: "Webb used his
six years in the US Senate to stand in the way of Democratic efforts to
combat climate change. Virginia, after all, is a coal state, and Webb regularly
stood up for the coal industry, earning the ire of environmentalists."[59] And
on issues of race, class, and identity, he was out of step with his party. At the
National Press Club, he talked about forgotten Americans, including ghetto
kids, but also addressed what would become Trump Country:

> Or if you're a kid growing up in the Appalachian Mountains of Clay County Ken-
> tucky, by most accounts the poorest county in America, which also happens to be
> 98 percent white, surrounded by poverty, drug abuse and joblessness, and you leave
> your home in order to succeed, and when you do you are welcomed with the cynical,
> unbelieving stares and whispers of an America that no longer understands your
> cultural journey, and policies that can exclude you from a fair shot at education and
> employment with the false premise that if you are white you by definition have
> begun with some kind of socioeconomic advantage, what are you going to think
> about the so-called fairness of your own government?[60]

One could speculate that the general election might have taken a different
turn if Democrats had nominated someone who could talk that way—and
whose combat record would have enabled him to stare down Trump on
national security issues. As with the outcome of a Biden candidacy, the question will remain open. If the Democratic primary electorate had looked like
the one that nominated Bill Clinton in 1992, Webb might have had a chance.

But it did not, and Webb never got traction. When asked in an October
debate which enemy they were proudest of, Clinton and O'Malley listed the
National Rifle Association, from whom Webb had a 92 percent positive rating; Webb cited the North Vietnamese soldier whom he killed in combat. His
valor may have earned him the Silver Star, but his answer earned him a
heaping of abuse from the alt-left. He left the race, concluding that the Democratic Party was not a fit for him.[61]

Last, but not least, she would keep her war chest full. Her 2008 campaign ran low on funds, and she eventually had to lend it $13 million out of her own pocket. Not eager to tap her savings again, she held dozens of high-dollar fundraising events in the summer of 2015. She also had support from several outside spending groups:

- Ready for Hillary, a super PAC, raised millions in 2013 and 2014, keeping the Clinton fires burning between her departure from the State Department and her formal announcement of candidacy. Since FEC rules forbid super PACs to use the names of announced candidates, this organization rebranded itself as Ready PAC once she officially entered the race.
- Priorities USA Action started in 2012 to support President Obama's reelection and later sided with Clinton. It ran sophisticated TV ads, which it financed with million-dollar checks from big names such as Steven Spielberg and George Soros.[68]
- Correct the Record, originally part of another super PAC called American Bridge, spun off so that it could do rapid response and opposition research. Super PACs are generally forbidden to coordinate with the campaigns they support, but Correct the Record found a loophole. The Federal Election Commission only regulates Internet activity when it appears on another entity's website for a fee. The group put all its material on its own website, so it contended that it could coordinate with the Clinton campaign.[69] And coordinate it did. In a July 2015 memo addressed to Clinton herself, her campaign laid out detailed plans for working with Correct the Record.[70]

Big money would simultaneously fuel her campaign and renew doubts about her character. In February 2015, the *Washington Post* reported on the Bill, Hillary and Chelsea Clinton Foundation. Created in 1997 to underwrite a variety of good works around the world, the foundation had raised nearly $2 billion. Much of the money came from corporations, particularly from the financial services sector, as well as foreign governments and businesses.[71] The *Wall Street Journal* revealed that least sixty companies that lobbied the State Department during her time as secretary had given a total of at least $26 million.[72]

Another issue would have more impact on the fall campaign than the primaries. In March, news broke that Clinton had used a personal email account to carry out government business as secretary of state. This practice appeared to violate requirements for retention of official correspondence. One expert told the *New York Times*, "It is very difficult to conceive of a scenario—short of nuclear winter—where an agency would be justified in allowing its cabinet-level head officer to solely use a private email communications channel for the conduct of government business."[73] Even more troubling, her use of a "home-brew" server raised security concerns that she had exposed secrets to Internet espionage.

Clinton tried to put the matter to rest with a hastily arranged press conference, but the effort failed. James Carville, who had served Bill Clinton in the 1990s, told a reporter, "Look, the problem here isn't about the emails; you guys are never going to be satisfied with whatever answers she gives. Y'all are just going to go out there and say, 'She raised more questions than she answered.' "[74] At the *New York Times*, Maureen Dowd reviewed controversies from the 1990s and concluded, "The Clintons don't sparkle with honesty and openness. Between his lordly appetites and her queenly prerogatives, you always feel as if there's something afoot."[75]

In the meantime, Bernie Sanders was drawing big and enthusiastic crowds full of students and other young voters. "Sanders offers what young people— and most Americans—want in political leaders," wrote columnist Brent Budowsky. "He offers authenticity and ideas; a politics of conviction and values that soars above the petty cash of political propaganda and political spin."[76] Sanders had a long history of supporting civil rights: during his own student days, he had attended Martin Luther King's 1963 "I Have a Dream" speech and been arrested at a civil rights demonstration in Chicago.[77] He also had a big problem in this respect. With African Americans making up only 1 percent of its population, Vermont is the second-whitest state in the Union, just after Montana. Sanders's ties to the African American community had atrophied during his many years in office, and few black activists rallied to his campaign. His supporters were youthful, zealous, and pale.

The impact of his demographic challenge would become evident later. For the time being, he was contemplating an unusual approach to fundraising. On March 9, 2015, he told the National Press Club, "[If] I was really enormously successful, and I had three million people contributing a hundred dollars each, three million people, that would be $300 million dollars [*sic*], an enormous sum of money, one-third of what the Koch brothers themselves are going to spend. So those are the issues that I'm trying to work on right now."[78] He was not kidding. The response to his famous 2010 Senate speech showed that he had an enormous potential cyber-constituency. His nascent campaign focused on the Internet. "From the beginning, we knew it was important to fund this campaign differently from most," he wrote. "We weren't going to receive a whole lot of support from wealthy donors and we didn't want a super PAC. In the end, 94 percent of our money came in online, and we not only talked the talk about campaign finance reform, we walked the walk."[79]

EARLY SKIRMISHES

Hillary Clinton formally announced her candidacy on April 12, 2015, and Sanders followed eighteen days later. For most of the year, the mainstream media assumed that the Democrats would not have much of a fight, and that the real action was on the GOP side. In 2015, the Tyndale Report found that Donald Trump dominated political coverage on the three broadcast networks' evening news programs, with 327 minutes (or nearly a third of the airtime) devoted to the presidential campaign. Clinton was the second most newsworthy candidate (121 minutes), with another 88 minutes going to her email controversy and 29 minutes to the probes into the Benghazi attack. The Democrat who got the second-greatest amount of coverage was not even running: the networks gave 73 minutes to Biden's decision to stay out of the race. Bernie Sanders got only 20 minutes.[80]

Still, there were signs of a serious Democratic contest. The release of FEC data in July showed that Clinton had raised about $45 million during the previous quarter, while Sanders had raised $15 million. Though his haul was smaller, he outperformed expectations and had a lower spending rate, so he could keep more of what he took in. Moreover, since his contributions mostly came in small amounts, he did not have to worry about contributors bumping against the legal contribution ceilings, and he could hit them up repeatedly. The next quarter was an even bigger surprise. At $25 million, Sanders's take was just $3 million behind Clinton's.[81]

Pressure from the left weighed on Clinton. During the Obama years, many liberal activists had grown increasingly critical of Israel in connection with Palestine and other regional issues. When Israeli prime minister Benjamin Netanyahu spoke to a joint meeting of Congress in March 2015 to make a case against the Iran nuclear deal, dozens of Democratic lawmakers stayed away.[82] In May of that year, Clinton policy aide Jake Sullivan wanted to include a strong statement of support for Israel in her standard stump speech. In an email exchange, pollster Joel Benenson disagreed: "Why would we call out Israel in public events now? The only voters elevating FP [foreign policy] at all are Republican primary voters. To me we deal with this in stride when [and] if we are asked about FP." Campaign manager Robby Mook added, "I'm w Joel. We shouldn't have Israel at public events. Especially dem activists."[83]

Her husband's administration had promoted NAFTA, and as secretary of state, she had praised international negotiations on the Trans-Pacific Partnership (TPP), a trade deal including nations in Asia and the Americas. The agreement was unpopular among Democratic liberals, and in the fall of 2015, she changed her position and came out against TPP.[84] She could not erase her history, however, and the issue would continue to dog her through November.

The party's ideological winds also moved her on the issue of the Keystone XL Pipeline. President Obama was about to reject a proposal to build a 1,179-mile leg to bring oil from Alberta to Nebraska. The project was popular among blue-collar workers in the Rust Belt but toxic to environmentalists. Clinton sided with the environmentalists. "The [building] trades are also hearing that HRC will put out a statement stating that she encouraged Obama to take this position," wrote Nikki Budzinski, Clinton's labor outreach director in an email that later leaked. "Politically with the building trades, this would be a very dangerous posture." Campaign chair John Podesta answered, "Your [*sic*] in trouble, girl. Seriously, doubt we'll say we 'encouraged' but assume we'll support if it goes that way."[85] Clinton came out against Keystone in September. Environmentalists cheered. Labor leaders grumbled but gave her a pass. Evan Halper of the *Los Angeles Times* offered a prescient warning: "For Democrats eager to capture key swing states in the Rust Belt and Rockies, Keystone is dangerous. The loud, persistent and growing opposition in Democratic strongholds like California hasn't taken hold in the parts of the country where the election will be hardest fought."[86]

On October 13, the candidates met for their first televised debate, in Las Vegas. CNN's Anderson Cooper raised the Clinton email issue, and, as expected, Clinton called it a distraction from policy concerns. Sanders made news by agreeing: "Let me say—let me say something that may not be great politics. But I think the secretary is right, and that is that the American people are sick and tired of hearing about your damn e-mails."[87] In the short run, Sanders helped Clinton by declining to probe a weakness, and he helped himself by looking high-minded. In the longer run, he may have inadvertently helped Trump.[88] Had he pushed the issue, Clinton would have had to build up her defenses, and it would have become old news to an easily bored electorate. Instead, he left the issue on the table, where Republicans could later grab it.

Sanders preferred to stick to the economy and political reform. Clinton provided him with plenty of material. On November 14, at the second Democratic debate in Des Moines, he went after her Wall Street contributors: "Well, why do they make millions of dollars of campaign contributions? They expect to get something. Everybody knows that." Clinton responded, "I represented New York on 9/11 when we were attacked. Where were we attacked? We were attacked in downtown Manhattan where Wall Street is. I did spend a whole lot of time and effort helping them rebuild. That was good for New York. It was good for the economy and it was a way to rebuke the terrorists who had attacked our country."[89] Clinton's remarks got a poor reception. One columnist wrote that "invok[ing] terrorist attacks and the subsequent rebuilding as any sort of defense for Wall Street having such potential influence is unbelievably tone deaf at best, and wildly offensive at worst."[90] At a Democratic barbecue the next day, Clinton campaign chair John Podesta tried to defend Clinton against charges that she was a corporate lackey, but a sharp-eyed reporter noticed that he was wearing a fleece jacket bearing the logo of Equilibrium Capital, a $1 billion investment firm.[91]

On January 1, 2016, the RealClearPolitics polling average put Clinton 23 points ahead of Sanders among Democrats nationwide. She had hundreds of endorsements from elected officials, whereas Sanders had only a few. The only members of Congress to support him at this point were Representatives Keith Ellison of Minnesota and Raul Grijalva of Arizona.[92] Clinton also led among unions and advocacy groups. Sanders, however, noticed that while Clinton did better when the executive boards decided the endorsement, he did better when the members got to choose. "In general, we did well with the rank and file, not so well with the Inside the Beltway leadership."[93]

IOWA AND NEW HAMPSHIRE

In 2008, Hillary Clinton never quite recovered from losing the Iowa caucuses. Eight years later, she poured time and resources into the state, in hopes of avoiding a repeat. She won, by the narrowest of margins. Iowa tallied its caucus by "state delegate equivalents" (SDEs) instead of the popular vote, and Clinton came out ahead by 700.47 SDEs to Sanders's 696.92, a difference of about two-tenths of one percent. Clinton got a numerical win of sorts and avoided a humiliating defeat. Sanders got a moral victory and a psychological boost.

Youth was the old man's secret weapon. Entrance polls showed that caucus-goers under the age of thirty (18 percent of the total) favored Sanders by an 84–14 percent margin. He also led among first-time participants (59–37 percent) and those who identified as "very liberal" (58–39 percent).[94] Several features of the Iowa contest favored Sanders. Iowa is almost as white as Vermont: Clinton was strong among African Americans, but they accounted for only a tiny percentage of the caucus vote. Sanders tended to do better among poorer voters, and the Iowa caucus electorate was relatively downscale. The state's Democrats have long leaned to the left: as noted earlier, a significant number openly embraced the "socialist" label. *New York*

Times election analyst Nate Cohn had a word of caution for Sanders support-ers: "National polls show him roughly tied with Mrs. Clinton among white voters, and it was the case here as well. It suggests that additional gains for Mr. Sanders in national polls will require him to do better than he did in Iowa, not that the close race in Iowa augurs a close one nationally."[95]

Eight years before, Clinton had won an upset victory in the New Hamp-shire primary, which enabled her to stay in the race. This time, the Clinton forces recognized that Sanders had a home-court advantage in the first pri-mary because he came from neighboring Vermont. The two states also shared demographic characteristics that favored Sanders, including a very small African American population. Still, the Clinton campaign decided to make a real effort. On February 4, she debated him in Durham, and the candidates had a lively disagreement over who was more liberal. Reflecting his state's affection for hunting, Sanders did not have a consistent record in favor of gun control. Clinton pounced: "You know, we have differences and, honestly, I think we should be talk[ing] about what we want to do for the country. But if we're going to get into labels, I don't think it was particularly progressive to vote against the Brady Bill five times. I don't think it was progressive to vote to give gun makers and sellers immunity." Sanders answered that "you can't be a moderate [and] a progressive."[96] The back-and-forth probably played well with the MSNBC audience, but it was less obvious that the more-liberal-than-thou debate positioned Clinton well for the general election.

As most expected, Sanders won the New Hampshire primary with 60 per-cent of the vote, to Clinton's 38 percent. As in Iowa, Sanders had crushing margins among voters under 30 (83–16 percent) and "very liberal" voters (67–33 percent).[97] One datum should have given pause to the Clinton cam-paign. About a third of voters said that the candidate characteristic that mat-tered most was "honest and trustworthy." Sanders won these voters 92–6 percent.

THE EMPIRE STRIKES BACK

Clinton reassured supporters that Iowa and New Hampshire were quirky states with atypical electorates. The next state, Nevada, was different. With significant numbers of Hispanic and African American voters, it was a chance for Sanders to show that his appeal extended beyond cold climates and light complexions. But he had made an early decision to focus on Iowa and New Hampshire, and by the time of the February 20 Nevada caucuses, the Clinton campaign had the organizational upper hand. Clinton won 53 percent of the county delegates—no landslide, but enough to restore her campaign's confidence. Entrance polls showed her winning most of the African American vote while losing the Hispanic vote to Sanders. Nate Cohn analyzed the caucus results and found Clinton ahead in heavily Hispanic areas, suggesting that the survey data were misleading.[98] It would not be the last such case in the 2016 campaign.

The morning after the caucuses, Sanders held a conference call with campaign aides, expressing regret that he had not build a stronger ground operation in the state. "If Clinton had lost Iowa, New Hampshire and Nevada, it would have been a devastating series of defeats that would have called into question her entire campaign," said Sanders adviser Tad Devine. "We had to shift our strategy. But no matter what, the nomination became tougher to win."[99] Devine was understating the case. A week after the Nevada caucuses came the South Carolina primary, where African Americans made up most the Democratic primary electorate. Sanders had attempted outreach to the black vote, but it was too little, too late. Clinton won with 73.5 percent to just 26 percent for Sanders.

March 1 was Super Tuesday, with a dozen Democratic contests. As explained earlier, Super Tuesday originated in the 1980s as a way to give a voice to conservative Southern Democrats. Over the years, the Super Tuesday roster had evolved, and so had the makeup of its Southern states. The conservative whites who had voted for Bill Clinton in 1992 had long ago left for the GOP, and African Americans were the dominant Democratic force in much of the South. In 2016, Clinton swept Alabama, Arkansas, Georgia, Tennessee, Texas and Virginia, and even narrowly carried Massachusetts, which Sanders had hoped to win. She also won the caucuses in American Samoa. Sanders won his own state, Vermont, together with Colorado, Minnesota, and Oklahoma.

On that night, Clinton effectively clinched the Democratic nomination. Though several months of campaigning were still ahead, Super Tuesday made it prohibitively difficult for Sanders to overtake her. The reason was proportional allocation of delegates. Under Democratic rules, each candidate's share of a state's convention delegates is roughly proportional to his or her vote share. Even if one candidate wins a plurality of the vote in a state, another candidate can still take a substantial number of delegates. So once one candidate builds up a sizable lead in delegates, it is very hard for rivals to erase it.[100] In 2008, this dynamic kept Obama ahead even after Clinton won some key contests later in the season. In 2016, Clinton was the beneficiary, and her delegate margin was larger than Obama's had been.[101] Campaign manager Robby Mook wrote in early April:

> Hillary Clinton has a lead of nearly 230 pledged delegates—and with each passing week, it's becoming increasingly unlikely that Senator Sanders will be able to catch

up. In order to do so, Sanders has to win the four remaining delegate-rich primaries—New York, Pennsylvania, California, and New Jersey—with roughly 60 percent of the vote. To put that in perspective: Sanders has thus far won only two primaries with that margin: Vermont and New Hampshire. Needless to say, the size and demographic makeups of New York, Pennsylvania, California, and New Jersey are decidedly different than Vermont and New Hampshire. And these figures don't even include superdelegates, where Clinton has an overwhelming lead.[102]

Spoiler alert: Clinton won New York, Pennsylvania, California, and New Jersey. She did have some unpleasant moments in the months after Super Tuesday, however. Despite polls showing a Clinton victory in the Michigan primary, Sanders won an upset victory. In hindsight, this result was another indicator that election surveys have become less reliable. (The same state would provide another reminder on the night of November 8.) Clinton had been counting on the black vote in the Detroit area, but she did not generate the same level of passion as Barack Obama, particularly among younger African Americans.

As the outcome of the nomination contest became clear, some Sanders supporters reacted with anger. One activist posted a database of personal information on superdelegates, with a graphic of a donkey in crosshairs. "These people are worried someone is going to come to their house," said Bob Mulholland, a California Democratic political operative in California who backed Clinton. "They have been put on a 'hit list.' "[103] The Nevada state Democratic convention dissolved into disorder after Sanders forces lost a rules dispute. The "Bernie Bros" did not stop when the convention ended. "It's been vile," said state Democratic chair Roberta Lange. "It's been threatening messages, threatening my family, threatening my life, threatening my grandchild."[104]

This period also generated some problems that were not apparent at the time. Democratic operative Donna Brazile, working as a commentator for CNN, improperly gave the Clinton campaign advance information about debate questions. Just before a Michigan debate, she sent an email saying that a woman from Flint would ask about the city's water contamination crisis. "One of the questions directed to HRC tomorrow is from a woman with a rash," Brazile said in the subject line. She continued, "Her family has lead poison and she will ask what, if anything, will Hillary do as president to help the ppl of Flint."[105] At most, the Clinton campaign got some marginal value from Brazile's messages. But once they leaked in the fall—probably as the result of Russian hacking—they supplied Donald Trump with yet another way to attack "Crooked Hillary."

That revelation was still in the future. In the spring, it still looked as if Clinton was on the road to becoming the first woman president. In early June, she locked up enough delegates to win the nomination. After her victory in the June 7 California primary, President Obama endorsed her. On June 24, Sanders said that he would vote for her.

WHOSE PARTY?

Bernie Sanders lost the nomination but won the party. He had defied the odds and stunned the political community by raising more than $200 million, mostly online via small donations. On the day that Clinton clinched the nomination, he had a higher net favorability rating among Democrats: 52 percent to Clinton's 39 percent.[106] His zealous base of supporters was a powerful force that no Democrat could ignore. As he recounted in *Our Revolution*, the 2016 Democratic platform reflected his influence:

> While we didn't get everything we wanted, we did get much of what we were fighting for. It was now the Democratic Party's policy to break up too-big-to-fail banks, pass a twenty-first-century Glass Steagall Act, make public colleges and universities tuition free for working families, enact a price on carbon and methane, raise the minimum wage to $15 an hour, abolish the death penalty, expand Social Security, close loopholes that allow corporations to avoid paying taxes, create millions of jobs rebuilding our crumbling infrastructure, eliminate super PACs, and pass a constitutional amendment to overturn Citizens United.[107]

In addition to making concessions to Sanders on the platform, Clinton tried to unify the party with her vice presidential selection. Tim Kaine was a nominal Southerner, representing Virginia in the U.S. Senate. He had been a civil rights lawyer and mayor of majority-black Richmond. He spoke Spanish, an outgrowth of his time as a Catholic missionary in Honduras. And he had an acceptably liberal voting record from the Americans for Democratic Action. In some ways, he was also like Clinton herself: he had a Midwestern upbringing and accent, a commitment to liberal religious values, and Ivy League law degree (Harvard). He was a good fit for the Democratic Party of 2016.

Throughout the convention, the roster of speakers repeated the themes of diversity and inclusion. Clinton herself discussed all the groups that would benefit from her policies and suffer under Trump's. "This was a strategic mistake," wrote scholar Mark Lilla of Clinton's emphasis on identity politics. "If you are going to mention groups in America, you had better mention all of them. If you don't, those left out will notice and feel excluded."[108]

The nomination process had left Clinton in a precarious position. To appeal to the Democratic liberals and counter the Sanders insurgency, she had moved to the left, where her stands on cultural and environmental issues might cause her trouble among working-class white voters in the fall. However, as Sanders's strong showing indicated, she had not totally closed the sale among core Democratic voters, either. Sanders had scored points by linking her to Wall Street. Al From, who founded the now-defunct DLC, explained why such a connection had become so toxic: "The circumstances are changed when you go through a depression like we did in 2008 and 2009, when you can point a finger at somebody. In this case, people point the finger at Wall Street. It's a different world. We needed Wall Street for investment to grow the economy so everybody could do better. Now they're the villains."[109]

Hillary Clinton had moved far beyond the Clintonism of the 1990s, but the past was still too much with her.

NOTES

1. Al From, *The New Democrats and the Return to Power* (New York: Palgrave Macmillan, 2013), 97.

2. Ibid., 111.

3. James Ceaser and Andrew Busch, *Upside Down and Inside Out: The 1992 Elections and American Politics* (Lanham, MD: Rowman & Littlefield, 1993), 55–56.

4. Ibid., 65, 78.

5. Gwen Ifill, "Clinton Won't Back Down in Tiff with Jackson Over a Rap Singer," *New York Times*, June 20, 1992, http://www.nytimes.com/1992/06/20/us/1992-campaign -democrats-clinton-won-t-back-down-tiff-with-jackson-over-rap.html.

6. Transcript, "Leaders 2," 1992, http://www.livingroomcandidate.org/commercials/ 1992.

7. H.R. 3734 (104th): Personal Responsibility and Work Opportunity Reconciliation Act of 1996, https://www.govtrack.us/congress/bills/104/hr3734.

8. Barry Latzer, *The Rise and Fall of Violent Crime in America* (New York: Encounter Books, 2016), chapters 3–4.

9. University of Albany, *Sourcebook of Criminal Justice Statistics Online*, http:// www.albany.edu/sourcebook/pdf/t31062012.pdf.

10. Steven M. Gillon, *The Pact: Bill Clinton, Newt Gingrich, and the Rivalry That Defined a Generation* (New York: Oxford University Press, 2008), xv.

11. In 1998, seven in ten Americans said that they did not believe that Clinton had high ethical standards. David S. Broder and Richard Morin, "Struggle Over New Standards," *Washington Post*, December 27, 1998, http://www.washingtonpost.com/wp-srv/ politics/special/clinton/stories/values122798.htm.

12. "Hillary's Cash Cows and Other Sweet Deals," *Newsweek*, April 3, 1994, http:// www.newsweek.com/hillarys-cash-cows-and-other-sweet-deals-186812.

13. William J. Clinton, "Statement on Signing the Iraq Liberation Act of 1998," October 31, 1998, http://www.presidency.ucsb.edu/ws/?pid = 55205.

14. William J. Clinton, "Address to the Nation Announcing Military Strikes on Iraq," December 16, 1998, http://www.presidency.ucsb.edu/ws/?pid = 55414.

15. Frank Newport, "Clinton's Job Approval Legacy," Gallup, January 4, 2001, http://www.gallup.com/poll/4657/clintons-job-approval-legacy.aspx.

16. William F. Connelly Jr. and John J. Pitney Jr., *Congress' Permanent Minority? Republicans in the US House* (Lanham, MD: Rowman & Littlefield, 1994), 156–58.

17. Matthew Cooper, "Beware of Republicans Bearing Voting Rights Suits," *Washington Monthly*, February 1987, 11–15, at http://www.unz.org/Pub/WashingtonMonthly-1987feb-00011.

18. John J. Pitney Jr., "Clinton and the Republican Party," in *The Postmodern Presidency: Bill Clinton's Legacy in US Politics*, ed. Steven E. Schier (Pittsburgh: University of Pittsburgh Press, 2000), 178.

19. Harry Enten, "Hillary Clinton Was Liberal. Hillary Clinton Is Liberal," FiveThirtyEight, May 19, 2015, http://fivethirtyeight.com/datalab/hillary-clinton-was-liberal-hillary-clinton-is-liberal/.

20. Senator Hillary Rodham Clinton, "Floor Speech of Senator Hillary Rodham Clinton on S.J. Res. 45, A Resolution to Authorize the Use of United States Armed Forces Against Iraq," October 10, 2002, https://web.archive.org/web/20081218155448/http://clinton.senate.gov/speeches/iraq_101002.html.

21. Andrew J. Taylor, *Elephant's Edge: The Republicans as a Ruling Party* (Westport, CT: Praeger, 2005).

22. Matt Bai, *The Argument: Billionaires, Bloggers and the Battle to Remark Democratic Politics* (New York: Penguin, 2007), 74.

23. Ronald Brownstein, *The Second Civil War: How Extreme Partisanship Has Paralyzed Washington and Polarized America* (New York: Penguin, 2007), 335–36.

24. Ibid., 214.

25. Harold Meyerson, "A Real Realignment," *Washington Post*, November 7, 2008, http://www.washingtonpost.com/wp-dyn/content/article/2008/11/06/AR2008110602571.html.

26. Ben Smith, "The End of the DLC Era," *Politico*, February 7, 2011, http://www.politico.com/story/2011/02/the-end-of-the-dlc-era-049041.

27. Lydia Saad, "Conservatives Hang on to Ideology Lead by a Thread," Gallup, January 11, 2016, http://www.gallup.com/poll/188129/conservatives-hang-ideology-lead-thread.aspx.

28. Michael Dimock et al., "Political Polarization in the American Public," Pew Research Center, June 12, 2014, http://www.people-press.org/2014/06/12/political-polarization-in-the-american-public/.

29. Carroll Doherty et al., "The Parties on the Eve of the 2016 Election: Two Coalitions, Moving Further Apart," Pew Research Center, September 13, 2016, http://www.people-press.org/2016/09/13/2-party-affiliation-among-voters-1992-2016/.

30. Carroll Doherty and Rachel Weisel, "A Deep Dive into Party Affiliation," Pew Research Center, April 7, 2015, http://www.people-press.org/2015/04/07/a-deep-dive-into-party-affiliation/.

31. Carroll Doherty, Jocelyn Kiley, and Bridget Jameson, "Wider Ideological Gap Between More and Less Educated Adults," Pew Research Center, April 26, 2016, http://www.people-press.org/2016/04/26/a-wider-ideological-gap-between-more-and-less-educated-adults.

32. Joe Klein, "One for All and All for One," *Time*, September 10, 2012, http://content.time.com/time/magazine/article/0,9171,2123309,00.html.

33. Jay Cost, "The Democratic Bench Is Shockingly Weak," *The Weekly Standard*, January 29, 2015, http://www.weeklystandard.com/democratic-bench-shockingly-weak/article/830664.

34. Chris Cillizza, "Republicans Have Gained More Than 900 State Legislative Seats Since 2010," *Washington Post*, January 14, 2015, https://www.washingtonpost.com/news/the-fix/wp/2015/01/14/republicans-have-gained-more-than-900-state-legislative-seats-since-2010.

35. Erica Orden, "Andrew Cuomo's Former Top Aide Indicted on Public-Corruption Charges," *Wall Street Journal*, November 22, 2016, http://www.wsj.com/articles/andrew-cuomos-former-top-aide-indicted-on-public-corruption-charges-1479849941.

36. At the start of 2015, her average poll rating was 51–28 percent unfavorable. "Nancy Pelosi Favorable Rating," *HuffPost Pollster*, December 14, 2016, http://elections.huffingtonpost.com/pollster/nancy-pelosi-favorable-rating.

37. Jeffrey M. Jones, "Biden Maintains Positive Image," Gallup, October 14, 2015, http://www.gallup.com/poll/186167/biden-maintains-positive-image.aspx.

38. Jennifer Hoar, "Biden's Comments Ruffle Feathers," CBS, July 7, 2006, http://www.cbsnews.com/news/bidens-comments-ruffle-feathers.

39. Mark Halperin and John Heilemann, *Double Down: Game Change 2012* (New York: Penguin, 2013), 71.

40. Byron York, "Joe Biden's Woman-Touching Habit," *Washington Examiner*, February 17, 2015, http://www.washingtonexaminer.com/joe-bidens-woman-touching-habit/article/2560311.

41. Nick Gass, "Barney Frank: Joe Biden 'Can't Keep His Mouth Shut or His Hands to Himself,'" *Politico*, March 24, 2015, http://www.politico.com/story/2015/03/barney-frank-joe-biden-no-discipline-116360.

42. James W. Ceaser, Andrew E. Busch, and John J. Pitney Jr., *Epic Journey: The 2008 Elections and American Politics* (Lanham, MD: Rowman & Littlefield, 2009), 121.

43. Jon Greenberg, "Hillary Clinton Says She and Bill Were 'Dead Broke,'" PolitiFact, June 10, 2014, http://www.politifact.com/truth-o-meter/statements/2014/jun/10/hillary-clinton/hillary-clinton-says-she-and-bill-were-dead-broke/.

44. Aaron Blake, "Hillary Clinton: Last Time I Drove Was 1996," *Washington Post*, January 27, 2014, https://www.washingtonpost.com/news/post-politics/wp/2014/01/27/hillary-clinton-last-time-i-drove-was-1996/?utm_term=.17c558d85f50.

45. Allison Graves, "Did Hillary Clinton Call African-American Youth 'Superpredators?'" PolitiFact, August 28, 2016, http://www.politifact.com/truth-o-meter/statements/2016/aug/28/reince-priebus/did-hillary-clinton-call-african-american-youth-su. The inventor of the term was political scientist John J. DiIulio Jr., who would go on to advise the George W. Bush administration. See John J. DiIulio Jr., "The Coming of the Super-Predators," *The Weekly Standard*, November 27, 1995, http://www.weeklystandard.com/the-coming-of-the-super-predators/article/8160.

46. Amy Chozick, "Bill Clinton Says He Regrets Showdown with Black Lives Matter Protesters," *New York Times*, April 8, 2016, http://www.nytimes.com/2016/04/09/us/politics/bill-clinton-apology-black-lives-matter-philadelphia.html.

47. Jonathan Chait, "Hillary Clinton Is Reliving Al Gore's Nightmare," *New York Magazine*, October 7, 2015, http://nymag.com/daily/intelligencer/2015/10/hillary-clinton-is-reliving-al-gores-nightmare.html.

48. Bernie Sanders, *Our Revolution: A Future to Believe In* (New York: Thomas Dunne Books, 2016), 17.

49. Gabriel Debenedetti, "Poll: Majority of Democrats Say Socialism Has 'Positive Impact,'" *Politico*, February 22, 2016, http://www.politico.com/story/2016/02/democrats -poll-socialism-219600.

50. John McCormick and Arit John, "Anti-Wall Street Sentiment Breaks by Party Line in Iowa Poll," *Bloomberg News*, January 15, 2016, https://www.bloomberg.com/ politics/articles/2016-01-15/anti-wall-street-sentiment-breaks-by-party-line-in-iowa-poll.

51. "Clinton in Commanding Lead Over Trump Among Young Voters, Harvard Youth Poll Finds," Harvard University, Kennedy School of Government, Institute of Politics, April 26, 2016, http://iop.harvard.edu/youth-poll/harvard-iop-spring-2016-poll.

52. Max Ehrenfreund, "A Majority of Millennials Now Reject Capitalism, Poll Shows," *Washington Post*, April 26, 2016, https://www.washingtonpost.com/news/wonk/ wp/2016/04/26/a-majority-of-millennials-now-reject-capitalism-poll-shows/?utm_term = .780f677af5fd.

53. Sanders, *Our Revolution*, 22.

54. Vermont does not have party registration. For an account of Trump's switches, see Joshua Gillin, "Bush Says Trump Was a Democrat Longer Than a Republican 'In the Last Decade,'" PolitiFact, August 24, 2015, http://www.politifact.com/florida/statements/ 2015/aug/24/jeb-bush/bush-says-trump-was-democrat-longer-republican-las.

55. Bernie Sanders, "Full Congressional Record Transcript of Sanders Filibuster," December 10, 2010, http://www.sanders.senate.gov/newsroom/press-releases/full-con gressional-record-transcript-of-sanders-filibuster.

56. Sanders, *Our Revolution*, 47.

57. Ibid., 52, 54.

58. Ben Jacobs, "Martin O'Malley, Tommy Carcetti and 2016," *The Daily Beast*, April 9, 2013, http://www.thedailybeast.com/articles/2013/05/09/martin-o-malley-tommy -carcetti-and-2016.html.

59. Patrick Caldwell, "Jim Webb Wants to Be President. Too Bad He's Awful on Climate Change," *Mother Jones*, December 22, 2014, http://www.motherjones.com/ environment/2014/12/jim-webb-climate-change.

60. Jim Webb, Remarks at National Press Club, Washington, DC, September 23, 2014, http://www.jameswebb.com/news/jim-webb-to-speak-at-national-press-club -luncheon-sept-23-watch-live.

61. Nick Gass and Daniel Strauss, "Jim Webb Drops Out of Democratic Race," *Politico*, October 20, 2016, http://www.politico.com/story/2015/10/webb-dropping-out -214952.

62. Chris Cillizza, "How Hillary Clinton Turned a Losing 2008 Campaign into a Winning 2016 One," *Washington Post*, June 7, 2016, https://www.washingtonpost.com/ news/the-fix/wp/2016/06/07/5-reasons-hillary-clinton-went-from-a-loser-in-2008-to-a -winner-in-2016/.

63. John Podesta, email, May 14, 2015, https://wikileaks.org/podesta-emails/emailid/ 10290.

64. Stephen Ollemacher and Hope Yen, "Big Nomination Lead for Clinton: Pocketing 'Superdelegates,'" Associated Press, November 13, 2015, https://www.yahoo.com/news/ clinton-early-commanding-delegate-lead-nomination-120111050.html.

65. Ceaser, Busch, and Pitney, *Epic Journey*, 111.

66. Emma Margolin, "Hillary Clinton: 'Yes, Black Lives Matter,'" MSNBC, July 23, 2015, http://www.msnbc.com/msnbc/hillary-clinton-yes-black-lives-matter.

67. Patrick Healy and Amy Chozick, "Hillary Clinton Relying on Southern Primaries to Fend Off Rivals," *New York Times*, September 5, 2015, http://www.nytimes.com/2015/09/06/us/politics/hillary-clinton-relying-on-southern-primaries-to-fend-off-rivals.html.

68. Melissa Yeager and Libby Watson, "Behind the Clinton Campaign: Mapping the Pro-Hillary Super PACs," Sunlight Foundation, December 1, 2015, http://sunlightfoundation.com/2015/12/01/super-pacs-dark-money-and-the-hillary-clinton-campaign-part-1.

69. Libby Watson and Melissa Yeager, "Behind the Clinton Campaign: Dark Money Allies," Sunlight Foundation, December 3, 2015, https://sunlightfoundation.com/blog/2015/12/03/behind-the-clinton-campaign-dark-money-allies/.

70. Lee Fang and Andrew Perez, "Hacked Emails Prove Coordination Between Clinton Campaign and Super PACs," The Intercept, October 18, 2016, https://theintercept.com/2016/10/18/hillary-superpac-coordination.

71. Rosalind S. Helderman, Tom Hamburger and Steven Rich, "Clintons' Foundation Has Raised Nearly $2 Billion—and Some Key Questions," *Washington Post*, February 18, 2015, https://www.washingtonpost.com/politics/clintons-raised-nearly-2-billion-for-foundation-since-2001/2015/02/18/b8425d88-a7cd-11e4-a7c2-03d37af98440_story.html.

72. James V. Grimaldi and Rebecca Ballhaus, "Hillary Clinton's Complex Corporate Ties," *Wall Street Journal*, February 19, 2015, http://www.wsj.com/articles/hillary-clintons-complex-corporate-ties-1424403002.

73. Michael S. Schmidt, "Hillary Clinton Used Personal Email Account at State Dept., Possibly Breaking Rules," *New York Times*, March 2, 2015, http://www.nytimes.com/2015/03/03/us/politics/hillary-clintons-use-of-private-email-at-state-department-raises-flags.htm.

74. Glenn Thrush and Gabriel Debenedetti, "Clinton: I Used Private Email Account for 'Convenience,'" *Politico*, March 10, 2015, http://www.politico.com/story/2015/03/hillary-clinton-email-press-conference-115947.

75. Maureen Dowd, "With the Clintons, Only the Shadow Knows," *New York Times*, March 7, 2015, http://www.nytimes.com/2015/03/08/opinion/sunday/maureen-dowd-only-the-shadow-knows.html.

76. Brent Budowsky, "Why Bernie Sanders Excites Students and Young Voters," *The Hill*, June 12, 2015, http://thehill.com/blogs/pundits-blog/presidential-campaign/244826-why-bernie-sanders-excites-students-and-young-voters.

77. Sanders, *Our Revolution*, 19–20.

78. Bernie Sanders, Remarks at National Press Club, March 9, 2015, http://www.press.org/sites/default/files/20150309_sanders.pdf.

79. Sanders, *Our Revolution*, 99.

80. Andrew Tyndale, "Campaign 2016 Coverage: Annual Totals for 2015," *The Tyndale Report*, December 21, 2015, https://web.archive.org/web/20160315160523/http://tyndallreport.com/comment/20/5773/.

81. Rebecca Ballhaus, "Hillary Clinton Raised $28 Million in 3rd Quarter, Edging Bernie Sanders," *Wall Street Journal*, September 30, 2015, http://www.wsj.com/articles/hillary-clinton-raised-28-million-in-3rd-quarter-edging-bernie-sanders-1443665690.

82. Alexandra Jaffe, "58 members of Congress skipped Netanyahu's speech," CNN,

March 3, 2015, http://www.cnn.com/2015/02/26/politics/democrats-missing-netanyahu -whip-list/.

83. Blake Hounshell, "Clinton Aides Struck Israel from Early Stump Speech," *Politico*, October 17, 2016, http://www.politico.com/live-blog-updates/2016/10/john-podesta -hillary-clinton-emails-wikileaks-000011#postid = 00000157-d599-ddff-a1d7-f7b947a 40000.

84. Lauren Carroll, "Hillary Clinton flip-flops on Trans-Pacific Partnership," Politi-Fact, October 8, 2015, http://www.politifact.com/truth-o-meter/statements/2015/oct/08/ hillary-clinton/hillary-clinton-now-opposes-trans-pacific-partners.

85. Nikki Budzinski and John Podesta, emails, August 20, 2015, https://wikileaks.org/ podesta-emails/emailid/2039.

86. Evan Halper, "Democrats Cheer Keystone Pipeline Setback, But It Could Hurt Them in Presidential Race," *Los Angeles Times*, November 3, 2015, http://www.latimes .com/nation/politics/la-keystone-pipeline-swing-states-20151103-story.html.

87. CNN, transcript of Democratic debate, Las Vegas, October 13, 2015, http://cnn pressroom.blogs.cnn.com/2015/10/13/cnn-democratic-debate-full-transcript/.

88. Jeet Heer, "Bernie Should've Attacked Hillary's 'Damn Emails,' " *New Republic*, May 26, 2016, https://newrepublic.com/article/133741/bernie-shouldve-attacked-hillarys -damn-emails.

89. Transcript of Democratic debate, Des Moines, Iowa, November 14, 2015, http:// www.cbsnews.com/news/democratic-debate-transcript-clinton-sanders-omalley-in-iowa/.

90. James Downie, "Hillary Clinton's Unbelievable Defense of Wall Street Contributions," *Washington Post*, November 15, 2015, https://www.washingtonpost.com/blogs/ post-partisan/wp/2015/11/15/hillary-clintons-unbelievable-defense-of-wall-st-contribu tions/?utm_term = .31e2d01503e6.

91. Hunter Walker, "Clinton Campaign Tries to Move Beyond Debate 9/11 Comment," Yahoo News, November 15, 2015, https://www.yahoo.com/news/clinton-cam paign-tries-to-move-beyond-debate-911-220736819.html.

92. Aaron Bycoffe, "The Endorsement Primary," FiveThirtyEight, June 7, 2016, http://projects.fivethirtyeight.com/2016-endorsement-primary/.

93. Sanders, *Our Revolution*, 109.

94. "Iowa Entrance Polls," *New York Times*, February 1, 2016, http://www.nytimes .com/interactive/2016/02/01/us/elections/iowa-democrat-poll.html.

95. Nate Cohn, "Why a 'Virtual Tie' in Iowa Is Better for Clinton Than Sanders," *New York Times*, February 2, 2016, http://www.nytimes.com/2016/02/02/upshot/how-the -virtual-tie-in-iowa-helps-hillary-clinton.html.

96. Transcript of Democratic debate, Durham, New Hampshire, *Washington Post*, February 4, 2016, https://www.washingtonpost.com/news/the-fix/wp/2016/02/04/sanders -clinton-debate-transcript-annotating-what-they-say.

97. "New Hampshire Exit Polls," *New York Times*, February 9, 2016, http://www .nytimes.com/interactive/2016/02/09/us/elections/new-hampshire-democrat-poll.html.

98. Nate Cohn, "No, the Polling Doesn't Prove Bernie Sanders Won the Hispanic Vote in Nevada," *New York Times*, February 21, 2016, http://www.nytimes.com/2016/02/ 22/upshot/why-clinton-not-sanders-probably-won-the-hispanic-vote-in-nevada.html.

99. Patrick Healy and Yamiche Alcindor, "Early Missteps Seen as a Drag on Bernie Sanders's Campaign," *New York Times*, April 3, 2016, http://www.nytimes.com/2016/04/ 04/us/politics/bernie-sanders-hillary-clinton.html.

100. Ceaser, Busch, and Pitney, *Epic Journey*, 94.

101. Nate Silver, "Clinton Is Following Obama's Path to The Nomination," FiveThirty-Eight, March 16, 2016, http://fivethirtyeight.com/features/clinton-is-following-obamas-path-to-the-nomination.

102. Robby Mook, "To Hillary Clinton Supporters: The Facts on Where the Race Stands," Medium, April 4, 2016, https://medium.com/hillary-for-america/to-hillary-clinton-supporters-the-facts-on-where-the-race-stands-87bf70654fbc#.ydalsqehm.

103. Evan Halper and Matt Pearce, "Sanders' Supporters Are Lashing Out, But Here's How They Might Be Hurting His Campaign," *Los Angeles Times*, April 15, 2016, http://www.latimes.com/nation/politics/la-na-bernie-sanders-supporters-20160415-story.html.

104. Alan Rappeport, "From Bernie Sanders Supporters, Death Threats Over Delegates," *New York Times*, May 16, 2016, http://www.nytimes.com/2016/05/17/us/politics/bernie-sanders-supporters-nevada.html.

105. Donna Brazile, email, March 3, 2016, https://wikileaks.org/podesta-emails/emailid/38478.

106. Frank Newport and Andrew Dugan, "Clinton Still Has More Negatives Among Dems Than Sanders," Gallup, June 6, 2016, http://www.gallup.com/opinion/polling-matters/192362/clinton-negatives-among-dems-sanders.aspx.

107. Sanders, *Our Revolution*, 181.

108. Mark Lilla, "The End of Identity Liberalism," *New York Times*, November 18, 2016, http://www.nytimes.com/2016/11/20/opinion/sunday/the-end-of-identity-liberalism.html.

109. Dan Balz, "Bill Clinton: Once Again in the Spotlight, But Before a Different Party," *Washington Post*, July 26 2016, https://www.washingtonpost.com/politics/bill-clinton-once-again-in-the-spotlight-but-before-a-different-party/2016/07/26/82837bd8-534c-11e6-b7de-dfe509430c39_story.html.

Chapter Three

Trumped

The Republican Nomination Contest

When Republicans surveyed the landscape after the 2014 midterm elections, they had many reasons to be hopeful. They had just added a Senate majority to the House majority they won in 2010 and had added considerable strength at the state level. Indeed, they had more seats in the House and more strength in state governments than at any time since the 1920s. As they looked ahead to 2016, they noted that their probable opponent, Hillary Clinton, had a number of serious deficiencies as a candidate, and would face the difficulty of trying to win for her party a third consecutive term in the White House, a feat accomplished only one time in five tries by a non-incumbent since 1960. (Another try for a third consecutive party term, by incumbent Gerald R. Ford in 1976, also ended in failure.) They could also be pleased that the field of probable contenders for the Republican presidential nomination was deep and talented, partly the consequence of the decimation inflicted by Republicans on congressional and state Democrats during the Obama years.

They could not know it at the time, but the deep Republican bench would prove to be more curse than blessing for the regular Republican Party, an ironic demonstration of the adage "too much of a good thing." When a brash celebrity businessman with a knack for getting in the news staked out a position with an unshakable core of support, the field never thinned quickly enough to allow anyone else to break out of the scrum. That candidate, Donald J. Trump, was on no one's radar screen in November 2014. By May 2016 he was the presumptive Republican nominee for president.

In this improbable story, to reach that position Trump had to fight his way through as many as sixteen opponents, many of whom were skilled and respected political figures—and all of whom had more experience in the political arena than did Trump. These contenders could be put into a number of categories:

The governors (and former governors): These candidates were or had been the chief executives of states across the country. They included former governor Jeb Bush of Florida and sitting governors Scott Walker of Wisconsin, Chris Christie of New Jersey, John Kasich of Ohio, and Bobby Jindal of Louisiana, who left office in January 2016. Bush, the son and brother of former U.S. presidents, was anointed by many as the front-runner in the race. Jindal was a wunderkind, having served as a member of Congress, an assistant secretary of Health and Human Services, and a two-term governor by the age of forty-five. Walker and Christie each had won election and reelection in states that had not voted for a Republican presidential candidate since the 1980s; Walker had also won a tough recall vote and plaudits from conservatives for waging a fight against Wisconsin's public sector unions. Before becoming the popular two-term governor of always-crucial Ohio, Kasich had served nine terms in the House of Representatives, where he helped usher in the balanced budgets of the late 1990s as chairman of the House Budget Committee. Former Virginia governor Jim Gilmore and three-term former New York governor George Pataki, first elected in 1994, rounded out the governors, but they were among the darkest of the dark horses.

The senators: A number of senators also offered themselves for the presidency, including Tea Party favorites Ted Cruz of Texas, Rand Paul of Kentucky, and Marco Rubio of Florida. Rubio and Paul had been elected in 2010, Cruz in 2012. Each had carved out a niche: Cruz was the hardliner who promoted a government shutdown in October 2013 in a bid to defund Obamacare; Paul angled for the libertarian constituency cultivated by his father, former Republican congressman and libertarian presidential candidate Ron Paul; and Rubio sounded the alarm against a weak Obama foreign policy while signing on to an ill-fated immigration reform bill in 2013. Another candidate from the Senate, Lindsey Graham of South Carolina, was a close ally of Senator John McCain.

The also-rans: Three aspirants in earlier Republican nomination races appeared again, hoping that their second time would be the charm. Rick Perry had been the longest-serving governor in Texas history, and he was making a second run at the White House after a failed bid four years earlier. Former Pennsylvania senator Rick Santorum also returned from a 2012 campaign in which he proved to be Mitt Romney's toughest competitor. Former Arkansas governor Mike Huckabee had run a strong race in 2008. Both Huckabee and Santorum had won the Iowa caucuses in their years and hoped to repeat the feat.

The outsiders: In a year of great dissatisfaction with politics as usual, three outsiders sought to make a mark. Former Hewlett-Packard executive Carly Fiorina was the only woman in the field and the least outside of the outsiders, having been the Republican nominee for U.S. Senate from California in 2010 and serving as fundraising chair for the Republican National Committee and an advisor to John McCain in 2008. Noted neurosurgeon Ben Carson, subject of the television drama *Gifted Hands*, hoped to capture the evangelical vote and to gain traction in an environment in which health care was an ongoing issue. Though a senator, Ted Cruz was a foe of the GOP establishment and would run a campaign drawing heavily on outsider themes. Finally, there was Trump himself.

Self-proclaimed billionaire Donald Trump (his actual wealth is hotly debated) had been a major name in the American cultural milieu for thirty years as a real estate mogul, author of the best-selling book *The Art of the Deal*, and host of the reality television shows *The Apprentice* and *The Celebrity Apprentice*, in which his role was to train and evaluate budding business associates—and to growl "You're fired!" several times a season. He had no political experience, but he did build a chain of luxury hotels and golf courses, a line of men's clothing, and several casinos, including some with strip clubs. A loud and colorful personality from New York City, Trump had periodically toyed with the idea of running for president since 1988. However, "The Donald," as he was sometimes known, had shown no long-term attachment to either the Republican Party or conservative principles. He had been loudly pro-choice on abortion, changed his party registration at least five times in his lifetime, had contributed to liberal Democrats including Hillary Clinton and Senator Chuck Schumer, and had called for the impeachment of President George W. Bush. He was thrice married, had boasted of his affairs with married women, and had been frequently enmeshed in lawsuits and bankruptcies related to his business dealings. His forays into politics, such as they were, had been unconventional. Most recently, in 2011, Trump had announced that he was financing a search for President Obama's African birth, an endorsement of "birtherism" that he would not set aside until September 2016. If his candidacy had been a turn of the wheel at one of his casinos, almost no one would have taken the bet. Indeed, Las Vegas odds of Trump winning the GOP nomination were rated 15–1 in August 2015; another firm gave him 100–1 odds of going all the way to the White House.[1]

Republican insiders thought of the candidates in different categories—filling "lanes" that pitted contestants for particular constituencies against each other until, by elimination, one would remain in each lane to fight it out for the ultimate victory. In this thinking, an "establishment" lane was led by Jeb Bush, who would compete against Lindsey Graham, John Kasich, and even Marco Rubio. The fact that Rubio, a Tea Party favorite in 2010 who defeated establishment candidate Charlie Crist in the GOP primary, was placed in the "establishment" lane was partly a testament to how mainstream the Tea Party had become. The Tea Party itself supposedly had a lane, shorn of Rubio, consisting of Ted Cruz and Rand Paul. A "social conservative" lane featured Ben Carson, Rick Santorum, and Mike Huckabee. And so on. Eventually, the concept of lanes would be reduced in the minds of both analysts and campaign strategists to just two: Trump and not Trump, with the remainder of candidates fighting among themselves to become the main opponent to Trump.

It is worth taking a moment to consider the contenders who ended up vying most seriously for the "not Trump" championship. Each had considerable strengths. They also turned out to have weaknesses, including a common incapacity to consolidate the "not Trump" lane. Bush began as the frontrunner, with high name recognition, a successful record as governor of Florida from 1999 to 2007, an ideological positioning as a moderate conservative, and an impressive national network of donors and organizers inherited from his father and brother. This inheritance, however, was a large part of his undoing, as he was clearly identified with a Republican establishment that was out of favor with too much of the party's base. More generally, he was a dynastic scion, brother of a president who had left office with a 34 percent approval rating. He was the ultimate insider in an outsider's year and sometimes seemed to exude a sense of entitlement, or at least indifference. "I might have to lose the primary to win the general election," he once mused, though no one who loses the primary makes it to the general election. Though he began with a lead, he also suffered from high negatives.

Marco Rubio, with his Hispanic surname, fluent Spanish, modest background, and strong defense of Reagan conservatism, had seemed to many a formidable candidate ever since his election to the Senate from Florida in 2010. He was featured on magazine covers as the great Republican hope, and had decided on a run in 2016 despite having to compete with his mentor in Florida politics, Jeb Bush. He was a fresh face, but had served longer in the Senate than Barack Obama had in 2008 and had been Speaker of the Florida House before that. He was a candidate who, in theory, could bridge varying factions in the party—Tea Party, business Republicans, social conservatives, foreign policy hawks. But for many he was too young (or looked too young, with a baby face that belied his years in politics), too glib, too "establishment," or too moderate in his tone. He had been badly hurt by his entanglement in the Gang of Eight immigration proposal and then his subsequent attempts to back away from it, and he had alienated some libertarian-leaning members of the Tea Party with his interventionist national security views.

Ted Cruz, on the other hand, had not allowed his Tea Party credentials to be undermined while in office. Like Rubio, he was young, smart, and well-spoken. Unlike Rubio, he also built a strong organization almost everywhere, and arguably made more and better use of data than anyone else in the Republican field. His campaign was aimed first and foremost at the True Conservatives who Cruz thought controlled the Republican primary process. In 2013, Cruz had been the driving force in using the budget process to try to defund Obamacare, a strategy that resulted in a brief government shut-down. He had largely avoided the taint of "insider" or "establishment" by making himself hated by Senate Republican leadership, starting with Mitch McConnell, whom he had called a "liar" on the floor of the Senate. However, his conservative positions and persona made it difficult for him to broaden his support. Finally, John Kasich had a resume that might have secured the nomination in other years. He was also governor of the crucial state of Ohio, and polled better against Hillary Clinton than any other major Republican contender. He brought together Middle America and Washington, D.C., and, like Bush, his record was somewhere on the moderate conservative side of the spectrum—where the real fulcrum of the Republican primary electorate usually resides, among the self-described "somewhat conservative." In a crazy year, Kasich could hope to appear as the "adult" in the race. However, in 2016, Washington was more of a drag than usual, and his Ohio experience had been tainted in the eyes of fiscal conservatives by his decision to accept Medicaid expansion as part of Obamacare. Moreover, he chose to position himself as an ideological renegade, in the mold of an Arlen Specter or Jon Huntsman—two notably unsuccessful aspirants—rather than where the bulk of his record would naturally put him.

On the outsider/ideological grid, Bush and Kasich were on the inside center, Cruz was on the outside right, and Rubio was on the middle of the inside-outside spectrum and the right of the ideological spectrum. Bush could never appeal to the Tea Party or the anti-establishment sentiment ultimately channeled by Trump. Rubio, rather than building bridges, was caught betwixt and between—too establishment for the Tea Party that had embraced him in 2010, too conservative for others. Cruz could appeal to some of Rubio's people but fewer of Bush's and Kasich's. Kasich was anathema to many of Cruz's people and some of Rubio's. Ultimately, winning the "not Trump" primary proved so difficult that no one did.

From the moment in June 2015 that Trump glided down the escalator at Trump Tower in New York to announce his candidacy for the Republican presidential nomination, he controlled the message and tempo of the contest, making bold statements in everyday language (what communications experts call "demotic rhetoric"). At the beginning, most of his competitors and nearly all analysts saw Trump as a colorful diversion from the real race between the serious candidates, at worst a buffoon who should be humored until he inevitably fell of his own weight. Trump's public relations consultant Stephanie Cegielski, who left the campaign early on, would later contend that Trump himself never expected to win and aimed to burnish his brand by finishing second in the Republican field as a protest candidate.[2] His opponents' biggest concern was not that he would win, but rather that he would lose, leave the party, and take his voters with him. To hem him in, the RNC brokered a pledge that each candidate would support the ultimate nominee. By the time most saw him for what he was—a serious threat—he had staked his claim to a powerful plurality and could not be dislodged.

In retrospect, it is tempting to criticize Trump's opponents for shortsightedness, but in reality almost no one got Trump right.[3] He was a mysterious candidate, committing a series of blunders that would likely have sunk any other candidate. His announcement statement at the beginning of his campaign achieved notoriety when he said of Mexican immigrants, "When Mexico sends its people, they're not sending their best. . . . They're sending people that have lots of problems, and they're bringing those problems with us. They're bringing drugs. They're bringing crime. They're rapists. And some, I assume, are good people."[4] Weeks later he ridiculed war hero and 2008 GOP presidential nominee Senator John McCain of Arizona for having been a prisoner of war, saying, "I like people who weren't captured."[5] After the first Republican presidential debate, Trump assailed moderator Megyn Kelly of Fox News, blaming her menstrual period for tough questions. He also mocked a disabled reporter.

Nevertheless, he struck a chord with voters, attacking both parties with gusto, calling American political leaders "stupid," and promising to "make America great again" (a slogan first used by Ronald Reagan in 1980) by bringing back lost manufacturing jobs, building a wall with Mexico and making them pay for it, and renegotiating trade agreements. "We're not winning anymore," Trump complained. Trump's wealth also worked to his benefit, giving him the appearance of a "winner" and allowing him to claim to know how to stop Washington corruption; he could not be bought, but rather was someone who had bought politicians himself! Some analysts were surprised that the billionaire could make a connection with working-class voters, but those voters, it turns out, resent condescending professionals much more than the super-rich, who they often admire and dream of emulating.[6] Trump, some suggested, might be the American version of former Italian premier Silvio

Berlusconi, a media magnate who parlayed his wealth and bold image into power.

Only days after Trump announced his candidacy, an illegal immigrant named Francisco Sanchez shot and killed Kate Steinle on a San Francisco pier, an incident that received national attention; Sanchez had previously been deported five times and admitted that he kept coming back to San Francisco because it had declared itself a "sanctuary" for the undocumented.[7] Trump may also have been fortunate that the front-runner at the time was Jeb Bush, offering a perfect foil for an outsider campaign—not only the consummate insider but also the next in line of the premier Republican family dynasty in America. Trump quickly took to calling Bush "low energy Jeb," a barb aimed at Bush's apparent diffidence at running for president. Bush also tripped when asked whether the Iraq War was a mistake, taking five days of incoherence to reach a conclusion. Trump ridiculed him for that, too, while asserting (against the evidence) that he had been a strong opponent of the war ("a terrible mistake") from the beginning. In one debate, Bush pushed back by defending his wife against a slight by Trump. Rick Perry and John Kasich took a few shots at Trump early. Otherwise, for the most part, Trump was unscathed in the fall of 2015, as his multitudinous rivals jockeyed against each other. Speaking for many, Marco Rubio's campaign manager Terry Sullivan admitted wrongly assuming "that gravity would take its course. Why would I engage in a fight with a skilled knife-fighter? Let someone else go and attack him."[8]

It was difficult for any of them to get noticed. Ted Cruz began as very complimentary of Trump, seeing that some of his issues were Trump's as well (especially immigration and a general disdain for the establishment). Cruz clearly hoped that being nice to Trump would make it easier to inherit his supporters whenever he collapsed. In the meantime, he worked to establish himself as the conservative candidate in the race by not allowing anyone to get to his right in any issue. Marco Rubio also tried to steer clear of Trump, though his participation in the unsuccessful Gang of Eight immigration proposal made him a target of Trump (as well as Cruz and others). Chris Christie, it was learned in late 2016, had reached by the fall of 2015 a modus vivendi with Trump, in which the two would look after each other and whoever dropped out first (Trump initially confided that he thought it might be him) would endorse the other.[9] Carly Fiorina had a moment of glory when she turned on Trump at a presidential debate, giving him a dose of his own medicine after he had attacked her appearance: "Women all over the country heard you loud and clear."[10] She gained a few points in the polls but quickly lost them.

Underscoring the degree to which it was shaping up as an outsiders' year, the one candidate other than Trump to gain noticeable traction in the fall of 2015 was Ben Carson, the famed neurosurgeon who was the only person in the field with as little political experience as Trump. Both nationally and in the first-voting state of Iowa, Carson came up quickly, challenging or even surpassing Trump's poll numbers. He did it by offering an undiluted outsiderism that was also free of Trump's vulgarities and moral irregularities. In October and November, Trump was sliding, and it seemed possible that the critics were right: maybe he was a transient meteor, whose flight across the sky was already crashing down.

Then events intervened. On November 13, ISIS supporters waged a mass terror attack in Paris; less than three weeks later, a married couple of radical Islamic terrorists attacked a local government holiday party in San Bernardino, California, killing fourteen before dying themselves. Trump seized on the moment, demanding a temporary complete halt to Muslim immigration. In contrast to the progressive pieties of the Obama administration, which could not even countenance the use of the term "Islamic terrorism," Trump's stand was noteworthy. To many Americans, it was shockingly extreme (even Ted Cruz politely disagreed with Trump's position). To many others, it represented a refreshing outburst of common sense and a rebuke to political correctness, another successful example of Trump's demotic rhetoric. However one saw it—and Trump himself would later back away from it—it reestablished the New Yorker as a force with momentum. The terrorist attacks also helped Trump by putting a premium on the appearance of strength, and it fatally undermined other candidates, especially Rand Paul, whose libertarian distrust of the National Security Agency suddenly seemed misguided and dangerous, and Ben Carson,[11] whose campaign manager would later say "There was an opportunity for a nice outsider to win until Paris came, and then all of a sudden (voters) needed 'strength' again."[12]

Other candidates never had momentum to lose and gain back again. Pataki, Jindal, and Gilmore never gained traction. The repeat contenders Perry, Huckabee, and Santorum also languished toward the bottom of the pack, unable to reprise past successes. Surprisingly, Scott Walker of Wisconsin, widely seen as a serious contender, was never able to translate his state labor successes into a broader agenda or broader support. Seeing the writing on the wall, he dropped out in September, warning that other candidates should do the same or they would be paving a road for Trump. Joining him on the island of non-survivors, candidates who quit the race before the end of the year included Rick Perry, Bobby Jindal, Lindsey Graham, and George Pataki.

Throughout the last half of 2015, most of the candidates did what candidates always do. They raised money, some more than others. If Jeb Bush was no longer the leader of the polls, he solidified his position as leader of the bank account. Bush raised more than any other candidate, and the super PACs backing him raised more than any other outside groups. The candidates debated, mostly in the placid, respectful, and rehearsed style to which they were accustomed. The candidates, or at any rate the ones who were not out of their league, built organizations, sought endorsements, and carefully honed their messages. While they prepared, Trump broke all the rules. He foreswore fundraising and spent little on the army of pollsters and consultants that traditionally surrounds every major campaign. He relied on rallies, Twitter, and free media to spread his message; by one estimate, he eventually received nearly $2 billion worth of free media coverage through mid-March 2016.[13] Though Fox News, Breitbart, and the Drudge Report were at the forefront of Trump's media extravaganza, more liberal outlets such as CNN and CBS joined, too, compelled by the colorful copy (and perhaps, some conservatives warned, by a secret desire to pump up Hillary Clinton's weakest opponent). CBS executive Les Moonves explained that Trump's candidacy "may not be good for America, but it's damn good for CBS. . . . The money's rolling in and this is fun."[14] Trump eschewed endorsements as a matter of necessity— there were few Republican officeholders willing to back him—though lack of endorsements also made him a more authentic outsider. He largely eschewed organization, relying instead on his ephemeral charisma. In and out of debates, he kept his opponents off balance by simply refusing to play by the rules of civility; he "punched down" at trailing contenders more than any other candidate.[15]

As 2015 turned to 2016, the campaigns prepared to meet the test of reality. The battle would move from planning to execution—and in Trump's case, from rallies to the voting booth. He could get people to wear his trademark red "Make America Great Again" hats, but could he get them to go to the polls and pull the lever? Many doubted that he could. In the cold of Iowa, they would soon have reason to doubt some more.

IOWA

As always, the first-in-the-nation Iowa caucuses were the focus of considerable candidate and media attention. For a time in the fall, Ben Carson led, but by December, the battle had resolved itself into two distinct contests: a struggle for first place between Donald Trump and Ted Cruz, and a contest for third place among a gaggle of candidates, including Carson, Marco Rubio, Rand Paul, and Jeb Bush. Cruz began his rise in early October, at the same time Carson did, but continued rising after Carson had peaked and fallen back. In early December, Cruz took the lead in the RealClearPolitics poll average, only to see Trump regain it in early January. In the back-and-forth, Cruz attacked the libertine Trump in down-home Iowa by tagging him with the label "New York values." Trump countered by citing the courage and patriotism of 9/11, but Cruz would not pay the full price for his comment until later. In the meantime, Rubio had passed Carson into third place in mid-December and had started a sharp climb the last ten days of January, propelled by an exchange with an atheist at a campaign event that went viral and brought many evangelical voters into his camp.[16] On January 31, the day before caucus day, the RealClearPolitics polling average showed Trump at 28 percent, Cruz at 23 percent, and Rubio at 17 percent, with others well behind.[17]

The results of the caucuses the next day demonstrated the difficulty of polling in a low-turnout contest decided by a largely invisible organization and last-minute trends. Cruz won with 28 percent, Trump finished second with 24 percent, and Rubio nearly snuck past Trump with 23 percent. As soon as the votes were counted, some commentators rushed to declare Trump dead, or at least severely wounded. At the very least, he had "underperformed" his polls, casting doubts on whether his professed supporters, many of whom were not regular voters, would show up to the polls. At the same time, Rubio maneuvered to take full advantage of his third-place showing, making the first "victory" speech of the evening and treating the result as a win worthy of serious momentum. Cruz's hope was that Trump had been proven a paper tiger; Rubio's hope was that neither Cruz nor Trump had broad enough appeal to go the distance, and his own third-place finish would focus attention on him as the most viable alternative.

However, the entrance polls also showed potential for Trump to remain a force in the race, especially as terrain shifted to other states with different demographics.[18] Trump won voters with high school education or less, while Cruz won those with some college and Rubio won college graduates and postgraduates. Cruz and Rubio both outdid Trump among those who had participated in caucuses before, but a very large number (45 percent) said they were new voters, and Trump won those decisively. Iowa was an open caucus, and one in five voters were independents; Trump and Rubio shared the win among them, with Cruz trailing. Cruz won a big plurality among self-described "very conservative" voters, Rubio won a solid victory among "somewhat conservative" voters, and Trump won among "moderate" voters. In heavily evangelical Iowa, where nearly two-thirds of Republican caucus-goers described themselves as "born-again or evangelical Christians," Cruz won the evangelical vote, as expected. However, Trump not only won the non-evangelical vote but also finished second among evangelicals, edging out Rubio. Rubio's opportunity and challenge were clear—he did well among a variety of groups (for instance, he was the only Republican to break 20 percent among both evangelicals and non-evangelicals), but he would have to make an extra move to go beyond being everyone's second choice.

The issue environment was not clarified in Iowa, either. Trump won a huge margin among voters citing immigration as their top concern, but that was only 13 percent of the voters. One in four said the economy was their top concern; Rubio won that group. One in four said terrorism and one in three said government spending were most important, and Cruz was their man. Interestingly, Rubio also beat Trump on terrorism. The December San Bernardino attack may have revived Trump's campaign nationally, but, at least in Iowa, it did not translate into votes. Among voters who put electability at the top of the list of things they were looking for in a candidate, Rubio had the edge; among voters looking for a nominee who shared their values, Cruz won decisively; among the one in three who wanted a candidate who "tells it like it is" or "can bring change," Trump prevailed, as he did decisively among those who wanted a candidate outside the establishment. (Trump also accumulated another insulting moniker for an opponent: "Lyin' Ted," he claimed implausibly, had won by falsely claiming that Ben Carson was about to leave the race.) The voters who preferred experience in politics split their votes between Rubio and Cruz, both first-term senators. If nothing else, it was clear that this was going to be an outsider year.

NEW HAMPSHIRE

Next would come the New Hampshire primary on February 8. Expectations by Cruz and Rubio that Iowa would push them into stronger contention in the Granite State were dashed. In the end, Cruz finished a distant third to Trump, and Rubio surged before crashing into fifth place after a disastrous few minutes in a televised debate the weekend before primary day.

For all of the drama provided by New Hampshire in the past, Donald Trump's eventual victory in 2016 was foretold by months of consistent polling. Indeed, Trump led the RCP polling average in New Hampshire from July 28, 2015, through the primary, most of the time by ten to twenty percentage points.[19] After Iowa, some analysts questioned whether the polling would hold up. One reporter observed among Republican activists and officials "a remarkable level of confusion, frustration, and just plain bewilderment at what is going on in their state's presidential race."[20] Incredulous long-time New Hampshire Republican activists asserted that they did not know any Trump supporters and doubted that his strength was solid. One veteran political operative noticed Trump signs in front of houses that had never displayed signs before. Trump was not the kind of candidate who had done well in New Hampshire in recent years—the John McCains and Mitt Romneys—nor was he doing what candidates normally do (i.e., building an organization and doing retail politics). He even had the temerity to insult the editor of the legendary *Manchester Union-Leader* when he failed to receive the paper's coveted endorsement.

Yet, at the end of the day, the polls were proven right: Trump won with 35 percent. John Kasich, his nearest competitor, kept his campaign alive with 17 percent. Ted Cruz held on to third with 12 percent. Jeb Bush scratched his way ahead of Marco Rubio with 11 percent to Rubio's 10.5 percent. A total of 3,157 votes separated Cruz from Rubio, and only 1,278 separated Bush from Rubio.

Other than Trump's victory, the biggest story of the primary was Rubio's failure to capitalize on Iowa. His campaign had laid out a plan (the "3-2-1 plan") predicated on a third-place finish in Iowa, a second-place finish in New Hampshire, building to a win in South Carolina that would propel him to the nomination. And, in line with this strategy, Rubio's RCP poll average in New Hampshire had gone from 9 percent and fifth place on January 29 to 16 percent and second place on February 5.[21] Then Chris Christie set his sights on Rubio. Christie complained that Rubio was a robot, programmed with scripted responses to every question. At the final pre-primary debate, Rubio fell into the trap. Arguing that President Obama had not been incompetent, but rather very competent at advancing a pernicious left-wing agenda, Rubio was challenged and repeated his argument, coming back to it yet again moments later nearly verbatim. Christie pounced on the "robotic" Rubio. Although by most accounts Rubio's debate performance was otherwise effective, it was these few moments that were replayed in the media over and over. Rubio's momentum was halted, his support shrank, and he was exiled back to fifth place. Christie had taken Rubio down but did himself no favors. Having done Trump's work for him, he finished sixth.

Overall, Trump was the big winner. Not only did he himself win by a large margin, but one of his most promising opponents was waylaid and John Kasich and Jeb Bush were encouraged to continue the fight, Kasich for several months. So what did Trump have going for him that the Republican pros of New Hampshire did not see?

First, though New Hampshire had recently favored establishment candidates, it has long had a dissident streak in both parties. On the Republican side, Ronald Reagan beat the establishment's George H. W. Bush in 1980, the Trump-lite Pat Buchanan gave Bush fits in 1992 then beat Bob Dole in 1996, and John McCain who won in 2000 was the maverick in the race. In the 1992 general election, Ross Perot won nearly 23 percent of the vote, above his national total of 19 percent. Even on the Democratic side, unexpected difficulties in New Hampshire helped convince both Harry Truman and Lyndon Johnson not to seek reelection. Trump was able to tap into this latent tendency.

Second, the demography of New Hampshire was much more fitted for Trump than Iowa. Most notably, while the Iowa Republican electorate had one of the largest percentages of evangelicals in the country, New Hampshire had one of the smallest—25 percent. As in Iowa, Trump did much better among the non-evangelicals than among the evangelicals, 38 percent to 27 percent.[22]

However, this explanation obscured the breadth of Trump's victory. Trump actually narrowly won the evangelical vote, too, with 27 percent to Ted Cruz's 23 percent and Marco Rubio's 13 percent. He broadened his coalition in other ways. He again decisively won the high school educated, but this time won other educational categories, including postgraduate, by smaller margins. He also won every income group, both men and women, and both first-time Republican primary voters and veteran voters (with a slight edge to the former). Two out of five voters in the primary were independents, but he won equal percentages among them and among Republicans.

In New Hampshire, Trump won among those most concerned with electability as well as those who most wanted a candidate who tells it like it is and those looking for an agent of change. Cruz edged out Kasich among those who wanted a nominee who shared their values, meaning that neither Kasich nor Rubio finished first in any category of candidate quality. Trump won voters who said the candidates' position on issues was most important and those who said leadership qualities were key. Not least, Trump won among every ideological group, even beating Cruz 36–23 percent among the self-described "very conservative." While Trump's victory was broad, he did best among those who said their families were falling behind and those who said they were "very worried" about the nation's economy. At the same time, his message seemed to evoke optimism, as he won 45 percent among the plurality who said life for the next generation of Americans would be better and only 31 percent among those who predicted it would be worse. Overall, 50 percent said they wanted someone from outside the establishment (versus 44 percent who preferred someone with experience), and Trump won a whopping 62 percent of that group. This sentiment was the engine pulling his otherwise multifarious and not entirely consistent train.

Other candidates could draw little comfort from a detailed analysis of the results. John Kasich finished second, but also demonstrated the limits of his appeal, winning 27 percent among self-described moderates but only 14 percent among the somewhat conservative and 6 percent among the very conservative. Kasich and Bush finished first and second among those looking for experience, but that was cold comfort in an outsider year. In that respect, both Cruz and Rubio appeared to fall between the stools, with too much experience to satisfy the outsider vote and not enough to compete for those who wanted experience. The greatest hope for anyone not named Trump was that the victory of the Orange was broad but not deep, netting just over one third of the vote. Kasich, Cruz, Bush, and Rubio had combined for over 50 percent, and this did not count the also-rans who littered spots six and below. Each nourished the possibility, perhaps even the expectation, that Trump had hit his ceiling in a favorable state, and that someone—preferably themselves—could beat him by consolidating the rest of the vote.

Within a few days after New Hampshire, the consolidating process had advanced. Huckabee, Paul, and Santorum had already left the race after Iowa. Now, in the wake of New Hampshire, Christie, Fiorina, and Gilmore departed. But would it be enough?

SOUTH CAROLINA

The next major contest was in South Carolina on February 20. Since 1980, South Carolina had been a critical primary for Republicans, the gateway to the South and a frequent "firewall" for the establishment. South Carolina had a significant evangelical vote, but also a large military vote and an active Republican business community. It was South Carolina that restored Bob Dole to political health in 1996, where George W. Bush regained his footing after losing New Hampshire to John McCain in 2000, and where McCain held the line against Mike Huckabee in 2008. Many outsiders had come into South Carolina with high hopes and left with a widening disaster on their hands.

Despite all of this, Trump had opened an early lead in South Carolina as he had around the country. Along with being a historically pro-establishment state, South Carolina was a state that remembered all the textile jobs it had lost to international competition, and had long been open to protectionist arguments on trade. The other candidates had opportunities. Kasich might have had appeal to South Carolina Chamber of Commerce Republicans. Cruz had placed great hopes in evangelical, conservative South Carolina, seeing a win there as a strategic necessity to opening up the South. Jeb Bush, whose father and brother had both owed their nominations in no small part to South Carolina, hoped to trade on family and the momentum, such as it was, from surviving New Hampshire. Rubio needed a strong showing if he was to have any hope of overcoming his New Hampshire setback. Ben Carson was already a spent force, having come within a couple of points of Trump in mid-November polls before collapsing.[23]

In the event, Kasich faded fast and Bush never expanded his meager support. Cruz built a stellar organization but treaded water in the polls. Rubio, however, engineered a comeback that put him back in the race. He, too, built an organization, and then he landed some key Republican endorsements in a state that values endorsements more than most: Governor Nikki Haley, Senator Tim Scott, and Congressman Trey Gowdy. Haley was the nation's first Indian American woman governor, while Scott was South Carolina's first African American senator since Reconstruction. At an event at the state capitol, Haley noted the ethnically diverse nature of the assembly on stage, saying "Take a picture of this, because the new group of conservatives that's taking over America looks like a Benetton commercial"[24]—an Indian American woman, a younger black man, and an older white man working for the election of a young Cuban American.

Meanwhile, Trump did what Trump did, holding rallies, tweeting, and making full use of free media. However, his position in South Carolina did not seem to have been bolstered by his win in New Hampshire, as his RCP polling average peaked at 38 percent on February 6 (three days before New Hampshire) and began a decline. A critical debate near the primary date also seemed to put Trump in jeopardy. Aligning himself with Code Pink and other victims of Bush Derangement Syndrome, Trump announced his view that George W. Bush had lied about weapons of mass destruction in Iraq and should be blamed for 9/11.[25] Cruz and Rubio teamed up effectively against Trump for the first time in the campaign. While Cruz waxed erudite on the Constitution, Rubio got on Trump's level, calling him a "con artist," ridiculing him for his ignorance about health care policy, and asserting that if Trump's father had not left him millions, he would have been hawking watches in Times Square. Rubio and Cruz had, together, gotten the better of Trump.

When the votes were counted, Trump remained in the lead, winning just under 33 percent. After lagging badly for most of the past several months, Rubio climbed into second place with 22.5 percent, about 1,100 votes ahead of Cruz. No one else came close. Bush, Kasich, and Carson, in that order, all clustered between 7.8 percent and 7.2 percent. Bush promptly exited the race, his campaign and associated super PACs having spent more than anyone, a large percentage of it on negative ads attacking Rubio.

The cross-ideological appeal Trump showed in New Hampshire was weakened, as Cruz beat him among the two in five voters who described themselves as "very conservative."[26] Although Trump performed the (for him) rare feat of doing better among evangelicals than non-evangelicals, he lost to Cruz among voters who said that shared religious beliefs mattered a great deal. Trump won among voters who said that immigration was their number one issue (10 percent), that the economy was their number one issue, and that terrorism was number one, but he had to settle for a three-way tie with Cruz and Rubio among the quarter of the electorate that saw government spending as the top issue. Rubio again won the voters looking for electability and Cruz the voters looking for someone who shared their values; Trump again won among those who said they wanted a candidate who "tells it like it is" and "can bring change." Rubio won among those who said they were "dissatisfied" with the federal government, Trump among those who called themselves "angry" with it. Finally, the electorate was split evenly between those who wanted experience and those who wanted someone outside the establishment; Rubio won the former, Trump the latter. Exit polls also showed that Trump had indeed faltered in the last week of the campaign, which was won by Rubio and Cruz. Trump had the votes of nearly half of those who had made their vote decision earlier, and only 17 percent of those who decided in the last week.

Had the field thinned enough to take on Trump? Had Trump peaked in New Hampshire and started his inevitable descent in South Carolina? Had voters realized after New Hampshire that a vote for Trump was not just a protest but could actually make Trump the Republican nominee? As these questions came to the fore, the race was about to turn away from retail politics to a national campaign.

SUPER TUESDAY

The next major event of the campaign was so-called Super Tuesday on March 1, on which twelve states, ranging from Vermont to Georgia and Minnesota to Texas, would vote. Leading up to Super Tuesday, Trump secured a solid win in the Nevada caucuses, his first win in the West and his first in a caucus state. As in South Carolina, Rubio finished second, slightly ahead of Cruz but far behind Trump.

Trump, as was often the case, was his own worst enemy. Just as many Republicans started to make peace with the idea of a Trump nomination, he declined in a February 28 interview to repudiate David Duke, the Louisiana politician who had been a member of the American Nazi Party and a grand dragon of the Ku Klux Klan. Though he did so several days later, Trump's reluctance to criticize Duke put a spotlight on other unsavory aspects of Trump's campaign. One, closely related, was the degree to which Trump seemed to be favored by white supremacists and the shadowy "alt-right," a loose online collection of hard-right nationalists whose targets were "globalists," which, it turned out, often meant Jews. The alt-right's tactics frequently included online harassment and merciless trolling. Another was the increasing tendency of violence to break out at Trump rallies, accompanied by the candidate's own exhortations to punch protestors in the nose or carry them out on stretchers.[27] One rally in Chicago had to be cancelled due to fears of violence. Late in the fall campaign, videos surfaced seeming to show that at least some of the violence had been deliberately stirred up by Democrats, who had hired provocateurs to infiltrate Trump rallies and start fights,[28] but scenes of rallies degenerating into chaos fed into another narrative: Trump as authoritarian.

Even if some concerns proved extreme—commentator Andrew Sullivan's long piece for the *Atlantic* positing that Trump was a neo-fascist was the prototype of an entire genre—Trump himself gave sufficient cause for worry. Aside from encouraging his supporters to beat up protestors, Trump had expressed admiration for Russia's Vladimir Putin as a "strong leader," declared that he hoped to make it easier to sue the media for libel, promised what sounded to many like a presidency unchecked by Congress or the Constitution, and told audiences that he could and would give them "everything." His "populism" was increasingly seen as coupled with a "strong-man" mentality, both from his end and from that of his most ardent fans. Republicans who were not anxious to hand him the keys to the party dug in.

Super Tuesday itself produced a mixed result, though one generally favorable to Trump. A widespread campaign stretched every campaign thin except Trump's, which was not based on organization or even local media buys but on national publicity and celebrity. Trump won Alabama, Arkansas, Georgia, Massachusetts, Tennessee, Vermont and Virginia. Cruz won Alaska, his home state of Texas, and Oklahoma. Rubio prevailed in the Minnesota caucuses. In the Colorado caucuses, no presidential preference poll was recorded; first-round delegates were selected, which ultimately led to national convention delegates. When that process concluded weeks later, Cruz had swept the Colorado delegation.

Trump did not break 50 percent in any of his wins, did best in the atypically liberal state of Massachusetts, and barely beat Cruz in Arkansas, Rubio in Virginia, and Kasich in Vermont. Even where Trump won handily, as in Georgia, Cruz and Rubio frequently combined for more votes, and Rubio could plausibly blame Kasich for keeping Virginia and Vermont out of his reach. In each state, the patterns laid down earlier mostly held, and differences in outcomes were more the result of different state demographics than any shift in momentum.

The contest had pretty clearly become a three-man race, but Kasich did not get the memo, and insisted on hanging on in hopes of winning Ohio and enough delegates to keep Trump from the convention majority in the splintered field. Indeed, the campaigns and the national media had caught on to the possibility that no candidate would achieve a majority before the convention met in Cleveland in July. From this point until early May, the candidates not named Trump believed they could force an open convention by staying in the race, at which point all bets would be off and anyone could, in theory, have a shot. Practically speaking, Cruz seemed best positioned to benefit, as his organization was quietly effective at collecting delegates even in states Trump had won.[29]

EARLY MARCH

Following Super Tuesday, the voters continued to decline to identify a clear winner, though there were some indications that Cruz had seized the momentum. Contests on March 5 produced Cruz wins in the Kansas primary and Maine caucuses and narrower than expected Trump wins in Kentucky and Louisiana, where Trump underperformed in polls and Cruz came in a close second and would have won handily with either Rubio's or Kasich's votes. On March 8, Trump came back with solid wins in Michigan and Mississippi and a narrow win in the Hawaii caucuses, while Cruz won decisively in Idaho. Still, Trump was unable to breach 50 percent; even in Michigan, Trump's 154,000 vote margin was eclipsed by Kasich's third-place 322,000 vote total.

In this moment of the campaign, three facts stood out. One was Trump's continued march forward on a broad front, despite difficulties. Another was Kasich's persistence despite not finishing higher than third in any of the eight most recent contests. The third was that Cruz had eclipsed Rubio as the main conservative alternative to Trump. Indeed, in these latest rounds of contests, Rubio had actually fallen to fourth place in Maine, Michigan, and Mississippi.

Rubio's sudden collapse was attributable to two factors. He had simply not won enough, and his voters began to sense that he was not viable in the primaries, though they continued to look forlornly at polls showing him beating Hillary Clinton handily in the fall. And he followed up his more aggressive debate approach by taking the bait that Trump had long been dangling to join him in the newly fetid gutter of American politics. Long abused by Trump as "little Marco," Rubio made a strategic decision to take on his tormentor, to fight fire with fire. He overstepped, ridiculing Trump with relish and noting his "small hands," in reference to an old wives' tale linking small hands to other small appendages. Trump then defended his manhood in the next debate, assuring the television audience that all of his appendages were appropriately sizable. Rubio and Trump had succeeded in bringing the presidential race down to a level not seen in living memory, but only Rubio paid a price. He had come into the race with higher positive ratings and lower negatives of any Republican candidate, and he had largely maintained that position until now. No one expected any better of Trump, but they had expected better of Rubio, and his excursion to the gutter was a deep blow to an already-struggling campaign.

MINI–SUPER TUESDAY

March 15 marked the next major event, mini–Super Tuesday. Rubio's Florida would be at stake, as would Kasich's Ohio. Also in play were Illinois, Missouri, and North Carolina. Kasich and Rubio needed home state wins to remain viable, Cruz wanted a win to maintain what momentum he had, and Trump was looking for the kill and collecting endorsements from Ben Carson and conservative lioness Phyllis Schlafly.

Kasich survived, winning Ohio handily. To no one's surprise, Rubio was trounced by Trump in Florida and formally ended his campaign. Trump ran the table elsewhere, winning Illinois in a blow-out, North Carolina by a few percentage points, and Missouri by a whisker. In the Show-Me State, Cruz lost by 1,700 votes while Kasich was collecting 93,000 and Rubio 57,000. Trump's percentages were inching upward, but were still well short of a majority, reaching 43 percent in Florida, 41 in Missouri, 40 in North Carolina, 39 in Illinois, and 36 in his loss in Ohio.

One week later, Trump and Cruz traded victories in the American Southwest, as Trump defeated Cruz 38–25 percent in Arizona and Cruz demolished Trump by a 70–14 percent margin in Utah (with Trump doing so badly that Kasich actually finished ahead of him, in second place). Trump's embarrassment in Utah was closely related to the fact that 2012 GOP presidential nominee Mitt Romney, the Republican Party's most famous Mormon, had intervened in the 2016 contest with a scathing speech critical of Trump. The New Yorker, Romney argued, was a fraud "who has neither the temperament nor the judgment to be president."[30] Opinion was divided over whether Romney's attack hurt Trump nationally or strengthened his position as an outsider who would shake up both parties' establishments, but in Utah the effect was clear.

The Romney speech drew attention to an increasingly bitter civil war on the right. Not only had the party's recent nominees from the center-right—Romney, John McCain, George W. Bush—been critical of Trump, but much of the conservative movement's intellectual core also found Trump philosophically, temperamentally, and morally unfit for the presidency. Arguably the two most high-profile conservative journals of opinion—*National Review* and *The Weekly Standard*—were firmly anti-Trump, as was RedState, one of the most widely read conservative websites. On March 17, a group of notable conservative activists held a conference call to try to plot a unified strategy to stop Trump. On the other side, pro-Trump intellectuals launched the *Journal of American Greatness*, trying to identify (or construct) a philosophical framework for Trumpism around a revival of nationalism. (It folded in June but was quickly replaced by *American Greatness*.) The intellectual debate was real, though one commentator would later note, "There is a profoundly asymmetrical relationship between Trump and the Trumpist intellectuals, who must formulate their doctrine without much assistance from its namesake."[31] Trump also had his share of supporters and opponents in the world of conservative talk radio, and evangelical leaders were, as usual, divided.

WISCONSIN

After the Arizona-Utah pairing, the candidates had two weeks to prepare for the next primary, in Wisconsin, which took on the character of a showdown. Trump saw Wisconsin as a prime target, a heavily white, working-class state with relatively few evangelicals. Cruz saw a great opportunity to seize the initiative in a state that had trended Republican recently. Cruz took full advantage of the state's unique conservative talk radio network, which was almost uniformly aligned against Trump (in contrast with much of conservative talk radio elsewhere).[32] He also benefited from the strong endorsement of Governor Scott Walker. The Texan pleaded with Wisconsin voters to stop the Trump tide, which he argued was doomed to defeat in November. Cruz also benefited from Trump's ham-handed Twitter attack on his wife, Heidi. (Cruz additionally accused Trump of planting a story with the *National Enquirer* alleging five extramarital affairs by Cruz—the first of at least three times during the campaign that Trump either fed or fed off of the *Enquirer*, whose publisher was a personal friend, as if it were a serious news source.[33])

When Cruz won a clear 48–35 percent victory in Wisconsin, it seemed possible that he had turned a corner. He had finally put together the coalition of very conservative and somewhat conservative voters that has dominated Republican nominations for decades. Trump won only among self-described moderates. Cruz won among all age groups, all education levels, and all incomes. He crushed Trump among evangelicals but also beat him among non-evangelicals. He won handily among Republican voters and tied Trump among independents. He won on the economy, terrorism, and government spending, and on both electability and values. He won among those who felt betrayed by GOP politicians as well as those whose did not. Notably, Cruz nearly drew even with Trump among those whose first priority was making change.[34] Wisconsin was nearly as broad and complete a victory for Cruz as New Hampshire had been for Trump a very long two months before. If he could replicate this success, perhaps with a unified Republican Party behind him, Cruz could win it all.

Those who anticipated an open convention were more convinced than ever that it would come to pass. Trump had thus far won only 37 percent of the total reported primary and caucus vote. Analysts feverishly calculated what outsized proportion of remaining delegates Trump would have to (improbably) win in order to prevail on the first ballot. It was widely assumed that if Trump did not win on the first ballot, he would not win at all. Fighting back, the Trump campaign loudly argued that the convention should automatically back whichever candidate received the most votes in primaries, even if he had fewer than the majority required by the rules. Polls of voters in Republican primaries showed that about two-thirds agreed. Going further, some Trump backers threatened to publicize the Cleveland hotel rooms of delegates who held a contrary position, raising the phenomenon of "doxing" to a new level.

THE END APPROACHES:
THE NORTHEAST PRIMARIES

It turned out that, far from Wisconsin being a turning point on Ted Cruz's way to the nomination, it was his last hurrah. The Republican leadership, still smarting from his jabs, did not coalesce behind him. John Kasich did not clear his way for a one-on-one battle against Trump. And geography was not his friend. He would not again run against Trump in a state as hospitable as Wisconsin. Instead, Cruz had to face Trump in the Northeast, starting with New York on April 19, followed by Pennsylvania and four other Northeastern states on April 26. The race would not return to the Midwest until the Indiana primary on May 3. By the time Indiana came around, the dynamic of the race had changed dramatically. Trump himself adjusted after Wisconsin, turning to new people and a somewhat more orthodox approach to regain his footing.[35]

As the New York primary loomed, it became clear that Cruz was in no position to compete there. His strong political conservatism, his Texas persona, and his cultural dismissal of New York combined to render him unviable. His remark denigrating "New York values," delivered to the voters of Iowa in January, was replayed endlessly. Cruz gamely tried to explain that he meant liberal Democratic Manhattan values, and that the poor, longsuffering Republicans of New York should understand what he meant, but to no avail. Hoping to scrape at least a few delegates out of the barrel, Cruz even campaigned in heavily black precincts in Brooklyn where a few hundred Republican votes might net him some district delegates. As a candidate, John Kasich was actually more suited than Cruz to New York, and he continued running his own vigorous campaign. But New York was Donald Trump's city, and it would not turn its back on its favorite son. Trump finally broke the 50 percent barrier in the New York primary, winning with 60 percent to Kasich's 25 percent and Cruz's 15 percent.

New York was a sign of things to come. Cruz got little traction in Pennsylvania, losing to Trump 58 percent to 22 percent (Kasich finished third with 20 percent). Trump also won by wide margins in Rhode Island (with 65 percent), Delaware (63 percent), Connecticut (59 percent), and Maryland (57 percent). In all four, Kasich finished second, with Cruz bringing up the rear with 20 percent or less. Over the previous two months, Trump had suffered many setbacks and had not yet consolidated Republican support, but he was the only candidate who had proven appeal in all parts of the country. Now, just when he had needed it the most following his Wisconsin debacle, the race had turned to his own backyard, and he made the best of it. The speed with which Cruz's position deteriorated was startling, not least to Cruz himself. His Wisconsin momentum extinguished, his claim to electability in tatters, and the breadth of his appeal exposed as inadequate, Cruz turned to Indiana on May 3 as one last hope.

INDIANA AND THE END

When the candidates returned to the heartland, it was a different race. Polling had been sparse, but an Indiana poll taken just after Wisconsin showed Cruz leading Trump by double digits. After Trump's Northeastern romp, the candidates had switched places.[36] Although Cruz's supporters continued to point to math showing how Trump could be stopped on the first ballot, his campaign began to exude a sense of desperation. Indiana would be make or break. It was reported that Cruz and Kasich finally made a deal to stop cutting into each other's support, and that Rubio had been involved in the talks. Kasich would give Cruz a clean shot in Indiana, while Cruz would back off from Oregon and New Mexico, the states next up. However, both candidates were already on the ballot in all of those places, and it was too late to be removed.

Then, trying hard to reenergize his campaign, Cruz used a maneuver not seen since Ronald Reagan had attempted it on the eve of the 1976 Republican national convention: he named his prospective vice presidential running mate and campaigned as a team. The name was Carly Fiorina, the former Hewlett-Packard executive who ran in the earliest primaries and had bloodied Trump's nose in an early debate. She was an unquestioned outsider, a determined fighter, and a woman, a helpful attribute in both the immediate fight against the misogynistic Trump and the long-term fight against the feminist icon Hillary Clinton. However, Fiorina brought no appreciable base of support—she had dropped out after securing 4.1 percent of the vote in New Hampshire, and had no obvious pull even in her former home state of California—and her early designation by Cruz seemed to many like the sign of a flailing campaign.

Cruz may have briefly closed the gap (one poll had him within two points) but he never restored his Wisconsin coalition. He did get the endorsement of Governor Mike Pence, but Pence waited until the last minute and made enough positive comments about Trump during the course of his statement that he had to issue a clarification reaffirming that he had, indeed, endorsed Cruz. On the day of the vote, Trump inflicted a final indignity, highlighting a photograph on the front page of the *National Enquirer* tabloid purporting to show Cruz's father, Rafael, with JFK assassin Lee Harvey Oswald. "I mean, what was he doing—what was he doing with Lee Harvey Oswald shortly before the death? Before the shooting?" Trump asked. "It's horrible."[37] Cruz fumed that Trump was a "pathological liar," "utterly amoral," and "a narcissist at a level I don't think this country's ever seen."[38] But the voting went on. When those votes were counted, Trump had prevailed, 43 percent to 32 percent, with Kasich in third with 15 percent. That night, Cruz threw in the towel, followed the next day by Kasich, though both notably declined to endorse Trump.

The exit polls showed a large gender gap, with men supporting Trump and women Cruz (men were 53 percent of the electorate). Trump won each income group; each educational category but postgraduate; Republicans, independents, and Democrats; both the moderate and the somewhat conservative (Cruz retained his stronghold among the very conservative); evangelicals and non-evangelicals; and the two-thirds who said immigration, terrorism, or the economy were the top issues (as usual, Cruz won among those who were most concerned about government spending). Trump also prevailed among those who most wanted electability (a reversal from Wisconsin), a candidate who tells it like it is, and a candidate who can bring change (Cruz held on to the values voters); those who were satisfied with the federal government, those who were dissatisfied, and those who were angry;

those who felt betrayed by Republican politicians and those who did not. Cruz won the vote of those who decided in the last week, but two-thirds had decided earlier, and they voted for Trump.[39] Cruz had predicated his campaign on the belief that there were enough "True Conservatives" in the country—especially in places like Indiana—that they could carry him to the nomination. It was a fatal miscalculation.[40]

Nine states voted after Indiana, but they were a formality, swept by Trump. The results, though never in doubt, exposed the degree to which many Republicans remained resistant to the Trump takeover. With every opponent having abandoned the fight, leaving only their names on ballots as a retreating army leaves its tents and broken-down jeeps as detritus of a lost battle, Trump nevertheless won only two-thirds of the vote in Nebraska, Oregon, and South Dakota, around three-quarters of the vote in West Virginia, California, Montana, and New Mexico, and around 80 percent in Washington and New Jersey. In those nine states, he averaged 73 percent. In other words, with no one running against him, anywhere from one in five to one in three Republican voters preferred no one. (Four years earlier, Mitt Romney had also faced an enthusiasm deficit, though doubtless among a different set of voters: in the eleven primaries after Romney cleared the GOP field, he had averaged 71 percent of the vote.)

Trump would clearly have his work cut out as he tried to unify the Republican Party behind him. In an NBC/Wall Street Journal survey taken just after the Indiana primary, only 72 percent of Republican voters nationwide said they intended to vote for him in November.[41] Complicating his task would be the #NeverTrump movement of Republicans, mostly conservatives, who saw Trump as flatly unfit to be president for both moral and political reasons. #NeverTrump followers could not abide Trump's nomination and sought ways through November 8 to liberate themselves from his anchor. First, they hoped to work through the convention to deny Trump a victory. Not since 1952 had a nominee been drafted at a national convention, but what made this hope slightly plausible was that Trump's campaign was very effective at communications but very ineffective at organization and mastering the rules of local delegate selection. Cruz's success in winning delegates in states that had voted for Trump had been the basis of his hopes for many weeks. Now Cruz was gone, but his delegates were not. The #NeverTrump organizers sought to adopt convention rules that would have unbound delegates on the first ballot, allowing the hidden Cruz delegates and others to nominate, if not Cruz (who showed little appetite for the plan), at least someone other than Trump. The rebels had the open support of hundreds of delegates, but failed to get sufficient votes on the convention rules committee to bring the proposal to a floor vote.[42]

Simultaneously, prominent Trump opponents such as *Weekly Standard* editor William Kristol took a different tack, trying to recruit an independent conservative candidate for president. Mitt Romney was asked to run, but he declined. Ditto for senators Ben Sasse of Nebraska (who had said Trump had the appeal of a "dumpster fire") and Tom Coburn of Oklahoma. Congressman Justin Amash, Rand Paul, John Kasich, Mark Cuban, Condoleezza Rice, and retired generals James Mattis and Stanley McChrystal were mentioned as possibilities, but they did not bite. After that, the effort drifted into obscurity, as *National Review* contributor David French was recruited, gave it serious consideration, and declined. Finally, Evan McMullin agreed. McMullin had been policy staff director for the House Republicans and, before that, a CIA special operations officer. He was young, well informed, conservative, and articulate—a perfect contrast with Trump. He was also completely unknown to the broader public.

Trump tried to tamp down the civil war on his right, first by issuing a list of possible Supreme Court nominations within days of his Indiana win. The list of conservative jurists was developed with assistance from the Heritage Foundation, and it sought to give conservatives a solid reason to be enthusiastic about Trump. Even if they had questions about Trump as president, they could hope that he would save the Court from liberal judicial activism. It was the first time he had fully leveraged the unique situation brought about by the death of Justice Antonin Scalia, which left a vacancy in the majority of what had frequently been a 5–4 Court. Weeks later, with the same objective—consolidating conservative Republican support—he named Mike Pence as his running mate. In between, though, he undid much of the benefit of his "pivot" to presidentialness by publicly attacking the judge in the Trump University civil case. Trump called Judge Gonzalo Curiel a "Mexican"—he was actually a second-generation American citizen born in Indiana—and wondered aloud if he could get a fair trial from him.[43] The remarks bought Trump a drop in the polls and considerable criticism from Republican officials. It was not the first time he stepped on his own lines, and it would not be the last. If the Court list had quieted his critics on the right, the Curiel comments inflamed them, showing Trump again to be a loose cannon who was about to be handed the party's nomination in an eminently winnable year.

It did not matter. RNC Chair Reince Preibus took pains to disclaim any desire to overturn the will of the primary voters. The convention met in Cleveland, swatted down the proposed #NeverTrump rules changes, nominated Trump and Pence without obstacle, and prepared for the fall. The major note of discord was introduced by Ted Cruz, who had been given a prime speaking slot just before Mike Pence's acceptance speech. Cruz congratulated Trump on his nomination, but refrained from endorsing him by name, calling on viewers to "vote your conscience." He left the stage to boos. Trump had succeeded in doing what almost no one thought possible when he announced his run a year earlier.

AN OVERVIEW OF THE SURPRISE

Overall, Donald Trump's victory in the Republican nominating contest was little short of astounding. He had defeated sixteen talented rivals and won more primary votes than any previous Republican aspirant despite having no political experience, breaking most of the received rules of presidential campaigning, being opposed by the vast majority of Republican officeholders and veteran activists, trampling on multiple tenets of traditional Republican doctrine, and polling worse against the probable Democratic nominee than all of his chief competitors.

Through his decisive win in Indiana, Donald Trump prevailed in twenty-seven state contests—twenty-five primaries and two caucuses—of the forty-two that were held. Ted Cruz won five primaries and six caucuses (if one includes Colorado, Wyoming, and North Dakota, where no first round results were tallied but Cruz was reported to have won the most delegates through the process), Marco Rubio one primary and one caucus, and John Kasich one primary. Through that point, Trump had won 40 percent of the total vote, Cruz 28 percent, and Kasich 14 percent.

Consequently, it is tempting to dismiss Trump as simply a minority nominee. No examination of his victory can ignore the fact that nearly two-thirds of the Republican primary and caucus vote went to someone other than Trump when it mattered. Trump was a singular figure whose unique campaign had the good fortune to be competing against sixteen more conventional opponents, at least half a dozen of whom were strong contenders. Even in Indiana, the last stand of the last holdouts, anti-Trump Republicans never got the one-on-one contest against Trump that might have stopped him. Not until mid-March did conservative leaders meet in Washington to formulate a strategy for unifying in the face of the Trump threat—too little, too late.

This recognition leads one to dwell on the potential importance of contingency. What if the GOP had swung behind Cruz after Wisconsin? If Kasich had left the race sooner? If Rubio had not been ambushed by Christie in New Hampshire? If Bush had not run, serving as an establishment lightning rod to Trump's lightning, or run but not trained most of his fire on Rubio? If the rest of the field had taken the fight to Trump in the fall before he consolidated his lead in state after state?

Though the fractured field is the beginning of understanding the Republican primary campaign, it cannot be the end. One still has to account for the 40 percent who supported Trump through Indiana and their enthusiasm. In this respect, it is clear that Trump's coalition was broader than many credited, and much broader than anyone else's. Geographically, he won in states including New Hampshire and Massachusetts, South Carolina and Alabama, Virginia and Tennessee, Michigan and Indiana, Nevada and Arizona, Missouri and Maryland, New York and Delaware—New England, the deep South, the peripheral South, the Midwest, Southwest, border states, and mid-Atlantic: industrial states, financial capitals, and agricultural heartland. Demographically and politically, Trump had a core support that he secured consistently: lower-income voters, the less educated, older voters, more secular voters, those angry with Washington and Republican leaders, and above all those who called change their first priority. But he often carried with him other groups as well. Likewise, he won the voters most concerned with immigration, but those were usually only around 10 percent of the electorate; he won the nomination by convincing the much larger number whose first issue was the economy or terrorism. Trump also pointed the way to a new kind of victorious Republican coalition, an alliance between the somewhat conservative and the moderates lubricated by his own ideological amorphousness and unspecificity on policy matters. It was the "Republican Party," not the "conservative party," Trump reminded people after Indiana.[44]

Trump's adversaries clearly misgauged his "ceiling" of support, which continued rising slowly through the primary season, and probably overestimated the degree to which the non-Trump vote was a reliably anti-Trump vote. Cruz, Rubio, and Kasich might have been right that each of the others were blocking them from forming an anti-Trump coalition, but it is far from obvious that the coalition each could have constructed would have included the supporters of all three candidates. By the end, exit polls showed that many Kasich supporters would not support Cruz and vice versa. Polls in a handful of states testing hypothetical two-way races against Trump showed Cruz winning three of five but Trump consistently beating Rubio or Kasich.[45] Moreover, Kasich's voters often bore a greater resemblance to Trump's than to Cruz's, especially ideologically.

Thus, the split field is not enough to explain Trump by itself. Nor is the prevalence of open primaries, sometimes blamed by Republicans for Trump's ascendancy. While Trump did well in open primaries among non-Republican voters, his vote percentages among Republicans beat his vote percentages among non-Republicans in seventeen of the twenty-six contests through Indiana for which there were exit or entrance polls; in another three, his Republican vote percentage matched his non-Republican vote. In every critical open primary that he won, Trump won among Republicans as well as among the interlopers.[46] While some analysts blamed racism or anti-government extremism in the GOP electorate for Trump's rise, a more plausible explanation would focus on his serendipitous role as the most outside option in a year ripe for outsiders, both inside and outside the Republican Party, and both inside and outside the United States. He was the only candidate wealthy enough and blunt enough to be independent from every establishment, political, economic, social, cultural, and media. And yet the media also showered $2 billion of free attention on him, though much of it was negative.

In the end, Trump won the Republican nomination because he jumped out to an early lead, consolidated it while his opponents were busy fighting among themselves, and held on despite late advances by others. The polling history of key primary states such as New Hampshire and South Carolina show a Trump lead that was established in the summer and fall of 2015. In the twenty-six states through Indiana that had exit or entrance polls, Trump won the vote, usually handily, among those who reported that they had decided their vote more than one month before. He lost the last week of the campaign in nineteen of the twenty-six states, averaging only 28 percent among these late deciders versus 56 percent among the early deciders.[47] In the delegate count, Trump seized the lead in New Hampshire and never gave it up. David Kochel, Jeb Bush's chief strategist, argued that, in retrospect, "At a certain point, probably in August (2015), Trump was Godzilla walking into a power plant. Everybody thought he'd blow up, and he just got stronger every time."[48]

To assess Trump's 2016 primary success, one must also take a longer view of politics, institutions, and society. For example, one has to take a deeper look at the respective party coalitions. Ever since the McGovernite takeover of the Democratic Party in 1972, Democrats have made inroads into the suburban professional class while repelling white working-class voters with policies ranging from forced busing to abortion on demand to anti-anti-communism. As a result, white working-class voters became an increasing proportion of the Republican vote. In 2002, John Judis and Ruy Teixiera, in their book *The Emerging Democratic Majority*, noted the importance of this trend to George W. Bush's 2000 victory over Al Gore.[49] However, for years Republicans had primarily appealed to this group on the basis of cultural issues, moral issues, or simple patriotism. Although a handful of Republican presidential aspirants such as Mike Huckabee or Rick Santorum experimented with economic themes, Donald Trump was the first to appeal to this group forcefully and wholeheartedly on the basis of economic concerns.

He was not only filling a vacuum within the Republican Party but also filling a vacuum in national politics more generally. Although there was often intra-party dissension at the congressional level on issues of trade and immigration, for decades there had been something of a cross-partisan consensus at the presidential level in favor of free trade and loose enforcement of immigration law. Millions of Americans had legitimate causes for concern. Although nearly all economists agree that free trade is a net benefit for the country as a whole, some individuals, regions, and sectors of the economy found themselves at the losing end. It can hardly be considered unproblematic that there are 11 million people residing in the United States in violation of the laws of the country. And then there was what seemed to many the suffocating pretensions of political correctness, a political culture of euphemism so feckless that self-evident acts of jihadism had to be discussed as "workplace violence." Yet there was no one at the presidential level speaking to those concerns—until Trump. Political analyst Michael Barone also noted that, through the end of March, Trump's greatest primary successes came in states with the lowest levels of social connectedness, his worst showings in states with the greatest social connectedness.[50] He was, like many populists (or demagogues) before him, speaking for people who felt disconnected from the dominant structures of society. In these respects, Trump's rise appears considerably less surprising.

Not least, Trump's rise was made possible, if not inevitable, by changes in the presidential nominating system that were inaugurated in the McGovern-Fraser reforms of 1972, which sought to make the system more "democratic" and more open to political outsiders. The party establishments, to use a term greatly in vogue in 2016, were stripped of much of their power to influence presidential nominations. Caucuses were made more open, primaries proliferated (though the McGovern-Fraser Commission did not explicitly call for an increase in primaries), and popular results of both caucuses and primaries were tied more closely to delegate outcomes. Gone was the role of the national convention as a mediating institution exercising judgment to pick the best candidate; gone was the ability of the party organization to block extreme or unqualified aspirants; gone, perhaps, were barriers to popular demagoguery. The "popular arts" feared by the Founders were to be rewarded rather than diverted.[51]

Although the reforms were undertaken with Eugene McCarthy's movement campaign in mind, it is far from clear that the reforms worked to the benefit of grassroots political movements. Movements thrive on organization. Candidates such as Barry Goldwater, George McGovern, Pat Robertson, and, in 2016, perhaps Ted Cruz were movement candidates. All did better in caucuses than in primaries, because organization is the coin of the caucus realm, but the reform system deemphasized caucuses and multiplied primaries. It has not been movement outsiders but what one might call "unconnected outsiders"—outsiders trading on personal charisma and often-vague promises to the alienated and not connected with an existing organized movement—that have seen their stock rise in the modern system. These candidates tend to do better in primaries, which can be won by ephemeral appeals through media, than in caucuses. In different ways, George Wallace and Jimmy Carter were early examples. Donald Trump was the most recent example, the unconnected outsider in purest form (even Wallace and Carter had been state governors).[52] To Trump's defenders, he had simply used the system to his benefit, as any candidate should be expected to do. To his detractors, he was the embodiment of the longstanding fear that the reformed nominating system was bound at some point to produce a dangerous demagogue or a popular but unqualified buffoon. Or both.

Demagogue, buffoon, budding statesman, or something else, Trump had defied the odds to become the Republican nominee. And the surprises were only beginning.

NOTES

1. Brett Steidler, "Vegas sets odds for Republican nomination," *Las Vegas Review-Journal*, August 7, 2015, http://www.reviewjournal.com/politics/elections/vegas-sets-odds-republican-nomination.

2. Stephanie Cegielski, "An Open Letter to Trump Voters from His Top Strategist-Turned-Defector," March 28, 2016, http://www.xojane.com/issues/stephanie-cegielski-donald-trump-campaign-defector.

3. An interesting exception can be found in Henry Olsen and Dante J. Scala, *The Four Faces of the Republican Party: The Fight for the 2016 Presidential Nomination* (London: Palgrave Pivot, 2016). The authors did not predict Trump's nomination but noted that he "throws a wrinkle into our analysis, as so far he draws from all factions of the party. The primary factor behind his rise is an outsider appeal to voters without a college degree" (142).

4. "Here's Donald Trump's Presidential Announcement Speech," *Time*, http://time.com/3923128/donald-trump-announcement-speech/.

5. Ben Schreckinger, "Trump Attacks McCain: 'I like people who weren't captured,'" *Politico*, July 8, 2015, http://www.politico.com/story/2015/07/trump-attacks-mccain-i-like-people-who-werent-captured-120317.

6. Joan C. Williams, "What So Many People Don't Get about the U.S. Working Class," *Harvard Business Review*, November 10, 2016, https://hbr.org/2016/11/what-so-many-people-dont-get-about-the-u-s-working-class.

7. Emily Shapiro, "San Francisco Shooting Suspect Says He Kept Coming Back to the City to Avoid Deportation," ABC News, July 6, 2016, http://abcnews.go.com/US/san-francisco-shooting-suspect-coming-back-city-avoid/story?id=32247731.

8. James Hohmann, "Trump's Pollster Says He Ran a 'Post-Ideological' Campaign," *Washington Post*, December 5, 2016, https://www.washingtonpost.com/news/powerpost/

paloma/daily-202/2016/12/05/daily-202-trump-s-pollster-says-he-ran-a-post-ideological
-campaign/5844d166e9b69b7e58e45f2a/.

9. Tom Davis, "Donald Trump Had Expected to Drop Out in 2015, Endorse Chris
Christie, New Book Says," http://patch.com/new-jersey/mendham-chester/donald-trump
-expected-drop-out-2015-endorse-chris-christie-0.

10. M. J. Lee, "Let the sparks fly: Carly Fiorina takes on Donald Trump," http://
www.cnn.com/2015/09/16/politics/republican-debate-cnn-2016/.

11. Paul's campaign manager, Chip Englander, argued at a panel discussion after the
election that the San Bernardino attack completely upended Paul's campaign strategy.
Hear the first panel on http://iop.harvard.edu/get-inspired/campaign-managers-confer
ence/campaign-president-managers-look-2016.

12. Hohmann, "Trump's Pollster Says He Ran a 'Post-Ideological' Campaign."

13. Nicholas Confessore and Karen Youresh, "$2 Billion Worth of Free Media for
Donald Trump," *New York Times*, March 15, 2016, http://www.nytimes.com/2016/03/16/
upshot/measuring-donald-trumps-mammoth-advantage-in-free-media.html?_r = 0.

14. Eliza Coillins, "Les Moonves: Trump's Run is 'damn good for CBS,'" *Politico*,
February 29, 2016, http://www.politico.com/blogs/on-media/2016/02/les-moonves-trump
-cbs-220001.

15. Justin H. Gross and Kaylee T. Johnson, "On Twitter, Trump 'punches down' far
more than any of his rivals," *Washington Post*, October 27, 2016, https://www.washing
tonpost.com/news/monkey-cage/wp/2016/10/27/trump-hurls-far-more-attacks-via-twit
ter-than-any-of-his-rivals-sad/?utm_term = .ce22af74721a.

16. Guy Benson, "Video: Atheist Voter Confronts Rubio in Iowa," http://townhall
.com/tipsheet/guybenson/2016/01/20/rubio-321-strategy-n2106714.

17. "Iowa Republican Presidential Caucus," http://www.realclearpolitics.com/epolls/
2016/president/ia/iowa_republican_presidential_caucus-3194.html.

18. See http://www.cnn.com/election/primaries/polls/IA/Rep.

19. New Hampshire Republican Presidential Primary, http://www.realclearpolitics
.com/epolls/2016/president/nh/new_hampshire_republican_presidential_primary-3350
.html.

20. http://www.washingtonexaminer.com/byron-york-gop-fear-and-loa thing-in-new
-hampshire/article/2581329.

21. http://www.realclearpolitics.com/epolls/2016/president/nh/new_hampshire_re
publican_presidential_primary-3350.html.

22. http://www.cnn.com/election/primaries/polls/NH/Rep.

23. South Carolina Republican Presidential Primary, http://www.realclearpolitics
.com/epolls/2016/president/sc/south_carolina_republican_presidential_primary-4151
.html.

24. Zeke J. Miller, "Rubio Endorsement Rally Shows a More Diverse Vision for
GOP," *Time*, http://time.com/4230230/marco-rubio-nikki-haley-tim-scott-endorsement
-diversity/.

25. Michael Grunwald, "Trump Goes Code Pink on George W. Bush," *Politico*, http://
www.politico.com/magazine/story/2016/02/trump-code-pink-bush-iraq-9-11-213630.

26. http://www.cnn.com/election/primaries/polls/SC/Rep.

27. Jeremy Diamond, "Donald Trump on protester: 'I'd like to punch him in the
face,'" CNN, http://www.cnn.com/2016/02/23/politics/donald-trump-nevada-rally

-punch/; Ben Mathis-Lilley, "A Continually Growing List of Violent Incidents at Trump Events," *Slate*, http://www.slate.com/blogs/the_slatest/2016/03/02/a_list_of_violent_incidents_at_donald_trump_rallies_and_events.html.

28. Alex Pfeiffer, "Hidden Camera Video Shows Democrats Sent Agitators to Trump Rallies," *The Daily Caller*, http://dailycaller.com/2016/10/17/hidden-camera-video -shows-democrats-sent-agitators-to-trump-rallies/.

29. Janet Hook and Reid J. Epstein, "Cruz's Stealth Delegate Hunt," *Wall Street Journal*, March 22, 2016, A1.

30. "Transcript of Mitt Romney Speech," *New York Times*, http://www.nytimes.com/ 2016/03/04/us/politics/mitt-romney-speech.html.

31. Kelefa Sanneh, "Intellectuals for Trump," *New Yorker*, January 9, 2017, www .newyorker.com/magazine/2017/01/09/intellectuals-for-trump.

32. Ashley Parkler and Nick Corasaniti, "6 Talk Radio Hosts, on a Mission to Stop Trump in Wisconsin," *New York Times*, April 4, 2016, http://www.nytimes.com/2016/04/ 05/us/politics/donald-trump-wisconsin-radio.html?_r = 0.

33. Eric Bradner and Gregory Kreig, "Ted Cruz: Trump team planted *National Enquirer* sex scandal story," CNN, March 29, 2016, http://www.cnn.com/2016/03/29/poli tics/amanda-carpenter-ted-cruz-allegations/.

34. http://www.cnn.com/election/primaries/polls/WI/Rep.

35. Jonathan Lemire and Jill Colvin, "After Wisconsin stumble Trump moves to reshape his campaign," Associated Press, April 9, 2016.

36. "Indiana Republican Presidential Primary," RealClearPolitics, http://www.real clearpolitics.com/epolls/2016/president/in/indiana_republican_presidential_primary-57 86.html.

37. Nolan D. McCaskill, "Trump accuses Cruz's father of helping JFK's assassin," *Politico*, http://www.politico.com/blogs/2016-gop-primary-live-updates-and-results/2016/ 05/trump-ted-cruz-father-222730.

38. David Wright, Tal Kopan, and Julia Manchester, "Cruz unloads with epic take-down of 'pathological liar,' 'narcissist' Donald Trump," CNN, http://www.cnn.com/2016/ 05/03/politics/donald-trump-rafael-cruz-indiana/.

39. Indiana Exit Polls, CNN, http://www.cnn.com/election/primaries/polls/IN/Rep.

40. Ross Douthat, "The Defeat of True Conservatism," *New York Times*, May 3, 2016, http://www.nytimes.com/2016/05/04/opinion/campaign-stops/the-defeat-of-true-conser vatism.html.

41. John Harwood, "Despite Divide, Trump Still Needs His Party," *New York Times*, May 10, 2016, http://www.nytimes.com/2016/05/11/us/politics/despite-divide-trump-still -needs-his-party.html.

42. Ed O'Keefe, "Dozens of GOP delegates launch new push to halt Donald Trump," *Washington Post*, June 17, 2016.

43. "Trump Says Judge's Mexican Heritage Presents 'Absolute Conflict,' " *Wall Street Journal*, http://www.wsj.com/articles/donald-trump-keeps-up-attacks-on-judge-gonzalo -curiel-1464911442.

44. David Rutz, "Trump: This Is the Republican Party, It's Not Called the Conserva-tive Party," *Washington Free Beacon*, http://freebeacon.com/politics/trump-republican -party-not-called-conservative-party/.

45. The states where these questions were asked included Michigan (Cruz over

Trump), Mississippi (Trump over Cruz), Missouri (Cruz), North Carolina (Cruz), and Ohio (Trump). Ohio was the only state where Kasich beat Trump one on one, and Rubio never did. "Republican exit polls," CNN, http://www.cnn.com/election/primaries/polls.

46. "Republican Exit Polls," CNN, http://www.cnn.com/election/primaries/polls.

47. "Republican Exit Polls," CNN, http://www.cnn.com/election/primaries/polls.

48. Hohmann, "Trump's Pollster Says He Ran a 'Post-Ideological' Campaign."

49. John B. Judis and Ruy Teixeira, *The Emerging Democratic Majority* (New York: Scribner, 2002).

50. Michael Barone, "Does lack of social connectedness explain Trump's appeal?" *Washington Examiner*, March 27, 2016, http://www.washingtonexaminer.com/does-lack -of-social-connectedness-explain-trumps-appeal/article/2586842.

51. James W. Ceaser, *Presidential Selection: Theory and Development* (Princeton, NJ: University of Princeton Press, 1979).

52. Andrew E. Busch, *Outsiders and Openness in the Presidential Nominating System* (Pittsburgh: University of Pittsburgh Press, 1997).

Chapter Four

Race to the Bottom

The General Election

Although neither nomination was made official until the party conventions in July, the race was on by May, when everyone knew who the contestants were going to be. It would be a contest between the two most-disliked major party nominees in the history of polling. By roughly a 10 percent margin, Hillary Clinton was disliked more than she was liked; Donald Trump's negative gap was twice that of Clinton. And about one in four voters reported disliking both major party nominees; in 2012, that had been true of only one in ten.[1] Despite ups and downs through the fall, those numbers did not fundamentally change. Frequently it seemed that each candidate's campaign boiled down to reminding voters that they were not the other.

It was, consequently, fitting that the unofficial opening of the general election campaign consisted of a black mark for each, the opening salvos in a downward spiral that produced perhaps the most uncivil, vulgar, and scandal-flecked campaign in living memory. Trump greeted his de facto nomination with the attack on Judge Gonzalo Curiel, which served to reduce his poll standing versus Clinton and light a new fire under the #NeverTrump movement in the Republican Party. Clinton prepared for her convention with a near-miss from the FBI and a direct hit from WikiLeaks.

After a several-month-long investigation of Clinton's non-secure email use while secretary of state, an investigation that offered five immunity from prosecution deals and led to rampant speculation about Hillary in an orange jumpsuit, FBI Director James Comey took the unusual step of announcing the bureau's non-binding recommendation to the Justice Department on July 5. Comey was clearly uncomfortable in his role, which amounted to electoral arbiter—should one of the two presumptive nominees who were likely to have a real shot at the White House be indicted?—and he split the difference. On one hand, he recommended against prosecution, saying "no reasonable prosecutor would bring such a case." He then proceeded to say that Clinton and her colleagues "were extremely careless in their handling of very sensitive, highly classified information" ("extreme carelessness" being essentially a synonym for "gross negligence," the statutory description of the offense being investigated) and indicated that it was not unlikely that "hostile actors" had gained access to Clinton's email system.[2] Two days later Comey testified before Congress that Clinton had made numerous false statements about her email use.[3] Hillary Clinton would escape prosecution—for now. Yet millions of Americans were left with the politically damaging impression that she was guilty and had only escaped because her last name was "Clinton," an impression furthered by the supposedly unplanned meeting between Attorney General Loretta Lynch and Bill Clinton at the Phoenix airport shortly before Comey's announcement. Days later, Republicans at their convention in Cleveland took up the cry "Lock her up!" and Trump had a new Twitter moniker to use for the rest of the campaign, to take the place of "Low-energy Jeb," "Lyin' Ted," and "Little Marco": "Crooked Hillary." Everyday language cutting through the clutter of politics.

The WikiLeaks revelations disrupted the Democratic convention and began a drip-drip-drip that plagued Clinton until November. The first round of documents was leaked emails from the Democratic National Committee that showed that the DNC had stacked the deck for Clinton in her primary battle against Bernie Sanders. DNC chair, Florida Congresswoman Debbie Wasserman Schultz, was forced to resign, and Sanders supporters at the convention felt the Bern again. For the next three months, WikiLeaks would periodically torment Clinton, revealing one embarrassing inside story after another.

The Democrats tried to counter by claiming that the DNC and Clinton campaign had been victims of a Russian hacking campaign aimed at interfering in the American election by aiding Donald Trump. This complaint had more than a small amount of plausibility to it. A number of national security experts came to believe that Russian hackers were behind the security breach, and could not have been so without the knowledge and endorsement of the highest levels of the Russian government. (Not until after the election was a more definitive report issued on the subject.) There was also evidence that Putin's army of professional internet trolls was employed on behalf of Trump.[4] For his part, Trump had spoken admiringly of Vladimir Putin as a "strong leader," his son seemed to give credence to allegations that he had substantial business dealings in Russia, and his people at the Republican convention had squashed a platform plank calling for weapons to be given to Ukraine for self-defense against Russian aggression—the only recorded instance of the Trump campaign caring about any portion of the GOP platform.[5] However, her critics could argue that Clinton might not have been a poor choice for the Kremlin, either, having been the architect of the naïve "reset" with Russia in 2009 and having signed off on the transfer of at least 20 percent of the U.S. uranium reserve to a Russian-owned company whose chairman had close ties with Bill Clinton and who had made large undisclosed donations to the Clinton Foundation.[6] Whatever the international intrigue around WikiLeaks, the short-term consequence was that Democratic unity was undermined and the image of Clinton as a corrupt insider grasping at power by any means necessary was reinforced.

The epic incidents at the beginning of the general election campaign, illuminating the tendencies and character of the individual candidates, renewed an important debate in political science. Are presidential elections mostly about "fundamentals," or mostly about "contingencies"? If they are mostly about the fundamentals, they are decided on the basis of the economy, the approval rating of the incumbent president, how unified each party is, broad contours of public opinion, and perhaps the stage in the political cycle (in 2016, the incumbent party trying to win three terms in a row). In that case, the candidates and the campaigns hardly matter, or matter only at the margins. If elections are mostly about contingencies, the candidates and the campaigns they run matter a lot, as do unpredictable national and world events—scandals, gaffes, debates, events outside the campaign that nevertheless affect the campaign. Perhaps the only thing typical about the election of 2016 was that, as usual, the election was actually shaped by the interaction of the fundamentals with the contingencies.

THE FUNDAMENTALS

One of the most fundamental of the fundamentals is the state of the economy. Here, the United States had officially been in a recovery since the summer of 2009. By October 2016, the unemployment rate had fallen to 5 percent. These happy statistics, however, had obscured other, less pleasant realities. Most notably, the Obama recovery had been the weakest economic recovery since World War II, with historically modest economic growth, job creation, wages, and productivity.[7] Real gross domestic product (GDP), the standard measure of economic growth, had grown at an annualized rate of only 1.4 percent in the second quarter of 2016 and had not reached 3 percent in any year of Barack Obama's presidency. The Gallup organization calculated the "real" unemployment rate, including part-timers who wanted full-time work and people who had dropped out of the job market, at closer to 10 percent.[8] At least three in five Americans saw the economic glass as half-empty, calling the economy poor or bad.

Obama himself had suffered through most of his presidency—and the entire time from May 2013 to June 2016—with approval ratings below 50 percent in the RealClearPolitics polling average. However, in summer 2016, Obama's average approval edged upward, finally going over 50 percent. On Election Day it was 53 percent.[9] Some analysts attributed this improvement to the slow but continuing improvement of economic statistics or to the quieting of some foreign policy crises. Others noted that Obama's approval rose as he was pushed out of the news by Trump and Clinton or speculated that he looked better to Americans when compared with those two. In any event, both the economy and the president's approval rating sent mixed signals and seemed to indicate a close election.

Perhaps the most immovable "fundamental" of the race worked against Clinton, and had to do with the election's place in the electoral cycle. Clinton would be working against the tendency of voters to want a change after two terms of the same party in the White House. In the last six decades, Richard Nixon in 1960, Hubert Humphrey in 1968, Gerald Ford in 1976, George H. W. Bush in 1988, Al Gore in 2000, and John McCain in 2008 had each tried to win a third consecutive term for their party. Nixon, Humphrey, Ford, and Gore had come agonizingly close, but only Bush had succeeded. Not coincidentally, the incumbent president he sought to follow, Ronald Reagan, was the most popular and successful of the recent presidents. Another way of thinking about political cycles was to ask whether a party's vote share was on the upswing or the downswing; here, too, Democrats were seemingly in trouble. Barack Obama's share of the vote fell from 53 percent in 2008 to 51 percent in 2012, as he became the only president to be reelected with a smaller total vote than he was elected with.

The broad contours of public opinion would reinforce that tendency toward change. Three in five Americans consistently said they thought the country was on the wrong track. The appetite for outsiders was strong, as had already been demonstrated in the Republican primaries (by Trump and Cruz) and in the Democratic primaries (by Sanders). Needless to say, Trump was better suited than Clinton to a contest driven by outsiderism.

Finally, party identification in the electorate and party unity (as expressed, among other ways, through primary election results) can be important fundamental factors, and here one would have to give the edge to Clinton going into the general election campaign. At the beginning of June, Gallup polls recorded that 48 percent of Americans identified as Democrats and 41 percent as Republicans if party-leaning independents were included.[10] She not only won well over 50 percent of the total Democratic primary vote but also obtained her main rival's endorsement at the convention. By contrast, Trump had won well under half of the Republican primary vote, his strongest rival did not endorse him at the convention, and the intellectual superstructure of the Republican Party was bitterly divided over Trump and Trumpism. On the face of it, Clinton appeared to have the stronger hand, though Democrats nursed their own deep divisions, stoked by WikiLeaks.

An entire school of political science is devoted to turning those fundamentals, in one way or another, into predictions of election outcomes. Of nine notable political scientists and economists who offered models based on some combination of the fundamentals, five—among them Yale economist Ray Fair, the unofficial dean of election models—predicted in the summer of 2016 that Trump would win a majority share of the two-party vote. One of the five dismissed his own estimate on the grounds that his model assumed that both sides featured candidates with broad appeal running reasonably competent campaigns, but Trump was a uniquely bad candidate. In other words, in this unusual circumstance, fundamentals could be overtaken by contingencies. The other four predicted that Hillary Clinton would squeak by with between 51.0 and 52.1 percent of the two-party vote. No one thought the fundamentals foretold a Clinton landslide.[11] Altogether, Michael Barone observed at the beginning of August, "It remains an open question how the seemingly irresistible force of public discontent will shift the seemingly immovable object of partisan deadlock."[12]

THE CONTINGENCIES

The candidates have both been sketched in detail. Now they can be juxtaposed: Clinton the prepared, the careful, the well organized, the cool (or, to her detractors, the cold), the co-head of an impressive political machine of national scope and a quarter-century duration. Trump the spontaneous, the unconventional, the volatile, the newcomer to politics who seemingly said whatever came into his mind. Clinton the consummate insider, Trump the ultimate political outsider. Clinton and Trump, distrusted by the ideological purists in their own parties as unprincipled opportunists; Clinton and Trump, each with their own plethora of scandals, distrusted and disliked by wide swaths of the American public. Trump's obvious weaknesses led Clinton campaign operatives to identify him early in the primary season as their preferred Republican opponent, so much that they crafted a media strategy to help promote his campaign.[13] Clinton's obvious shortcomings led Republicans to see her as eminently beatable, but also to fear that Trump was not the one to do it. For its part, Trump's campaign saw but a narrow path to victory.

Each campaign was a reflection of its candidate. Clinton's was professional and amply staffed, leaving nothing to chance. Trump's was lean and disorganized, with frequent turnover in top spots. Clinton's was well funded, spending in the end more than twice what Trump spent. Clinton opened field offices across the country, demonstrating a commitment to the "ground game" by out-officing Trump by 489–207 by early October.[14] Clinton also ran a full-fledged air campaign, a veritable barrage of television advertising, outspending her rival by $145 million to $32 million through October 4; Trump's campaign was late on the air and significantly outspent in advertising overall, though it was competitive with Clinton in the last couple of weeks.[15] Sometimes Trump's campaign seemed to consist of little more than tweets and rallies, though his digital campaign turned out to be stronger than it appeared; headquartered in San Antonio, far off the beat of most political reporters, it stayed under the radar until late in the campaign.[16]

If the Clinton camp had the advantage when going down the checklist of normal presidential campaign prerequisites, Trump had some compensating strengths. For all his apparent weaknesses, Trump's campaign had an intangible spark that Clinton's well-oiled machine seemed to lack, and a correspondingly higher level of enthusiasm among its supporters. While Clinton's strategists fought to maximize her popular vote advantage, assuming that if they did so, the Electoral College would take care of itself, Trump's planners crafted an electoral vote strategy.[17] Since the election was to be decided by the electoral vote, this gave Trump something of a strategic edge. Trump's demotic rhetoric gave him an edge in the race to break through the noise in a memorable way; free media coverage, though often negative, carried his message nonetheless. Above all, in an election in which voters seemed to be craving change, Clinton was the candidate of the status quo.

One cannot survey the candidates of 2016 without addressing the wild cards, the three independent (or third-party) candidates who had a potential to affect the race significantly. Two of these were nominees of minor parties that had worked for years to gain a share of the limelight. Gary Johnson was the Libertarian Party candidate, nominated in 2016 as he had been in 2012. Johnson was the former Republican governor of New Mexico, where he had gained fame by promoting legalization of marijuana. He was on the ballot in all fifty states and hoped to take advantage of what some analysts had called the "libertarian moment" in American politics, especially an alleged tendency of millennials to favor a combination of fiscal conservatism and social liberalism. Johnson expected to draw from both anti-Trump Republicans and anti-Clinton Democrats, and he picked William Weld, the former Republican governor from Massachusetts, as his running mate.

Jill Stein was the Green Party nominee, also repeating a 2012 run. Running on a far-left platform, Stein, who was on the ballot in forty-five states, had little appeal to Republicans but might hope to draw significant numbers of disappointed Bernie Sanders Democrats and left-leaning independents. No one could forget Ralph Nader's Green Party run of 2000, when he won 3 percent of the national vote and may very well have tipped Florida to George W. Bush.

Finally, there was the conservative independent Evan McMullin, the standard-bearer of the #NeverTrump movement. His proximate aim was to give conservatives a candidate they could vote for with satisfaction. Having gotten a late start, he was on the ballot in only eleven states and was a registered write-in in about two dozen more, so he had less opportunity to win votes. However, unlike the other two, McMullin had at least one theoretically possible, though highly improbable, path to the presidency. McMullin was Mormon, and hoped to take advantage of Utah's deep dislike of Trump (recall that he was beaten 69–14 percent by Ted Cruz in the GOP caucuses there) to be competitive in that state. If he could eke out a win in Utah, with its six electoral votes, and if Clinton and Trump were close enough otherwise, he might prevent either of the major candidates from winning an outright majority in the Electoral College. The choice would then go to the House of Representatives, which would choose from between the top three vote-getters—Clinton, Trump, and McMullin. With Republicans in the House majority (Republicans, not incidentally, for whom McMullin had been policy staff director) and no love lost between them and Donald Trump, McMullin could dream.

On balance, the match-up between candidates and campaigns was tilted toward Clinton for the duration of the race, until the last day. From January 1 until November 8, Clinton led the RealClearPolitics poll average every day except for three days in late May just before Trump's Curiel comments, when they were essentially tied, and four days in July between the Republican and Democratic national conventions, when Trump led by about one percentage point. Trump also briefly drew to within one point in late September. Otherwise, Clinton was ahead by anything from eleven points in March to three in much of September and just before Election Day.[18] She also consistently led in estimates of the Electoral College vote. As a result, Clinton was the prohibitive favorite in the election prediction markets, which generally considered her a 70–80 percent probable winner. The famed Nate Silver also made her the odds-on favorite to win throughout the fall, though he was more cautious; at the end, he gave her a two-in-three chance of winning. There were a few notable exceptions. Dilbert creator and blogger Scott Adams predicted a Trump win, as did film-maker Michael Moore, who declared in October that "This wretched, ignorant, dangerous part-time clown and full time sociopath is going to be our next president."[19] Clinton's numerical advantage among prognosticators may not have been quite as lopsided as Thomas Dewey's edge over Harry Truman in 1948, when fifty experts were polled by *Newsweek* magazine and unanimously agreed that Dewey would win, but it was not far off.[20]

What the experts tended to ignore was that Clinton's lead was not solid enough to justify the level of certainty they often exuded. While she led most national polls, she never broke 50 percent after March 2016, and there were more undecided voters than usual. Even in late October, there were three times as many undecideds as at the same point in the 2012 race.[21] More crucially, except for a few days in late October when she hit 272, RCP consistently estimated her electoral votes below the magic number of 270 needed to elect. That meant that Election Day would be suspenseful—and could even be surprising, if Donald Trump "ran the table" in important states. Clinton led all the way, but her lead was never big enough to be out of reach. When Election Day arrived, she had not yet closed the sale.

Every time Hillary Clinton seemed to be on the verge of doing so, something new would upend the race. Every time Donald Trump seemed on the verge of overtaking her, something new, usually self-inflicted, would reverse his momentum. Every few weeks would bring some new reason to dislike or distrust one of the candidates. They took turns on this roller-coaster, this race to the bottom, all the way to November 8.

BACK AND FORTH

The first stage of this back and forth came when, in the immediate aftermath of the Democratic national convention, Trump attacked the mother and father of a dead U.S. Marine who had spoken at the convention. In his remarks, Mr. Khizr Khan, a Muslim, criticized Trump for his proposal to temporarily ban Muslims from entering the United States, asking, "Have you even read the United States Constitution?"[22] While Khan and his wife, Ghizala, were being interviewed on CNN, Trump responded by tweeting "Mr. Khan, who does not know me, viciously attacked me from the stage of the DNC and is now all over TV doing the same. Nice."[23] He then engaged in a running social media battle with the Khans and their supporters for several days. Clinton was shocked, her strategists were secretly delighted, and key Republicans again took a step back. His one-point pre-convention lead suddenly became an eight-point deficit by August 8. In this case, Trump's tweets were devastating—to himself.

Over the next month, Trump slowly climbed back into contention, but was still three points down on September 11. He and some of his media allies (including the *National Enquirer*) had been raising questions about Hillary Clinton's health—she had suffered a concussion in 2012 and recently had several extended coughing fits during speaking engagements—when she collapsed and had to be helped into her vehicle at the end of a 9/11 anniversary observance in New York. Her campaign then whisked her off to an undisclosed location and provided little information for several hours. Finally, the campaign disclosed that she had been diagnosed with pneumonia several days before. The incident did two things, both of them bad from Clinton's perspective. First, her demonstrated health travails seemed to validate concerns that had been raised by Trump and raised further questions. Second, perhaps more damaging, her campaign's obfuscation reminded people of the Clintons' historic penchant for secrecy and dishonesty. If Clinton had been suffering from pneumonia for days, they asked, why couldn't the campaign have just said so?

If Clinton's fall on September 11 gave reason for some voters in the middle to doubt both her capacity and her veracity, two days earlier she had already given Trump supporters reason to write her off. In a private fundraiser in Manhattan—what better setting?—she attacked Trump supporters as racists and rubes, saying that half of Trump's voters consisted of a "basket of deplorables." Her immediate target was the "alt-right," but by anyone's reckoning the alt-right represented far less than half of Trump's support, and when her speech became public Trump supporters across the country inevitably took the remarks as a broad-brush assault on them. For the rest of the campaign, they wore the "deplorable" label as a badge of honor, an indication of Clinton's liberal snobbery. Clinton's comments may also have hurt her with voters in the middle, as it undercut her claim to be a national unifier and her general election slogan of "stronger together." Clinton's comments quickly entered the ranks of private fundraiser gaffes, alongside Barack Obama's 2008 dissection of those who "cling bitterly to their guns and their religion" and Mitt Romney's 2012 denunciation of the "47 percent" takers. Between the "deplorables" and the health episode, Clinton's lead fell to one percentage point on September 17.

Then the tide turned again. Clinton regained her footing and a bit of her lead by the time of the first debate on September 26. Historically, the first debate has been the best opportunity for the challenger—in this case, one could say Trump—to make gains on the "incumbent"—who was not quite Clinton, but almost. In addition, pressure was on Clinton to show that she was in good health. This time, it was the candidate of the status quo who seemed to do best. Trump landed some early blows on trade and the economy, and he kept coming back to this central question: Clinton had been in Washington for "thirty years" (actually twenty-four), and what did she have to show for it? Clinton, though, remained poised and hit back hard on Trump's long affair with "birtherism," which he had finally foresworn only days before; his ill treatment of contractors on his real estate projects; the possibility that he had paid no income taxes for eighteen years (an allegation Trump seemed to confirm by saying it had been "smart business"); and Trump's insulting comments toward Alicia Machado, Miss Venezuela in a Trump beauty pageant some years before. Trump was frequently rude or flummoxed and nearly always vague, and he did himself no favors when he spent the next week replaying the Khan blunder by fighting it out with Alicia Machado on Twitter. Analysis by commentators tended to see Clinton as the winner, and post-debate polls confirmed it (except for self-selected online polls, where the enthusiasm of Trump's supporters showed itself).

Clinton's lead grew to three points by October 2. The Republican ticket may have briefly stabilized the situation with a sharp performance by Mike Pence against Tim Kaine in the vice presidential debate. Here, Pence was self-assured and focused on issues while it was Kaine who constantly interrupted. But the reprieve was short-lived. On October 7, a bombshell burst that must have seemed to Clinton like the final blow from which Trump could not recover. A decade-old tape from an *Access Hollywood* interview between reporter Billy Bush and Trump became public, showing Trump on a hot mic making extremely lewd comments about women. In the interview, Trump talked about kissing a variety of women, grabbing them by their private parts, and trying to have sex with them, claiming "when you're a star, they let you do it."[24] The reaction was immediate and severe. An avalanche of Republicans condemned Trump's comments. Some prominent figures withdrew their endorsements, including Senator John McCain of Arizona and Senator Kelly Ayotte of New Hampshire, who said she would write in Mike Pence for president. House Speaker Paul Ryan, who had only endorsed Trump reluctantly, cancelled a joint campaign appearance. Altogether, by October 9, some three dozen Republican leaders had called on Trump to depart the race altogether. Former Utah governor and ambassador to China Jon Huntsman, who had previously endorsed Trump, said, "In a campaign cycle that has been nothing but a race to the bottom—at such a critical moment for our nation—and with so many who have tried to be respectful of a record primary vote, the time has come for Governor Pence to lead the ticket."[25] There were serious discussions in online media about whether it was feasible for Republicans to replace Trump at the top of the ticket with only a month to go.[26] There were even rumors reported on the anti-Trump conservative website RedState that Pence himself was wavering about remaining on the ticket.[27] It was a measure of the degree to which Republicans had been pulled onto the Trump train against their will that so many were still eager to find a new candidate at this late date. And those were just the Republicans.

Trump issued a pro-forma apology for his comments, saying, "I said it, I was wrong, and I apologize." However, never one to linger in introspection, he quickly went on the attack, saying the tape was "a distraction from the issues we are facing today." He also compared his "foolish" comments to Bill Clinton's abuse of women and Hillary Clinton's record of having "bullied, attacked, shamed and intimidated his victims."[28] He then held a media event showcasing several of Clinton's female victims before the second presidential debate on October 10. At that debate, Trump was lured into claiming that there were no women who could say that he had ever actually acted as he suggested in the *Access Hollywood* video. Within days, this claim was shattered, as, one after another, women came forward to allege that he had indeed kissed them, groped them, or otherwise attempted to force himself on them. At this point, Trump's campaign seemed to be in freefall. On October 17, Clinton led by seven percentage points in the RealClearPolitics average and was poised to break through the 270 mark in electoral votes for the first time since the end of August.[29] A huge gender gap seemed to be in the offing, with the possibility of mass defections among Republican women. Swing states that Trump desperately needed, such as North Carolina, Pennsylvania, and Ohio, were swinging Clinton's way. Republican strongholds like Georgia, Arizona, and even Texas seemed like they could be in play. In Utah, polls showed Evan McMullin moving to within striking distance of Trump, forcing the Republican campaign to dispatch Pence to the state that was normally one of the most Republican in the country. The only remaining question seemed to be whether Trump would lose respectably or in a landslide, and whether he would drag the Republican Congress down with him.

This put Trump in roughly the same position that Harry S. Truman was in three weeks before the 1948 election, when pollsters thought his situation so hopeless that they stopped polling. Having learned their lesson sixty-eight years before, they did not stop polling, but most stopped believing it was a real race. Perhaps Hillary Clinton and her campaign were among that contingent. Certainly there were observers who claimed to notice a slackening effort. Indeed, throughout the fall campaign, Clinton held many fewer campaign events than Trump—fifty-two events to Trump's eighty-eight between August 1 and October 10—a decision, according to analysts, that "reflected Clinton's risk-averse style and her campaign's calculation that she benefits by receding from the spotlight and allowing it to shine on Trump's scandals and incendiary remarks."[30] According to reports published after the election, the Clinton campaign's confidence in its data analytics operation also led it to forego polling during the last month in crucial states, some of which hardly saw the candidate in person or on the air.[31] Clinton made zero campaign visits to Wisconsin in the general election.

Then the final turn of the wheel came. It may have started, almost imperceptibly, with the third debate on October 19. It was almost certainly the most substantive of the three debates, and the one in which Trump came off best. Trump was widely disparaged for refusing to promise in advance to accept the results of the election, a refusal that fed the political conversation for days. However, he successfully hammered, as before, on Clinton as the insider, status-quo candidate, saying, "Hillary has experience, but it's bad experience." He hit her on emails, on ISIS, on the Supreme Court, on gun control, and on late-term abortion, and he drew some blood. (It also did not go unnoticed that, for the second debate in a row, Clinton offered a lengthy answer to a question about the Supreme Court without ever using the word "Constitution" except to reference the Senate's role in confirmation of judges.) For many skeptical Republicans watching the debate, Trump may have given the first real indication that he spoke their language. He also exercised more self-control than in past debates.

Although Trump amplified his claims that the election was "rigged," he also built on his improved debate performance with a policy-heavy speech—one of his few—in Gettysburg, where he promised, among other things, to support term limits for Congress, a federal hiring freeze, elimination of two regulations for every new regulation enacted, rescission of Barack Obama's unconstitutional executive orders, the end of federal funding to "sanctuary cities," the deportation of two million alien criminals, approval of the stalled Keystone XL Pipeline, repeal of Obamacare, and tax cuts and simplification, along with repeal of NAFTA, cancellation of the Trans Pacific Partnership, and other protectionist measures. As one conservative columnist noted, "As part of his Contract with the American Voter, Trump pledged to take 18 major steps on January 20, 2017. Most of these give center-right voters excellent reasons to support Trump at the polls."[32] Characteristically, he stepped on his lines by using the beginning of the speech to threaten to sue the most recent of his female accusers, and it is hard to say how much of the content of the speech penetrated the national consciousness, but it was another move in the direction of convincing the wavering—especially Republicans and conservative independents—that he met the necessary threshold of seriousness.

The real world also intervened, not least through the announcement during the last three weeks of the campaign of massive health insurance rate increases tied to Obamacare. The Affordable Care Act appeared less affordable than ever, as voters in a number of swing states faced rate increases of 20, 30, or 50 percent. The president's promise that people could keep their insurance if they liked it had gone defunct three years before; the fact that his promise that health care reform would reduce premiums by $2,500 per family was similarly shredded. Clinton, who had chosen to tie herself to Obama's mast, shared ownership of that failure. It did not help that her husband had publicly declared that Obamacare was leading to a situation—"the craziest thing in the world"—in which hard-working people were facing huge premiums and deductibles.[33]

At nearly the last moment, one final event fed Trump's momentum. On October 28, FBI Director James Comey announced that the investigation into Hillary Clinton's unauthorized email use as secretary of state would be reopened. The route by which this occurred was circuitous and sordid. Clinton's top personal aide was Huma Abedin, whose estranged husband was Anthony Weiner, former Democratic congressman from New York. Weiner had been forced to resign in 2011 after he admitted to sexting with multiple women. In 2016, a new round of Weiner sexting, this time directed at a fifteen-year-old, led to an investigation. In the process of examining the former congressman's laptop, the FBI came across a new batch of emails from Clinton to Abedin. Comey, who had clearly wanted to split the difference in July, was forced to decide in October. If he reopened the investigation before Election Day, he would be accused of tilting toward Trump. If he kept the 650,000 emails on Weiner's laptop under wraps until after Election Day, he would be accused of covering up for Clinton and keeping important information away from the voters. After receiving considerable heat in recent weeks as details emerged that seemed to show the original FBI investigation might have been corrupted to let Hillary off the hook, Comey decided to go the other way.[34] Democrats, who had praised Comey in July, were apoplectic. What Comey giveth, Comey could taketh away.

The FBI worked overtime to process the emails, developing new software to try to identify which emails had not yet been seen in previous reviews. Two days before Election Day, Comey sent yet another letter to Congress, indicating that the reopened investigation was, again, closed. But damage was done. Clinton's seven-percentage-point lead of October 17 had already fallen to 4.5 percent on October 27, and it narrowed further to 1.6 percent by November 4. Correspondingly, her brief moment of glory atop 270 electoral votes at the end of October ended in a freefall. By November 8, RealClearPolitics estimated Clinton's electoral votes at only 203, with Trump's count at 164 and a decisive 171 too close to call. Although national polls tended to show a slight recovery for Clinton at the end, it was clear that the last phase of the campaign belonged to Trump. No longer were Texas and Utah tossups;

rather, the last weekend saw Clinton rushing to Michigan, long thought safe for the Democrats, and Pennsylvania, which they thought had been locked up a few weeks before. Clinton spent November 7 campaigning with Barack and Michelle Obama, Bon Jovi, and Bruce Springsteen at a Philadelphia rally that drew 30,000.[35] In a whirlwind befitting his entire campaign, Trump traveled to Florida, North Carolina, Pennsylvania, New Hampshire, and Michigan, promising to "drain the swamp" and end the "betrayal" of America by the political class.[36] The experts averted their gaze, putting their faith in national polls that continued to show Clinton with a narrow lead. Prediction markets gave her a four-in-five chance of winning.

For their part, the third-party candidates had mostly faded, falling victim to the longstanding tendency of the electorate to move toward the major party choices as Election Day draws near in order to avoid "wasting" a vote on a sure loser.[37] Despite having a golden opportunity to draw the disaffected from both major parties, Gary Johnson's Libertarian effort had peaked above 9 percent in the RCP average in mid-September but suffered steady decay since then, abetted by the candidate's failure to identify "Aleppo" (the town in Syria that had been the focus of a widely publicized humanitarian crisis for months) or any foreign leader he admired and by his running mate's frequent paeans to Hillary Clinton. Johnson fell short of the 15 percent national poll average required for inclusion in the debates, complained, and got nowhere. Jill Stein had peaked at nearly 5 percent in late June but had been on a downward slope since then. Evan McMullin's national appeal was blunted by his obscurity and limited ballot access, and even his drive to win Utah was apparently stalled, as the last polls showed Trump pulling away.

Now all that was left was to vote, and wait.

RESULTS

Not since Harry Truman beat Thomas Dewey in 1948 did the final results of a presidential election surprise so many participants and observers. Perhaps none were more surprised than the Democrats who turned out to Hillary Clinton's "victory party." In 1948, one correspondent reported that "Republicans who stayed up all night at national headquarters to celebrate looked at dawn today like haggard brides left waiting at the church."[38] Democrats in 2016 knew the feeling, as they turned from confidence to cautious optimism to concern to despair. Donald Trump took an early lead in popular votes that held up from the first East Coast results to the border of California. More important, he also took an early electoral vote lead and never gave it up.

As results came in, Trump won the key big eastern swing states: Florida,

North Carolina, and, surprisingly easily, Ohio. He pushed Clinton to the limit in Virginia before losing it in the end, another early warning sign for Democrats. It was when reports headed west, though, that panic began to set in at Clinton headquarters. Unexpectedly—except perhaps to Trump strategists, who had long seen this as their man's path to the White House—Trump jumped out to leads in Wisconsin and, more narrowly, in Michigan. He never relinquished them. Then, decisively, after the Philadelphia vote had delivered a large (but not large enough) lead to Clinton, the rest of Pennsylvania came in. In the middle of the night, returns from rural Pennsylvania put Trump on top, where he stayed. Pennsylvania, Michigan, and Wisconsin together were enough to give Trump well above the electoral vote majority he needed. (Though little noticed in the hoopla, he also came within 1.5 percentage points of taking Minnesota, which had not gone Republican since 1972.) He had brought down the vaunted "blue wall" of Midwestern states that Democrats had long counted on. Clinton won in the swing states of Colorado, Nevada, and New Hampshire, the last of which was not called for several days, but it did not matter. Clinton declined to concede publicly during the night, perhaps too shocked or emotionally spent to face the cameras and the crowd. The next morning, she spoke to the nation, acknowledged her loss, and withdrew to nurse her wounds.

Altogether, Trump won thirty states worth 306 electoral votes, while Clinton prevailed in twenty states plus the District of Columbia with 232 electoral votes. He flipped a total of six states from blue in 2012 to red in 2016 (Florida, Iowa, Michigan, Ohio, Pennsylvania, and Wisconsin). Trump's electoral vote total was the most for a Republican candidate for president since George H. W. Bush was elected in 1988. As commentators noted, one could drive from the tip of Florida to the border crossing with Canada in Idaho without ever touching a state that voted for Hillary Clinton.

Yet, as absentee and mail-ballot votes continued coming in from California, Washington State, and New York City, Clinton gained and then expanded a lead in the nationally aggregated popular vote. By the time states were done counting their votes, Clinton had won 48 percent to Trump's 46 percent. Her lead reached about 3 million votes nationally, which was more than accounted for by her 4.3 million vote advantage in California, one of the few states where she won a higher percentage than Barack Obama had in 2008 or 2012. So, as Republicans celebrated a presidential win, Democrats noted that 2016 represented the sixth election of the last seven in which the Democratic candidate had won more votes nationally than the Republican. Indeed, Trump received a smaller percentage of the total vote than Mitt Romney in 2012 (47.2 percent) and only slightly higher than John McCain in 2008 (45.6 percent). However, as a share of the two-party vote, Trump bested Romney by nearly a point and a half nationwide, improving the Republican presidential share in forty states. Though leading Trump, Clinton had suffered a fall-off of nearly three percentage points of the total vote since Obama had won 51 percent four years earlier. Although Democrats complained bitterly about losing in the Electoral College, their defeat was the result of the hyper-concentration of Democratic votes in coastal urban centers—or, to put it another way, the lack of Democratic appeal in a broad enough swath of the country. Clinton "ran up the score" in places she already had well in hand, while Trump's votes were spread more efficiently. And the Democrats' problem was getting worse: In 2000, Al Gore led George W. Bush by 500,000 votes while barely losing the Electoral College. Clinton led by 3 million and still soundly lost the electoral vote. Overall, looking at county-level results, the 2016 election was the most geographically polarized of the last six elections, with a higher proportion of votes coming from counties giving more than two-thirds of the vote to the winning candidate.

The third-party and independent candidates limped across the finish line. Gary Johnson finished with 3 percent of the national vote, Jill Stein with 1 percent, and Evan McMullin with half of a percent. Johnson had pockets of greater strength, including his home state of New Mexico, where he polled 9 percent, and a number of prairie and Pacific Northwest states where he won 5–6 percent. Stein had a universally dismal night, breaking 2 percent in only the hippie strongholds of Hawaii, Oregon, and Vermont. McMullin ended with 21 percent in Utah, 7 percent in Idaho, and a smattering everywhere else people could vote for him. Overall, third-party candidates gained almost 6 percent of the national vote, three times the rate in 2012 but less than one-third what Ross Perot polled in 1992, in the last full-scale outbreak of outsiderism. Maybe the third parties did not do as well in 2016 because many voters saw Trump as a third-party candidate himself, operating under a Republican label.

So how did Trump win?

The answer fixated on by analysts was that Trump had broken through, as he had throughout the Republican primaries, with white working-class voters. Given how frequently this group was referenced in 2016, it might be surprising to note how difficult it is to define and identify it. One common way is by education; here, white voters without college degrees—fully one third of the electorate—gave Trump 66 percent of their votes.[39] In the crucial states that he took away from the Democratic column, these voters represented an even larger share of the electorate. In Iowa, they were half of the electorate, in Wisconsin nearly half, and in Michigan and Pennsylvania two in five. Another is by income. Trump's best income groupings were among those who made between $50,000 and $200,000, the great middle of the American income distribution. In comparison with 2012 results, however, Trump did better than Romney in the below-$50,000 group and worse than Romney above it. As usual, the Republican candidate did better in the top one-third of the income distribution, the Democrat in the bottom one-third—but the gap between the two was much smaller than usual.[40] Results in some key working-class and rural counties demonstrated the general tendency: from 2012 to 2016, Juneau County, Wisconsin, went from a seven-percentage-point Obama win to a twenty-six-point Trump win; Macomb County, Michigan, shifted from a four-point Obama edge to an eleven-point Trump advantage; Lackawanna County, Pennsylvania, saw Obama's twenty-seven-point win turned into a four-point Clinton win; counties like Michigan's Huron and Tuscola, which had given about 55 percent of their votes to Romney, gave two-thirds to Trump. Moreover, working-class and rural counties and counties with a larger proportion of voters aged fifty-five and older saw increased turnout, up 1.4 million in four years.[41] In 2012, Romney enthusiasts had pointed to the missing white working-class vote in Ohio and elsewhere as the key ingredient in Romney's loss, and 2016 may well have proven their point. Conversely, Clinton expanded on Obama's margins in places dominated by affluent professionals such as Montgomery County, Maryland, and Fairfax and Loudon counties in Virginia, as well as college towns like Boulder, Colorado, and Charlottesville, Virginia.

However, Trump's strength among working-class whites is far from the only factor behind his win, as the exit polls yielded several other crucial (and sometimes surprising) results outside of Trump's domination of the white working class. Along with Trump's strength where it was widely expected, at least two things did not happen that were expected by analysts.

The women's vote did not turn against Trump with sufficient strength to give the election to Clinton. To be sure, there was a gender gap—Trump defeated Clinton 53–41 percent among men and lost to Clinton 54–42 percent among women—but it was basically a wash. In contrast, Obama had beaten Romney by 11 percent among women in 2012, while only losing by 7 percent among men. While Clinton did a single percentage point better than Obama among white women, she still lost them badly overall. Among white women without college degrees, Trump won a whopping 61 percent; among married women, he almost broke even. Clinton also did slightly worse than Obama among black women and significantly worse than Obama among Latinas. Nor was there a mass rebellion of Republican women against their party's nominee: Trump won 90 percent of the Republican men and 89 percent of the Republican women. Columnist Naomi Schaefer Riley contended in the aftermath of the election, "If the left learns nothing else from this election, perhaps they should understand that there's no such thing as female solidarity—not, at least, as they envision it . . . [women's] experiences in life and their views on policy issues tend to be shaped more by whether they went to college, whether they live in a city or suburb or rural area, whether they live in a blue state or a red state, how much money they make and how they identify themselves racially and ethnically."[42]

Another earthquake that did not happen was the widely expected outpouring of minority mobilization against Trump. In particular, it was hypothesized early in the campaign that Latinos, outraged by Trump's characterizations of Mexican immigrants as rapists and his dismissal of Judge Curiel, would rise up en masse to block him from the White House. In actuality, Trump did slightly better among racial minorities than Mitt Romney had four years before. Hillary Clinton got the support of 66 percent of Latinos in 2016 compared with Obama's 71 percent in 2012, and 89 percent of blacks versus Obama's 93 percent in 2012. Moreover, while the Hispanic share of the electorate edged up slightly, the African American share fell by the same percentage. There were some states where Latinos did mobilize—for example, adding to Clinton's big California margin by giving her 71 percent there. But, though there were some snap assumptions to the contrary, upon examination it turned out that Clinton's southwestern swing-state wins were not the result of an unusual outpouring of Hispanic support, which did not happen. In Nevada, Clinton only garnered 60 percent of the Latino vote, and in New Mexico only 54 percent. Red states for which Democrats had briefly entertained hopes fell through with similar results, with only 61 percent Latino support for Clinton in Arizona and Texas. Clearly, Latino voters, like women voters, were not a monolithic bloc.[43]

A third pillar of Barack Obama's coalition had been the young and the first-time voters. Clinton's struggles with younger voters were well documented during the Democratic primaries, when Bernie Sanders swept millennials, and continued in the general election. In 2012, Obama won eighteen-to twenty-nine-year-olds by a 60–37 percent margin; in 2008 he won by even more, 66–32 percent. In 2016, Clinton won among those eighteen to twenty-nine years of age by a 55–36 percent spread. Again, Trump had run in place, but Clinton had lost ground for the Democrats. When Obama won his change election in 2008, he swept first-time voters, winning nearly seven in ten. Clinton won them, too, but by a much reduced margin of 57–38 percent. In the twenty-five states for which exit poll data was available showing the eighteen- to twenty-nine-year-old vote, Clinton only won fourteen states decisively, with more than 50 percent. In four states Trump won the eighteen-to twenty-nine-year-old vote; in another two states Trump tied Clinton for the lead; and in the remaining five states Clinton won narrowly with less than 50 percent of the vote. A reprise of 2008 it was not.

Overall, a key question of the Obama years was whether his winning coalition was a Democratic coalition, transferrable to any other Democratic candidate, or just an Obama coalition. In 2016, the outlines held, but not the same outsized levels of support. There was a regression to the mean that exposed the chief deficiency of the "coalition of the ascendant": in order to succeed, Democrats had to win unnaturally high proportions of the vote in their target groups. Hillary Clinton was simply not as appealing as Obama to minorities or the young, and women were not swayed as a bloc by her historic status.

A supplementary question during the Obama era was whether his campaigns' technological edge and superior ground games would persist and bear fruit for the Democrats when he was no longer on the ticket. However, by the 2014 midterm elections it was apparent that Republicans were catching up on the technological front, and Clinton's vaunted ground game did not come through in critical places including Philadelphia, Pittsburgh, Detroit, and Milwaukee. Indeed, some published reports indicated that the Clinton campaign might have inadvertently turned out Trump voters. According to Becky Bond and Zach Exley, "Volunteers for the Clinton campaign in Pennsylvania, Ohio and North Carolina have reported that when reminding people to vote, they encountered a significant number of Trump voters. Anecdotal evidence points to anywhere from five to 25 percent of contacts [that] were inadvertently targeted to Trump supporters."[44]

Trump did not just win because Clinton failed to re-create the Obama coalition in its full might. He also performed well among other groups that are typically in the Republican coalition but were thought for a time to be wobbly in 2016. Most notably, a majority of college-educated whites wound up voting for Trump by a 48–45 percent margin, and white evangelicals voted overwhelmingly for Trump, despite his failings. At 80 percent support, Trump did better among evangelicals than Mitt Romney (78 percent), John McCain (74 percent), or George W. Bush (78 percent in 2004). Evangelicals were also a larger share of the electorate than in 2004, when their influence on the election alarmed secular liberals across the country. Other groups normally in the Republican coalition remained strong, as Trump won big among those who attend religious services weekly, among veterans, and in rural communities. Clinton held on tight to highly secular voters, single women, those with postgraduate degrees, and voters in big cities—the "coastal elites." But Trump narrowly won some critical swing groups, including suburbanites (49–45 percent) and Catholics (50–46 percent), and improved the Republican vote share among the unmarried.

In the fall, as in the spring, Republican leaders and conservative intellectuals were deeply divided over Trump. Some continued seeing him as unfit. Some fifty former foreign policy officials in past Republican administrations signed an open letter denouncing him, while the party's living ex-presidents—both named Bush—and recent losing nominees—McCain and Romney—remained aloof or in opposition. The elder Bush made it known he would vote for Clinton, while his son reportedly voted for neither major party nominee.[45] Others, represented by Publius Decius Mus, saw the election as a "Flight 93 moment," a last opportunity to save the republic from progressive destruction by "charging the cockpit"—backing an admittedly risky venture (Trump) as the only viable alternative to certain national doom.[46] In the end, the overwhelming majority of Republicans heeded the call to charge the cockpit. Post-election polls showed that two of three Trump voters thought the 2016 election was the last chance to turn the country around.[47] Party loyalty won out on both sides of the aisle. Overall, Trump won 88 percent of Republicans, and Clinton 89 percent of Democrats. The Democratic advantage in the electorate shrank from six points in 2012 to three points in 2016, and Trump won the independent or unaffiliated vote by 46–42 percent.

BEYOND HOW TO WHY

This may be *how* Trump won, but it leaves the important question of *why* Trump won. What caused voters to cast their ballots in sufficient numbers in the right places to send him to Washington?

There are a number of plausible causes, many of them mutually reinforcing. Here the debate of fundamentals versus contingencies returns with force. It also becomes clear that the debate assumes a dichotomy that is easier to assert than to delineate.

In the realm of fundamentals—or at least perception of fundamentals—by a 62–36 percent margin, voters said the economy was poor rather than good or excellent. By a nearly identical margin, they said the country was on the wrong track. And a 48–46 percent plurality judged Trump better able to handle the economy than Clinton.

It was, moreover, clear that a change election was prepared in deep wells of public opinion. In the view of a 50–45 percent plurality, the federal government should do less rather than more. Nearly half wanted the next president to be more conservative than Barack Obama, while only 17 percent wanted a president more liberal than Obama, as Clinton promised. Nearly seven in ten were dissatisfied or angry with the federal government, and they sided heavily with Trump; Clinton won the minority who were enthusiastic or satisfied with Washington. It was not a propitious time to be seeking a third consecutive term for the incumbent party.

Then there were the contingencies. After giving them a low-grade fever for most of the last seven years, Obamacare erupted again as a disaster for Democrats weeks before the election; exit polls showed 47 percent thought Obamacare had "gone too far"; only 18 percent that it "was about right." Trump won the former heavily. A majority thought the fight against ISIS was "going badly"; Trump won two-thirds of those voters. Trump's attention to the issue of the Supreme Court, made more salient by the death of Justice Antonin Scalia in February, paid dividends. Nearly one in five voters declared the Supreme Court the most important factor in their vote choice, and 56 percent of them favored Trump. An additional half of the electorate called the Court "an important factor." Of the nearly 70 percent in these two groups, Trump won a plurality. Voters who identified the economy (52 percent) or foreign policy (13 percent) as the most important issue facing the country tilted toward Clinton; those prioritizing terrorism (18 percent) or immigration (13 percent) went even more heavily for Trump. However, only one-quarter of voters thought illegal immigrants should be deported, and only four in ten supported building a wall on the Mexican border. Immigration by itself did not carry Trump to the White House.

Not least, the candidates themselves evoked strong, and largely negative, reactions. Hillary Clinton was viewed unfavorably rather than favorably by a 55–43 percent margin, only to be out-unliked by Donald Trump, whose unfavorable ratings outpaced his favorable opinions by 60–38 percent. Some 61 percent called Clinton untrustworthy, while 64 percent said the same of Trump. Nearly two-thirds said Clinton's use of private email bothered them; 70 percent said Trump's comments about women bothered them. A solid majority of voters said they would be either concerned or scared if Clinton won, and an even larger majority said the same if Trump won. In this race to the bottom, Trump fared even worse than Clinton. A total of 47 percent called Clinton "unqualified" to be president, an unusually high number; 61 percent said the same about Trump. And Clinton held a clear edge on the question of which candidate had the right temperament to be president: 55 percent said Clinton did, while only 35 percent said that Trump did. Overall, there has been no presidential election in recent memory in which both major party candidates were held in such low esteem.

Trump's strategy pinpointed areas of Clinton's weakness—biographical weakness, in her long insider resume and scandal sheet; political weakness, as an avatar of unpopular liberal policies; and geographic weakness, as an unappealing candidate outside of the coasts. Clinton had a flawed strategy, which took for granted the Rust Belt, counted on reassembling the Obama coalition in full, and positioned her as a status-quo candidate in a change year. She and her party swung too far to the left, doubling down on Obama-ism rather than creating space to run in the middle. Trump, by contrast, ran what his advisers called a "post-ideological" campaign that promised change,[48] and his everyday rhetoric dominated the discussion and the airwaves. His advisers also held that his bold rhetoric was not meant to be taken literally but established general principles that people could understand and rally around.[49] Not least, his wealth made it plausible for him to claim that he was a genuine outsider—that is, someone who could not be bought. Representative Tim Ryan (D-OH), who would unsuccessfully challenge Nancy Pelosi for leadership of House Democrats, argued that "while they [voters] look at us [Democrats] as trying to appeal to the donor class and the elites and the coasts and all that stuff, (Trump) said, '*I don't need anybody's money.*' If you want to resonate with people here who want to change the system, that one line did it."[50] Together, it proved just enough to overcome voters' deep doubts about him and his capacity to be president.

For his part, Trump and his team attributed his improbable election to a mandate from the American people. Yet, at the end of the day, Trump polled 3 million fewer votes than Clinton. His supporters were correct to note that a Clinton popular vote plurality in an Electoral College–based system would not necessarily translate into a Clinton win in a popular vote system. The rules of the game—270 electoral votes to win—controlled each candidate's strategic choices about where to buy ads, where to send the candidate, where to open field offices, and so on. If you change the rules, you change the game. No one knows how the popular vote would have turned out in a system in which Trump or Clinton would leave New Hampshire to its devices and troll for votes in Texas or California instead. Having said that, it is still difficult to argue for a sweeping mandate after having not only lost the popular vote but also posted the lowest two-party popular vote percentage of any winner in modern times. Contrary to his boasts, even Trump's electoral vote percentage ranked only seventh of the ten presidential election winners since 1980, twenty-sixth of the thirty-one winners since 1896, and forty-sixth of all the fifty-eight winners since 1788. Trump's numbers were not even impressive in the much smaller group of seven opposition party candidates since 1920 who deprived the incumbent party's non-incumbent nominee of a third term, placing fifth of seven in the electoral vote, sixth in the total popular vote, and seventh in the two-party vote.

The Clinton camp and its supporters offered a variety of similarly flawed theories for their candidate's loss. One was that third-party candidates took votes away from Clinton, making the difference in critical states like Wisconsin, Michigan, and Pennsylvania. In particular, Clinton enthusiasts noted that Jill Stein received more votes than Clinton's margin of defeat in those states. However, as Aaron Blake explained in the *Washington Post*, "Exit polls showed 60 percent of Stein backers said they would have stayed home if she weren't on the ballot. Among the rest, Clinton led by about a two-to-one margin—27–13, to be specific—but Trump took a fair amount of voters. Applying those numbers to the totals above means Clinton would have gained about 4,300 votes in Wisconsin and about 6,400 in Pennsylvania—not nearly enough to change the results."[51] National exit polls also showed that in a two-person race, Trump and Clinton would have tied at 47 percent each, with the remaining voters choosing not to vote at all.[52] To put it another way, had the third-party candidates been removed from the race, Clinton would have gone from leading by two points to being tied with Trump. This implies that their net effect was not damaging to Clinton and may have even helped her a bit. In any event, the appeal of the third-party candidates was itself due largely to Clinton's (and Trump's) weaknesses as a candidate.

Another explanation offered by Clinton herself no sooner than the ink was dry on the *Chicago Tribune* headline "Clinton Defeats Trump" was that FBI Director James Comey's two late letters played a decisive role in her defeat. Certainly, Trump's last-minute polling gain partly coincided with the letter announcing reopening of the email investigation. Nate Silver has endorsed this hypothesis.[53] However, there are many reasons not to put too much emphasis on this factor. For one thing, Clinton's polling lead had actually peaked on October 17, eleven days before the first letter, and had been receding since then. Trump was already closing fast, and he may have continued doing so even without the reopening of the investigation. It may be significant that Trump's most positive free media coverage and biggest paid media buys were in the final two weeks of the campaign. Most of his late gain was among 2012 Romney voters who were "coming home."[54] When voters were asked in exit polls when they had decided for whom to vote, Trump was the winner among those who had decided in September (48–46 percent), those who had decided in October (51–37 percent), and those who had decided in the last week (49–41 percent). Clinton won among the 60 percent who had decided before September and tied Trump among the 8 percent who said they had decided in the last few days. If this is true, the second Comey letter may have helped her more than the first one hurt. In any case, most voters had heard about the email scandal and, to a large extent, had probably already factored it into their vote decision. Perhaps Comey and *Access Hollywood* cancelled each other out. In any case, the scandals and gaffes of the fall tended to reinforce the negative views that voters had of the candidates more than to change views.

Some argued that Trump won because of Russian interference on his behalf. Starting with the Debbie Wasserman Schultz revelations in July, WikiLeaks dribbled a steady stream of damaging information about Hillary Clinton, the Clinton campaign, and the Democratic National Committee. To cite three examples, one WikiLeaks release provided the transcripts of Clinton's highly paid speeches to Goldman Sachs, transcripts that Bernie Sanders had unsuccessfully demanded in the spring. They showed Clinton reassuring the finance executives that, although she had to be tough with them in public, there was a difference between her public and private politics.[55] On several other occasions, emails were leaked suggesting that the Clinton Foundation had been an elaborate pay-to-play scheme that foreigners funded to get favors from Clinton's State Department. And in October, WikiLeaks revealed emails among Clinton campaign staffers disparaging evangelical Christians and conservative Catholics and showing John Podesta to be involved in a partisan attempt to influence the doctrine of the Catholic Church.[56] The U.S. intelligence community concluded that Russia was behind the hacking of the documents that were exposed, though analysts debated the purpose of the exposures, both before and after the election. Some thought that Vladimir Putin wanted to help Trump win, judging him to be friendlier to Russia's interests; some thought he assumed Clinton would win, but aimed to sow chaos in the American political system; Michael McFaul, the U.S. ambassador to Russia from 2012 to 2014, contended that Putin simply aimed to exact revenge on Clinton for what he saw as her interference in Russia's 2011 parliamentary elections while she was secretary of state.[57] A partially declassified intelligence report released in January 2017 claimed that Putin originally aimed to help Trump with a broad influence campaign including propaganda and hacking and distribution of damaging information about Clinton; he later concluded that Trump was going to lose and shifted the objective to simply undermining the incoming president Clinton.[58] In any event, it was difficult to untangle how much effect any given revelation had, much less all of them together. Even Clinton campaign operatives dismayed by the Russian hacking were unable to identify any single particular effect. Of course, in a close election, everything can matter, but these complaints amounted to saying that Clinton might have won if only her misdeeds and character flaws and those of her top campaign staff had been more effectively covered up by DNC cybersecurity.

Finally, there were a number of versions of the theory that Trump owed his victory to racism in the electorate, as Clinton communications director Jennifer Palmieri argued in December 2016.[59] In this view, the central feature of Trump's campaign was his attack on Mexicans and Muslims and the support he received from the alt-right. There is no question that Trump was supported by white supremacists such as David Duke and Richard Spencer, though he ultimately disavowed them. On balance, this explanation for Trump's win is also difficult to sustain. Most important, exit polls showed that Trump had won slightly higher percentages among racial minorities and slightly lower percentages among white voters than Mitt Romney in 2012. The proximate cause of his win in the Electoral College was his ability to flip states such as Pennsylvania, Michigan, Wisconsin, Ohio, and Iowa; he flipped those states because he was able to convince a large number of white working-class voters who had voted for Barack Obama in 2008 and 2012 to vote for him in 2016. In other words, the decisive bloc of voters in the decisive states consisted of whites whose most recent votes were cast for the nation's first black president.

If third parties, FBI directors, Russians, and racists are not really satisfactory explanations for Trump's win, can anything else be offered to help understand this surprising election? An alternative story might be built around world trends, rioters, a weak president, and rampaging progressives. Though it, too, would be speculative, this story weaves together elements that help explain how Trump, who was never a regular Republican, nevertheless managed to hold together most of the traditional Republican coalition.

International Trends

Throughout the industrial world, voters in 2016 were rejecting supra-national elites and defending national sovereignty. Nowhere was this more dramatic than in Britain, which voted on June 23 to exit the European Union and where some of the same issues were in play, including uncontrolled immigration, centralized over-regulation, and loss of a sense of self-government. Trump consciously embraced Brexit, congratulating the British on their decision, and was in turn embraced by some of Brexit's most outspoken leaders. In June, pundits briefly considered the possibility that Trump's rise was part of a broader international trend and that the Brexit vote might foretell Trump's electoral success in November. The pundits soon moved on, but perhaps the voters did not. After the election, some commentators returned to this proposition, allowing that it was possible that "Trump's win is part of a global phenomenon of populist and nationalistic policies and leaders that have caught fire with voters worried about the ongoing threats of international terrorism, increased immigration and economic inequality."[60]

Law and Order

Background noise throughout the 2016 campaign included a sharp rise in the homicide rate nationally, accompanied by violence connected with the radical Black Lives Matter (BLM) movement. Examples of this breakdown of order and respect for police were seen in the assassination of five Dallas police officers in July and in the swing state of North Carolina in early September, when Charlotte police shot black motorist Keith Scott and BLM responded with protests and riots despite the fact that Scott was proven to be armed and resisting arrest.[61] Throughout the campaign, Trump made a point of praising police and was endorsed by a number of important law enforcement organizations, including the Fraternal Order of Police and the National Immigration and Customs Enforcement Council, the union for ICE employees.[62] Like Obama, Clinton praised BLM, incorporating the group into the Democratic national convention. A "silent majority" backing the police may have been swayed into Trump's corner; Gallup reported at the end of October that Americans' respect for the police had surged 12 percentage points since 2015 and was near record highs.[63]

Obama Weakness

Starting with the 2009 worldwide "apology tour," as critics dubbed it, Barack Obama made a deliberate policy of reducing the U.S. footprint abroad. For the remainder of his presidency, many Americans bemoaned what they saw as weakness exuded by the president, as in 2013 when he promised military action against Syria if its dictatorship used chemical weapons in the ongoing Syrian civil war and then backed off of enforcing the "red line" when it was crossed. The 2016 campaign months saw continued examples, such as U.S. ransom payments made to Iran and an episode in China in which President Obama was forced to exit from the rear of Air Force One in violation of diplomatic protocol, a breach the Chinese themselves would never have accepted. In separate incidents in the fall of 2016, the governments of Turkey, Russia, and the Philippines showed blatant disrespect to Obama with no visible consequences.[64] A seemingly unending series of Islamist terror attacks also coincided with the presidential campaign, including Paris (November 2015); San Bernardino (December 2015); Brussels (March 2016); Orlando (June 2016); Istanbul (June 2016); Nice (July 2016); Wurzburg, Germany (July 2016); Gaziantep, Turkey (August 2016); New York City (September 2016); and St. Cloud, Minnesota (September 2016). The nuclear deal with Iran, consummated under Secretary of State John Kerry but endorsed by Hillary Clinton, was another symbol of weakness, with opponents in the public outnumbering supporters by a 2–1 margin.[65] In this context, Trump's appearance of strength appealed to many, and it may have been his single most attractive quality to voters (though others feared that he promised too much strength).[66]

Religious Liberty

Finally, an issue simmering not far beneath the surface, and which gave the Supreme Court particular importance in the minds of many, was the fear of millions of traditionalist religious believers that progressives were aiming not only to win political battles, and not only to radically redesign the nation's moral compass, but also to drive them from public life altogether—in the words of one analyst, "run them out of their jobs, close down their stores and undermine their institutions."[67] Two key exhibits—though there were many more examples available—were Obamacare regulations that sought to force even private Catholic charities such as Little Sisters of the Poor to pay for contraceptive and abortifacient coverage against their consciences, and the unremitting campaign by gay activists to silence and drive out of business those not conforming to the new order of same-sex marriage. It was arguably this fear for the future of religious liberty that accounted for Trump's 81 percent share among white evangelicals and his narrower victory among Catholics despite his multiple divorces, affairs, strip clubs, and evident biblical illiteracy.

What held many of these issues together was a theme of nationalism and citizenship, as did the issues of immigration and trade that had long played a more open role in Trump's campaign. After the votes were counted, Corey Lewandowski, Trump's first campaign manager, argued, "We didn't have a traditional campaign of coalitions. It was the same message for everybody . . . 'I'm going to make America great again' . . . We just stuck to the same message the entire time. It was so simplistic, and it didn't target any specific demographic."[68] As twenty-four-year-old Shannon Goodin of Owosso, Michigan, explained, "Clinton would go out of her way to appeal to minorities, immigrants, but she didn't really for everyday Americans."[69]

Within days of his election, analysts asked: Could anyone but Trump have beaten Clinton? On one side, Trump's advocates, including the pseudonymous Publius Decius Mus, argued that no one else in the Republican field could have beaten Hillary Clinton.[70] They pointed to Trump's unusual strength among white working-class voters and held that the key states that flipped from blue to red could not have been flipped by anyone else.

There is no way to know with certainty, but there are two shortcomings with this line of reasoning. First, it is far from clear that no other Republican candidate could have won as Trump did, via the Rust Belt. To the contrary, a number of Republicans have done well there in recent years: John Kasich was the second-term governor of Ohio and trounced Trump in his home state primary, and Ohio senator Rob Portman, running for reelection in 2016, significantly outpaced Trump's general election vote in Ohio without ever endorsing him. Republican Scott Walker was the second-term governor of Wisconsin and endorsed Ted Cruz, who trounced Trump in his state primary. Michigan and Iowa also had Republican governors. Of the key Rust Belt flips, only Pennsylvania did not have a GOP governor, and Republicans controlled both houses of the state legislature there, as they did in Ohio, Michigan, and Wisconsin; Iowa had a split legislature. At the presidential level, the Midwestern states' approval of President Obama had declined relative to other states. As analyst Harry Enten noted, the Midwest in general has been trending Republican; Trump did not create the trend—he rode it.[71] Indeed, Pennsylvania, Michigan, and Wisconsin had been on Republican target lists as potential pickups for several election cycles. George W. Bush's campaign thought he had Wisconsin locked up in 2000 before losing 47.8 percent to 47.6 percent. John McCain, employing Sarah Palin, made a play for Michigan in 2008, and Pennsylvania has been the perennial dream of Republicans. There, they fell short by only four percentage points in 2000, two and a half points in 2004, and five points in 2012. Bush actually did win Iowa in 2004, and Ohio in both of his elections. Clinton's opposition to the Keystone XL pipeline and support for the EPA's anti-coal regulatory campaign would have hurt her across the Midwest and Rust Belt against almost any Republican.

Second, even if it is true that no one but Trump could have won the way he did, through the Rust Belt, it does not follow that no one else could have won by any other avenue. For example, it is not difficult to imagine a Marco Rubio or a John Kasich winning Virginia, New Hampshire, Colorado, and Minnesota, worth thirty-six electoral votes and enough to pass 270 with room to spare even without Pennsylvania, Michigan, and Wisconsin. More generally, in the spring of 2016, head-to-head polls showed Kasich and Rubio beating Clinton soundly and Cruz beating her sometimes, although Trump trailed in almost every matchup versus Clinton. At this point one might also recall Trump's toxic public image on Election Day, with two-thirds seeing him unfavorably, two-thirds calling him dishonest, 61 percent calling him unqualified, and only 35 percent saying he had the right temperament to be president. It seems unlikely that this candidate was the only Republican who could have beaten the most disliked Democratic presidential nominee since polling began.

In the end, most of the political science models that attempted to estimate the vote share of the major party candidates on the basis of the fundamentals were close to the mark, well within normal error. If anything, Trump underperformed the models on average (remember that five of nine predicted a Republican popular vote win), implying that the contingencies, including relative candidate and campaign quality, worked against him. Nate Silver also noted during the campaign that Trump was underperforming, given the fundamentals, and ascribed the gap to Trump's "increasingly abnormal campaign and appeals to a narrow slice of the electorate."[72] Less scientifically, in late October Peggy Noonan, anticipating a Trump loss, held that a "sane Trump would have won in a landslide."[73] It may be better to ask whether there was any potential Democratic nominee other than Clinton who could have lost to Trump. Of course, one would first have to ask whether the Democratic Party, its bench depleted by the electoral catastrophes of the Obama era, had any other plausible nominees *period*. President Donald Trump may have been Barack Obama's parting gift to his party.

The race to the bottom that was the 2016 general election campaign featured what may have been the most unsatisfying choice ever offered to American voters. If it had been a boxing match, it would have ended in a split decision, with Trump winning on points. If it had been a football game, it might have been a come-from-behind win from an underdog Trump team that had trailed all game on a last-second field goal that bounced in off the goalpost—following five consecutive fumbles by alternating teams. Had the sport been baseball, Trump might have prevailed 12–11 in extra innings, with the winning run coming in from third base on a balk. After a spate of penalties on each side, Clinton might have lost a soccer match 1–0 with an own-goal in the final minute.

Trump's win in the general election was no thing of beauty, but it was a win—a win that surprised most of the political world. Defying the odds, outsiderism had prevailed against the ultimate insider. House Speaker Paul Ryan, who had a strained relationship with Trump, declared that Trump had won because he "heard a voice out in this country that no one else heard."[74] The country had defeated the court. Almost no one had given Trump a chance when he opened his campaign in June 2015. He had just been elected president of the United States.

NOTES

1. Frank Newport and Andrew Dugan, "One in Four Americans Dislike Both Presidential Candidates," Gallup, July 12, 2016, http://www.gallup.com/opinion/polling-matters/187652/one-four-americans-dislike-presidential-candidates.aspx.

2. "Text of F.B.I. Director's Remarks on Investigation into Hillary Clinton's Email Use," *New York Times*, July 5, 2016, http://www.nytimes.com/2016/07/06/us/transcript-james-comey-hillary-clinton-emails.html?action = click&contentCollection = Politics&module = RelatedCoverage&region = Marginalia&pgtype = article.

3. Nick Gass, "Comey challenges truthfulness of Clinton's email defenses," *Politico*, July 7, 2016, http://www.politico.com/blogs/james-comey-testimony/2016/07/clinton-untrue-statements-fbi-comey-225216.

4. Natasha Bertrand, "It looks like Russia hired internet trolls to pose as pro-Trump Americans," *Business Insider*, July 27, 2016, http://www.businessinsider.com/russia-internet-trolls-and-donald-trump-2016-7.

5. Amelia Warshaw, "All the Times Donald Trump Sucked Up to Vladimir Putin,"

The Daily Beast, July 25, 2016, http://www.thedailybeast.com/articles/2016/07/25/all-the-times-donald-trump-sucked-up-to-vlaldimir-putin.html.

6. See Jo Becker and Mike McIntire, "Cash Flowed to Clinton Foundation Amid Russian Uranium Deal," *New York Times*, April 23, 2015, http://www.nytimes.com/2015/04/24/us/cash-flowed-to-clinton-foundation-as-russians-pressed-for-control-of-uranium-company.html. See also "Memo Sheds New Light on Clinton-Russia Uranium Scandal," Powerline, August 26, 2016, http://www.powerlineblog.com/archives/2016/08/memo-sheds-new-light-on-clinton-russia-uranium-scandal.php.

7. Eric Morath, "Seven Years Later, Recovery Remains the Weakest of the Post–World War II Era," *Wall Street Journal*, July 29, 2016, http://blogs.wsj.com/economics/2016/07/29/seven-years-later-recovery-remains-the-weakest-of-the-post-world-war-ii-era/.

8. "Real Unemployment," Gallup, http://www.gallup.com/poll/189068/bls-unemployment-seasonally-adjusted.aspx.

9. "President Obama Job Approval," RealClearPolitics, http://www.realclearpolitics.com/epolls/other/president_obama_job_approval-1044.html.

10. "Party Affiliation," Gallup, http://www.gallup.com/poll/15370/party-affiliation.aspx.

11. The five predicting a Trump majority were Fair, Professor Alan Abramowitz, Professor Helmut Norpoth, Professor Drew Linzer, and Professor Ray Cuzan. However, Abramowitz repudiated his own model. The four models estimating a Clinton majority were from Professor James Campbell, Professor Robert Erikson, Professor Andrew Gelman (utilizing Douglas Hibbs's model), and the team of Michael Lewis-Beck and Charles Tien. One other model was prospective, using public opinion surveys on most important issues and leadership skills, and it projected a Clinton win. Another was essentially a combination of polls of the public, experts, prediction markets and so on. It also predicted a Clinton win.

12. Michael Barone, "The Coming Electoral Crack-Up?" *The American Interest*, August 1, 2016, http://www.the-american-interest.com/2016/08/01/the-coming-electoral-crack-up/.

13. Gabriel Debenedetti, "They Always Wanted Trump," *Politico*, November 7, 2016, http://www.politico.com/magazine/story/2016/11/hillary-clinton-2016-donald-trump-214428.

14. Joshua Darr, "Where Clinton Is Setting Up Field Offices—And Where Trump Isn't," FiveThirtyEight, October 7, 2016, http://fivethirtyeight.com/features/trump-clinton-field-offices/.

15. Adam Pearce, "Trump Has Spent a Fraction of What Clinton Has on Ads," *New York Times*, October 21, 2016, http://www.nytimes.com/interactive/2016/10/21/us/elections/television-ads.html; Michael Levenson, "Clinton keeps the public schedule light in home stretch," Boston Globe, October 17, 2016, https://www.bostonglobe.com/news/politics/2016/10/16/hillary-clinton-shuns-spotlight-donald-trump-spirals/u3RTMhaaAW2ojlJcv6Cy8O/story.html.

16. Joshua Green and Sasha Issenberg, "Inside the Trump Bunker, With Days to Go," *Bloomberg Business Week*, October 27, 2016, www.bloomberg.com/news/articles/2016-10-27/inside-the-trump-bunker-with-12-days-to-go.

17. Peter Augustine Lawler, "Trump's Mandate," *National Review*, November 27, 2016, http://www.nationalreview.com/corner/442489/electoral-college-trump-popular-vote-mandate.

18. http://www.realclearpolitics.com/epolls/2016/president/us/general_election_ trump_vs_clinton-5491.html.

19. Michael Moore, "5 Reasons Why Trump Will Win," http://michaelmoore.com/ trumpwillwin/; Ben Dolnick, "No One Understands Donald Trump Like the Horny Narcissist Who Created Dilbert," *Slate*, http://www.slate.com/articles/news_and_politics/poli tics/2016/09/dilbert_creator_scott_adams_gets_trump_like_no_one_else.html.

20. For an extended discussion about the expert assumption that Truman would lose, see Andrew E. Busch, *Truman's Triumphs: The 1948 Election and the Making of Postwar America* (Lawrence: University Press of Kansas, 2012), 152.

21. Nate Silver, "Election Update: Where Are the Undecided Voters?" FiveThirty-Eight, October 25, 2016, http://fivethirtyeight.com/features/election-update-where-are -the-undecided-voters/.

22. "FULL TEXT: Khizr Khan's Speech to the 2016 Democratic National Convention," ABC News, August 1, 2016, http://abcnews.go.com/Politics/full-text-khizr-khans -speech-2016-democratic-national/story?id = 41043609.

23. Callum Borchers, "Donald Trump uses Twitter to fight with Khan family while they're live on CNN," *Washington Post*, August 1, 2016, https://www.washingtonpost .com/news/the-fix/wp/2016/08/01/donald-trump-uses-twitter-to-fight-with-khan-family -while-theyre-live-on-cnn/.

24. David A. Farenthold, "Trump recorded having extremely lewd conversation about women in 2005," *Washington Post*, October 8, 2016, https://www.washingtonpost.com/ politics/trump-recorded-having-extremely-lewd-conversation-about-women-in-2005/20 16/10/07/3b9ce776-8cb4-11e6-bf8a-3d26847eeed4_story.html.

25. Aaron Blake, "Three dozen Republicans have now called for Donald Trump to drop out," *Washington Post*, October 9, 2016, https://www.washingtonpost.com/news/the -fix/wp/2016/10/07/the-gops-brutal-responses-to-the-new-trump-video-broken-down/.

26. John Fund, "Early Voting Has Made It Impossible to Replace Trump," *National Review*, October 9, 2016, http://www.nationalreview.com/node/440896.

27. Betsy Rothstein, "Reports: Rumors Swirl That Pence Wants Off the Ticket," *The Daily Caller*, October 9, 2016, http://dailycaller.com/2016/10/09/reports-rumors-swirl -that-pence-wants-off-the-ticket/.

28. Farenthold, "Trump recorded," *Washington Post*, https://www.washingtonpost .com/politics/trump-recorded-having-extremely-lewd-conversation-about-women-in-20 05/2016/10/07/3b9ce776-8cb4-11e6-bf8a-3d26847eeed4_story.html.

29. "Battle for White House: State Changes," RealClearPolitics, http://www.realclear politics.com/epolls/2016/president/2016_elections_electoral_college_map_race_changes .html.

30. Levenson, "Clinton keeps the public schedule light in home stretch."

31. Charlie Cook, "How Analytical Models Failed Clinton," *National Journal*, December 26, 2016, https://www.nationaljournal.com/s/646194?unlock = O0PSAHTAH F7G58Y1.

32. Deroy Murdock, "Trump's Gettysburg Address Overflows with Conservative Ideas," *National Review*, October 26, 2016, http://www.nationalreview.com/article/44 1458/donald-trump-contract-american-voter-gettysburg-address.

33. Nancy Cook and Brianna Ehley, "Bill Clinton's Obamacare remarks put Hillary on the hot seat," *Politico*, http://www.politico.com/story/2016/10/bill-clinton-obamacare -crazy-229100.

34. See, for example, Kerry Pickett, "EXCLUSIVE: FBI Agents Say Comey 'Stood in the Way' of Clinton Email Investigation," *The Daily Caller*, October 17, 2016. http://dailycaller.com/2016/10/17/exclusive-fbi-agents-say-comey-stood-in-the-way-of-clinton-email-investigation/. Also Jeremy Lott, "Clinton ally funneled money to wife of FBI agent who oversaw emails," *Washington Examiner*, October 23, 2016, http://www.washingtonexaminer.com/clinton-ally-funneled-money-to-wife-of-fbi-agent-who-oversaw-emails/article/2605371.

35. Heidi M. Pryzbyla, "As Election Day Looms, Clinton Joins Forces with Obamas in Philadelphia," *USA Today*, November 7, 2016, http://www.usatoday.com/story/news/politics/elections/2016/11/07/hillary-clinton-campaign-last-day/93410200/.

36. David Jackson, "Trump Conducts Election Eve Marathon," *USA Today*, November 7, 2016, http://www.usatoday.com/story/news/politics/elections/2016/11/07/donald-trump-campaign-final-day/93412700/.

37. See "Four Way: Trump vs. Clinton vs. Johnson vs. Stein," RealClearPolitics, http://www.realclearpolitics.com/epolls/2016/president/us/general_election_trump_vs_clinton_vs_johnson_vs_stein-5952.html.

38. Hal Boyle, "GOP Headquarters a Scene of Gloom," Associated Press, November 3, 1948, in Robert J. Dinkin, ed., *Election Day: A Documentary History* (Westport, CT: Greenwood Press, 2002), 160.

39. This and subsequent voter preference data, unless otherwise noted, is drawn from "Presidential Election Exit Polls," CNN, http://edition.cnn.com/election/results/exit-polls/national/president.

40. Andrew Gelman, "19 Things We Learned From the 2016 Election," Statistical Modeling, Causal Inference, and Social Science, December 8, 2016, ndrewgelman.com/2016/12/08/19-things-learned-2016-election/.

41. Lerigh Ann Caldwell and Benjy Sarlin, "How Trump Won," NBC, http://www.nbcnews.com/specials/donald-trump-republican-party/presidency.

42. Naomi Schaefer Riley, "Killing the 'sisterhood': Why identity politics didn't work for Clinton," *New York Post*, November 13, 2016,

43. Fernanda Santos, "In Arizona County Where Latinos Have an Edge, So Did Trump," *New York Times*, December 13, 2016, http://www.nytimes.com/2016/12/13/us/politics/yuma-county-arizona-latinos-trump.html?ref = todayspaper&_r = 0.

44. Becky Bond and Zach Exley, "Hillary Clinton's Vaunted GOTV Operation May Have Turned Out Trump Voters," *Huffington Post*, November 11, 2016, http://www.huffingtonpost.com/entry/hillary-clintons-vaunted-gotv-operation-may-have-turned-out-trump-voters_us_582533b1e4b060adb56ddc27.

45. Darren Samuelsohn, "George H. W. Bush to vote for Clinton," *Politico*, September 19, 2016, http://www.politico.com/story/2016/09/exclusive-george-hw-bush-to-vote-for-hillary-228395; "George W. Bush Didn't Vote for Trump or Clinton," *The Daily Beast*, http://www.thedailybeast.com/cheats/2016/11/08/george-w-bush-voted-for-neither-trump-nor-clinton.html?via = desktop&source = copyurl.

46. Publius Decius Mus, "The Flight 93 Election," *Claremont Review of Books*, September 5, 2016, http://www.claremont.org/crb/basicpage/the-flight-93-election/.

47. Phillip Bump, "Two-thirds of Trump voters viewed the election as America's last chance," *Washington Post*, December 2, 2016, https://www.washingtonpost.com/news/the-fix/wp/2016/12/02/two-thirds-of-trump-voters-viewed-the-election-as-americas-last-chance/.

48. James Hohmann, "The Daily 202: Trump's Pollster Says He Ran a 'Post-Ideological' Campaign," *Washington Post*, December 5, 2016, https://www.washington post.com/news/powerpost/paloma/daily-202/2016/12/05/daily-202-trump-s-pollster-says -he-ran-a-post-ideological-campaign/5844d166e9b69b7e58e45f2a/.

49. Ibid.

50. James Hohmann, "The Daily 202: Rust Belt Dems broke for Trump because they thought Clinton cared more about bathrooms than jobs," *Washington Post*, November 22, 2016, https://www.washingtonpost.com/news/powerpost/paloma/daily-202/2016/11/22/ daily-202-rust-belt-dems-broke-for-trump-because-they-thought-clinton-cared-more -about-bathrooms-than-jobs/58339cf3e9b69b7e58e45f1b/?utm_term = .7fe59f05a432.

51. Aaron Blake, "3 election stats liberals love that don't mean as much as they seem," *Washington Post*, December 13, 2016, https://www.washingtonpost.com/news/the -fix/wp/2016/12/13/3-election-stats-liberals-love-that-dont-mean-as-much-as-they-seem/.

52. "Presidential Election Exit Polls," CNN.

53. Jay Caruso, "Nate Silver Says Comey Letter Cost Hillary the Election But Nothing Suggests That," RedState, December 12, 2016, http://www.redstate.com/jaycaruso/ 2016/12/12/nate-silver-says-comey-letter-cost-hillary-the-election/.

54. Dan Hopkins, "Voters Really Did Switch to Trump at the Last Minute," FiveThirtyEight, December 20, 2016, http://fivethirtyeight.com/features/voters-really -did-switch-to-trump-at-the-last-minute/.

55. Amy Chozick, Nicholas Confessore, and Michael Barbaro, "Leaked Speech Excerpts Show a Hillary Clinton at Ease with Wall Street," *New York Times*, October 7, 2016, http://www.nytimes.com/2016/10/08/us/politics/hillary-clinton-speeches-wiki leaks.html.

56. Sarah Pulliam Bailey, "WikiLeaks emails appear to show Clinton spokeswoman joking about Catholics and evangelicals," *Washington Post*, October 13, 2016, https:// www.washingtonpost.com/news/acts-of-faith/wp/2016/10/12/wikileaks-emails-show -clinton-spokeswoman-joking-about-catholics-and-evangelicals/; "Clinton campaign chief helped start Catholic organisations to create 'revolution' in the Church," *Catholic Herald*, October 12, 2016, http://www.catholicherald.co.uk/news/2016/10/12/clinton-campaign -chief-helped-start-catholic-organisations-to-create-revolution-in-the-church/.

57. Jessie Hellman, "Former ambassador to Russia: Putin wanted 'revenge' against Clinton," *The Hill*, December 11, 2016, http://thehill.com/homenews/sunday-talk-shows/ 309854-former-ambassador-to-russia-putin-wanted-revenge-against-clinton.

58. Greg Miller and Adam Entous, "Declassified report says Putin 'ordered' effort to undermine faith in U.S. election and help Trump," *Washington Post*, January 6, 2017, https://www.washingtonpost.com/world/national-security/intelligence-chiefs-expected-in -new-york-to-brief-trump-on-russian-hacking/2017/01/06/5f591416-d41a-11e6-9cb0-54 ab630851e8_story.html?utm_term = .00eab2ded554.

59. Karen Tumulty and Philip Rucker, "Shouting match erupts between Clinton and Trump aides," *Washington Post*, December 1, 2016, https://www.washingtonpost.com/ politics/shouting-match-erupts-between-clinton-and-trump-aides/2016/12/01/7ac4398e -b7ea-11e6-b8df-600bd9d38a02_story.html.

60. Caldwell and Sarlin, "How Trump Won."

61. See Richard Foussett and Alan Blinder, "Charlotte Officer 'Justified' in Fatal Shooting of Keith Scott," *New York Times*, November 30, 2016, http://www.nytimes.com/ 2016/11/30/us/charlotte-officer-acted-lawfully-in-fatal-shooting-of-keith-scott.html.

62. Louis Nelson, "Trump wins endorsement from Fraternal Order of Police," *Politico*, September 16, 2016, http://www.politico.com/story/2016/09/trump-fraternal-order-of-police-endorsement-228296.

63. "Americans' Respect for Police Surges," Gallup, October 24, 2016, http://www.gallup.com/poll/196610/americans-respect-police-surges.aspx.

64. John Robson, "John Robson on Barack Obama: The Incredible Shrinking President," *National Post*, September 12, 2016, http://news.nationalpost.com/full-comment/john-robson-on-barack-obama-the-incredible-shrinking-president.

65. "After Nuclear Deal, U.S. Views on Iran Remain Dismal," Gallup, February 17, 2016, http://www.gallup.com/poll/189272/after-nuclear-deal-views-iran-remain-dismal.aspx?utm_source = alert&utm_medium = email&utm_content = heading&utm_campaign = syndication.

66. See Hohmann, "Trump's Pollster Says He Ran a 'Post-Ideological' Campaign."

67. David Bernstein, "The Supreme Court oral argument that cost Democrats the presidency," *Washington Post*, December 7, 2016, https://www.washingtonpost.com/news/volokh-conspiracy/wp/2016/12/07/the-supreme-court-oral-argument-that-cost-democrats-the-presidency/.

68. Hohmann, "Trump's Pollster Says He Ran a 'Post-Ideological' Campaign."

69. Nancy Gibbs, "The Choice," *Time*, December 19, 2016, 71.

70. Publius Decius Mus, "Dear Repentant NeverTrumpers: No One Else Could Have Won," American Greatness, November 13, 2016, http://amgreatness.com/2016/11/13/dear-repentant-nevertrumpers-no-one-else-could-have-won/.

71. Harry Enten, "It's Not All About Clinton—The Midwest Was Getting Redder Before 2016," FiveThirtyEight, December 9, 2016, http://fivethirtyeight.com/features/its-not-all-about-clinton-the-midwest-was-getting-redder-before-2016/.

72. Nate Silver, "Election Update: Where the Race Stands with Three Weeks to Go," FiveThirtyEight, October 16, 2016, http://fivethirtyeight.com/features/election-update-where-the-race-stands-with-three-weeks-to-go/.

73. Peggy Noonan, "Imagine a Sane Donald Trump," *Wall Street Journal*, October 20, 2016, http://www.wsj.com/articles/imagine-a-sane-donald-trump-1477004871.

74. Ian Schwartz, "Paul Ryan: Trump 'Heard a Voice Out in This Country That No One Else Heard,'" RealClearPolitics, November 9, 2016, http://www.realclearpolitics.com/video/2016/11/09/paul_ryan_t rump_heard_a_voice_out_in_this_country_that_no_one_else_heard.html.

Chapter Five

Red Down the Ballot

Congressional and State Elections

Before the election, one party controlled the House and Senate, and the other party held the presidency. Voters decided to change parties in the White House and keep the majorities on Capitol Hill, with some marginal shifts. Unified government was back, and after years of widespread complaints about gridlock, the new president looked forward to legislative victories.

As you may have guessed, this description fits both the 1992 and the 2016 elections. There was a major difference, though, when it came to downballot races. In 1992, the congressional majorities were Democratic, which struck many academics and political professionals as the natural order of things. Republicans had not won a majority in the House since 1952, and their six years of Senate control (1980–1986) looked like a fluke stemming from the Reagan landslides and a run of good luck in small states.[1] Though Republicans had sometimes done well in the overall tally of governorships, it had been decades since they had held more than half of state legislative seats. Because the legislatures were the key "farm club" for congressional races, Democrats felt confident that they could hold onto their dominance for many years to come.

Nevertheless, Republicans had won five of the past six presidential elections, and political science developed a cottage industry devoted to Americans' apparent preference for divided government. One explanation was that voters liked Republicans on the broad issues on which presidents take the lead (national security, economic prosperity) while preferring Democrats on distributional issues (Social Security, health care) that made up the congressional wheelhouse.[2] The joke was that the people elected Democratic lawmakers to give them stuff and Republican presidents so that they would not have to pay for it. Another explanation was that Republicans ran inferior candidates on the wrong side of the issues that voters cared about in down-ballot races.[3] The assumption was the GOP's limited-government ideology made public service unattractive to its best and brightest. As one Wisconsin legislative leader told journalist Alan Ehrenhalt, "The Republicans hate government. Why be here if you hate government? So they let us run it for them."[4] The South was yet another purported reason for Democratic success: although Southern states had been trending Republican in presidential elections since Eisenhower, Democrats seemed to hold the residual loyalty of Southern voters in other races. After the 1992 election, for instance, Democrats controlled every Southern state legislative chamber except for the Florida Senate. As Bill Clinton of Arkansas took the oath of office, Southern Democrats looked healthy.

The next twenty-four years turned these assumptions upside down and inside out. In the seven presidential elections between 1992 and 2016, Republicans won the aggregated popular vote for president only once, in 2004. But they took control of the House in 1994 and, except for the elections of 2006 and 2008, they kept their House majorities through the beginning of the Trump years. They also controlled the Senate during most of this time. As of the 2016 election, Republicans dominated state governments as well, and, in a nearly complete reversal from the 1992 outcome, they controlled every state legislative chamber in the South. As Trump might say, there's something going on.

RED OVER BLUE

The end of the old order started abruptly in 1994, when a unique confluence of events triggered a Republican sweep in the midterm election. The 1992 defeat of George H. W. Bush had freed the GOP from having to defend an unpopular administration, and it also simplified the choices before the voters: the best way to register discontent with the state of the nation would be to vote Republican.[5] The early missteps of the Clinton administration and the ethics scandals on Capitol Hill gave them much to be discontented about. A couple of years before, moreover, the 1990 reapportionment and redistricting had created many winnable seats in the House and state legislatures. The Republican National Committee and Newt Gingrich's outside group GOPAC had done a skillful job exploiting these opportunities and recruiting a strong class of Republican candidates.

By undercutting the assumption that the Democrats were the "natural governing party," the 1994 election supplied long-term benefits to the GOP. First, it made fundraising easier. Access to a "permanent minority" had little value to interest groups, but now they had a strong material incentive to make friends with Republicans. Second, it showed that ideology was not as big a barrier to GOP recruitment as some had thought. There were many right-leaning and politically ambitious young people, but up until now, the GOP had often looked like a poor vehicle for their aspirations. Why bear the costs of a congressional or legislative campaign if there was no hope of ever serving in the majority? As of the mid-1990s, however, it made more sense for them to run as Republicans instead of conservative Democrats.

The 1996 election confirmed that the GOP majority was not a one-off. For the first time since 1928, voters reelected a Republican majority in the House. The second book in this series, *Losing to Win*, explained that President Clinton and the congressional GOP effectively used each other as foils.[6] Clinton ran ads against "Dole-Gingrich" while Republicans were portraying themselves as a check on a Democratic president. One GOP TV spot started a voiceover by asking, "What would happen if the Democrats controlled Congress and the White House? Been there, done that." It showed headlines from 1993 and 1994 about taxes, government waste, and Clinton's unpopular health care proposal. "The liberal special interests, aligned with Clinton," the voiceover continued, "desperately want to buy back control of Congress."[7]

Despite a public backlash against the Clinton impeachment, Republicans clung to their majorities in the 1998 midterm. In the "perfect tie" election of 2000, they barely held the House while ending up with a 50–50 split in the Senate. One senator's switch from the GOP briefly tipped the majority to the Democrats, but Republicans won it back in 2002. They took political advantage of the "rally around the flag" effect in the wake of the 9/11 attacks and the impending invasion of Iraq, thereby inverting the losses that the president's party usually suffers in a midterm. Additional GOP gains in 2004 led some scholars to fret that Republicans had a nefarious mojo that threatened democracy.

In 2006, these fears proved unfounded when the Democrats regained majorities in the House and Senate. The deepening unpopularity of the Iraq War intensified the usual midterm effect, and congressional Republicans had brought additional political woes upon themselves. In 1994, they had run as outsiders against a corrupt political establishment. Then they fell into the fundamental trap of outsiderism: when outsiders repeatedly win reelection to positions of power, they become insiders. There is more to this problem than a simple matter of definition. Over time, insiders come to value power for its own sake, and they fall prey to all kinds of temptations. Paul Ryan, who went on to become Speaker of the House, recalled in 2010:

And then slowly but surely, as the conference matured, they started to recruit career politicians as opposed to citizen legislators. They brought in more machine-like people. And I think our leadership changed and adopted the position that, well, we beat the Democrats' machine, now it's time to create a Republican machine to keep us in the majority. And out of that came this earmark culture.[8]

In the "earmark culture," GOP House members earmarked appropriations for local projects on the basis of political favor rather than merit. In 2005, Duke Cunningham (R-CA) pleaded guilty to taking bribes for earmarks, and as a sentencing memo revealed, he had brazenly written out a menu listing how much he expected in return for contracts of various sizes.[9] Shortly before the 2006 election, news broke that a GOP member had sent sexually charged text messages to minors working as congressional pages, and that the party leadership had looked the other way.

Republicans lost even more ground in 2008. "The conservative movement brought about by the Gingrich revolution has been crushed," said Democratic pollster Stanley Greenberg. "There has been a change in the way we think about society and the economy, and Democrats have a huge advantage."[10] The 2010 midterm shook such confidence. President Obama's signature health care law turned out to be unpopular, and his policies failed to bring about a quick recovery from the Great Recession. Republicans regained control of the House and, just as important for the long run, picked up twenty state legislative chambers. Not since the modern redistricting era began in the 1960s had they been in a stronger position to draw favorable district lines. GOP gerrymanders in Ohio, Pennsylvania, Michigan, and North Carolina would help entrench party majorities for the rest of the decade.

The 2012 election kept the partisan battlefield mostly in place, leaving Obama with a shrunken vote share and congressional Republicans with slightly fewer seats. Democrats thought that they had stemmed the GOP tide, and President Obama adopted a strategy of accepting gridlock until Democrats could regain the majority in the House. Noting that their party won a plurality of total popular votes cast for House candidates in 2012, some Democrats maintained that they could defy historical patterns and overtake the House GOP in the 2014 midterm.[11] For a while, this scenario seemed plausible.

When the 2010 midterm election gave the GOP a majority in the House, it brought many "Tea Party" Republicans who wanted to slash the size of government. Like generations of outsiders before them, the Tea Party Republicans took an aggressive stance against what they saw as a corrupt political establishment. They were suspicious of the new speaker, John Boehner (R-OH), even though he had started his own House career as a conservative outsider. They opposed any compromise in their fight to defund the president's health care law, and in October 2013, their hard line led to a partial government shutdown. The public scorned the GOP's actions, and polls showed Democrats pulling ahead in the generic congressional ballot.[12] *The New Republic* ran an article titled "The Last Days of the GOP" with the subheading "We could be witnessing the death throes of the Republican Party."[13]

For once, Republicans stanched their own bleeding. A short-term deal ended the shutdown in mid-October, and a longer-term compromise in December effectively precluded a shutdown before the 2014 election. In the meantime, the glitchy rollout of Obamacare gave the GOP a reprieve: by November, the ongoing problems of the program's website had overshadowed the shutdown and was cutting into public support for the Democrats. The broader issue of health care was not the political bonanza that Democrats had expected: most polls showed that the public opposed the new law.

The president's party usually sheds seats in midterm elections, but the scope of the Democrats' 2014 defeat was remarkable. Not only did they lose their Senate majority, but their House membership also dwindled to its lowest point in decades. Instead of gaining governorships, as they had expected, they suffered a net loss of three, including deep-blue Massachusetts, Maryland, and Illinois. They now held full control of just eleven state legislatures, their fewest since Reconstruction.[14]

These results reflected long-term trends as well as short-term fluctuations. The reddening of Southern white voters was one such long-term trend. Statistical journalist Harry Enten illustrated this point by analyzing data from the Cooperative Congressional Election Study (CCES). In the 2006 House elections, the first for which CCES data are available, he found that Republicans won Southern white voters 58 percent to 41 percent. In 2014, Southern whites voted Republican 70 percent to 28 percent, a much bigger shift toward the GOP than in the national electorate. Enten writes, "To put that in perspective, people are making a big deal over some Midwestern states—Michigan, for example—going from slightly more Democratic than the nation to slightly more Republican between the 2012 and 2016 presidential elections. What's occurred in the House over the past decade is a political earthquake by comparison."[15]

Arkansas is a vivid example. When Bill Clinton left the governorship to become president, his Democratic lieutenant governor succeeded him. Democrats controlled both chambers of the state legislature by big margins, as well as both of the state's U.S. Senate seats and two of its four House seats. Democrats held onto most of this strength through the first decade of the new century, but the state's blue wall crumbled during the 2010, 2012, and 2014 elections. By 2015, Arkansas Republicans held every constitutional office, every House seat, and both Senate seats. They also had large majorities in both chambers of the legislature.[16]

Race is one obvious explanation for the change, and some white Southerners turned away from the Democratic Party because it brought forth the nation's first African American president. It is possible to make too much of the racial angle, however. Whereas Gore and Kerry carried no Southern states at all, Obama won Virginia and Florida twice, and North Carolina once.

Broader changes were at work. During the first two years of the Clinton administration, Southern conservatives could look at Democratic elected officials and see people that they could like. Obviously, the president and vice president both spoke with drawls and often took centrist positions on issues such as welfare reform. The party's Senate leadership included moderates Wendell Ford of Kentucky and David Pryor of Arkansas. Pro-military Sam Nunn of Georgia chaired the Senate Armed Services Committee and pro-petroleum J. Bennett Johnston of Louisiana chaired the Energy and Natural Resources Committee. On the House side, moderate William Natcher of Kentucky chaired the powerful Appropriations Committee. As discussed in the chapter on the Democratic nomination process, the party then underwent a self-reinforcing cycle that made it much less appealing to Southern conservatives. As Republicans started to replace Democrats in elected office, the party became less Southern and more liberal. The Blue Dog Coalition, a group of moderate-to-conservative House Democrats, mostly from the South, went from a peak of fifty-four members after the 2008 election to just fourteen members after the 2014 midterm. Meanwhile, the very liberal Progressive Caucus grew to sixty-seven members.[17]

The public face of the congressional party consisted of House Democratic leader Nancy Pelosi, a San Francisco liberal, and Senate Democratic leader Harry Reid of Nevada, a former moderate who moved leftward as he climbed the party ladder.[18] Neither had much of a fan club in Dixie. In the 114th Congress, one event symbolized the party's problems with the South. House Democrats staged a sit-in on the chamber floor to protest the GOP majority's refusal to schedule a vote on gun control. The demonstration got considerable publicity and rallied the party's liberal core, but did nothing to reach out to voters that had moved to the GOP. In 2015, Gallup found that Republicans, conservatives, gun owners, and opponents of strict gun control laws were the most likely to say that a candidate had to share their views on gun control. A smaller fraction of gun-control supporters said that they would vote only for a candidate who agreed with them.[19] The political problem was especially intense in the South, where whites were much more likely to have a gun at home than in other regions.[20] Democrats would have been better off if they had made a flamboyant stand on behalf of job creation or aid to senior citizens, positions that might have rallied the Southern voters whom they had lost. Instead, they picked an issue that was sure to alienate them even more.

The same was true of cultural issues such as abortion. The South was the most anti-abortion region, in large part because of the presence of so many conservative evangelical Christians.[21] At the national level, the Democratic Party seemed to dismiss their concerns. Michael Wear, who headed faith outreach in President Obama's 2012 campaign, noted that more and more secular young operatives and politicians were taking key roles in the party: "They grew up in parts of the country where navigating religion was not important socially and not important to their political careers. This is very different from, like, James Carville in Louisiana in the '80s. James Carville is not the most religious guy, but he gets religious people—if you didn't get religious people running Democratic campaigns in the South in the '80s, you wouldn't win."[22]

The party's difficulties extended beyond the region. In recent decades, highly educated white liberals have made up a growing portion of the Democratic vote, and they have increasingly clustered in large urban areas. Together with African American and Hispanic voters, they have turned these areas into blue islands where Democratic candidates win by rubble-bouncing margins. The result is "unintentional gerrymandering," in which the Democratic vote clusters in a relatively small number of constituencies while the GOP vote has a more efficient distribution.[23] Journalist Alec MacGillis offers an example:

> That hyper-concentration of Democratic votes has long hurt the party in the House and state legislatures. In Ohio, for instance, Republicans won 75 percent of the United States House seats in 2012 despite winning only 51 percent of the total votes. That imbalance can be explained partly by Republican gerrymandering. But even if district lines were drawn in rational, nonpartisan ways, a disproportionate share of Democratic votes would still be clustered in urban districts, giving Republicans a larger share of seats than their share of the overall vote. Winning back control of state legislatures in Pennsylvania and Michigan could help Democrats in redistricting after 2020. But it would help more if their voters were not so concentrated in Philadelphia and Pittsburgh, Detroit and Ann Arbor.[24]

President Obama was popular in those cities, but in much of the country, he was a drag on his party's candidates. "What's happened on the ground is that voters have been punishing Democrats for eight solid years—it's been exhausting," said South Carolina state senator Vincent Sheheen, who twice ran against Republican governor Nikki Haley. "If I was talking about a local or state issue, voters would always lapse back into a national topic: Barack

Obama."[25] Congressional Democrats complained that he focused more on his own standing than his party's health down the ballot. He did not help matters when he installed Representative Debbie Wasserman Schultz (D-Florida) as chair of the Democratic National Committee. She proved ineffective at both articulating party positions and building its organization at the grassroots.[26] "We built this beautiful house, but the foundation is rotten," said South Carolina Democratic Chairman Jaime Harrison. "In hindsight, we should have looked at this and said, 'Maybe the state parties should be strong.'"[27] At the last press conference of his administration, President Obama acknowledged as much, though with an undertone of defensiveness:

> And I think that that the thing we have to spend the most time on—because it's the thing we have the most control over—is how do we make sure that we are showing up in places where I think Democratic policies are needed, where they are helping, where they are making a difference, but where people feel as if they're not being heard and where Democrats are characterized as coastal, liberal, latte-sipping, politically-correct, out-of-touch folks. We have to be in those communities. And I've seen that when we are in those communities, it makes a difference.
>
> But that requires a lot of work. It's been something that I've been able to do successfully in my own campaigns. It is not something I've been able to transfer to candidates in midterms and sort of build a sustaining organization around. That's something that I would have liked to have done more of, but it's kind of hard to do when you're also dealing with a whole bunch of issues here in the White House.[28]

The GOP's organizational status was a reverse image. As the Democrats grew stronger in the cities, the GOP retreated. As of late 2016, only three of the nation's twenty-five largest cities had Republican mayors, and few other GOP elected officials represented densely populated urban areas.[29] With an assist from outside groups, Republicans did a much better job in organizing in suburbs and rural areas between the Pacific coast and the Northeast corridor.

At one time, organized labor would have enabled the Democrats to counter these Republican advantages. At the high point of their influence many years ago, they supplied the people who worked the phones, stuffed the envelopes, and walked the precincts on behalf of the Democrats. In some states, they still were a significant force, but, overall, they were on the wane. Between 1983 and 2015, union membership as a share of employed workers plunged by almost half, from 20.1 percent to 11.1 percent.[30] Not coincidentally, the drop-off was steepest in five industrial states that voted Republican in the 2016 presidential race (see table 5.1).

In a couple of these states, Republicans gave unions a hard shove down the cliff. Wisconsin governor Scott Walker signed controversial legislation in

Table 5.1. Change in Union Density, Selected States, 1983–2015

	1983	2015	Change
Wisconsin	24.2	08.4	−15.8
Michigan	30.8	15.3	−15.5
Indiana	25.2	10.1	−15.1
Pennsylvania	27.7	13.4	−14.3
Ohio	25.3	12.4	−12.9

Figures are percentages.

Source: Barry T. Hirsch and David A. Macpherson, "State Union Membership Density 1964–2015," http://unionstats.gsu.edu/State_Union_Membership_Density_1964-2015.xlsx; Barry T. Hirsch, David A. Macpherson, and Wayne G. Vroman, "Estimates of Union Density by State," *Monthly Labor Review* 124, no. 7 (July 2001), http://unionstats.gsu.edu/MLR_7-01_StateUnionDensity.pdf.

2011 that denied collective bargaining rights to most public employee unions. The following year, the law stuck when Walker survived a labor-backed recall effort. In Michigan, once the home of mighty auto worker unions, Governor Rick Snyder signed a "right to work" bill forbidding employers from requiring union membership and payment of dues as a condition of employment. "When you chip away at one of the power sources that also does a lot of get-out-the-vote," says Tracie Sharpe, president of the conservative State Policy Network, "I think that helps—for sure."[31]

SENATE ELECTIONS

Notwithstanding all the GOP advantages, most of the smart money was on the Democrats to take control of the Senate in 2016. The reason was the peculiar cycle of U.S. Senate elections. Whenever a party wins a large haul of seats, it must defend them six years later under different political conditions. The winnings of a midterm election come up again during a presidential election, and vice versa. This phenomenon has often resulted in reversals in party fortunes. In the 1974 Watergate midterm, Senate Democrats won a smashing victory, but during the Reagan landslide six years later, they lost so many of these seats that the GOP took control of the chamber. In 1986, the GOP tide flowed out again, and the Democrats regained the majority. Similarly, the big Democratic victory of 2008 set the party up for defeat in 2014. In 2016, the Democrats saw a chance to avenge themselves. Thanks to GOP gains in 2010, they were defending just ten seats, whereas Republicans had two dozen. Seven of those twenty-four Republican seats were in states that President Obama had carried twice: Florida, Illinois, Iowa, New Hampshire, Ohio, Pennsylvania and Wisconsin.[32]

Even better from the Democratic perspective, Republicans had earlier shown a knack for throwing away opportunities. In 2010, inept candidates cost them Senate races in Colorado, Delaware, and Nevada. Two years later, Republicans went down in Indiana and Missouri because they made offensive comments about rape, pregnancy, and abortion. Also in 2012, Montana Republicans failed to counter an obvious Democratic effort to siphon GOP votes to a Libertarian spoiler. Had Republicans taken all the winnable races in 2010 and 2012, they would have ended 2014 with a supermajority of sixty seats.

Unfortunately for Democrats, the Republican establishment noticed this problem and had commenced action during the 2014 cycle.[33] Senate GOP leader Mitch McConnell said of Tea Party primary candidates who could put seats in jeopardy: "I think we are going to crush them everywhere."[34] His own reelection campaign cut off challenger Matt Bevin by telling GOP vendors and operatives that if they worked for Bevin, "it will be the last job you ever have in this business."[35] (The rivals reconciled in 2015, when McConnell supported Bevin's successful campaign for governor.) In Kansas, opposition researchers for the National Republican Senatorial Committee (NRSC) learned that Dr. Milton Wolf, who was challenging incumbent Pat Roberts, had posted photos of gunshot victims on Facebook, along with odd jokes. After the committee leaked the information to the media, Wolf faded. NRSC executive director Rob Collins defended the committee's involvement in the Kansas race and other primaries: "We're not anti-conservative. We're just anti-people-who-can't-win."[36]

The effort continued during the 2016 cycle. Representative Mike Pompeo, a hardline conservative, considered a primary race against Senator Jerry Moran of Kansas. NRSC discouraged conservative groups from even considering financial support to Pompeo, and it sent opposition researchers to Wichita. Reid Wilson reported at *The Hill*, "And the retired FBI agents didn't bother to cover their tracks; it would help the NRSC's cause if Pompeo knew the campaign arm was preparing a thick binder of opposition research."[37] In April, Pompeo declined to run against Moran, complaining of "legacy Republican leaders" whose aim was the "retention of office."[38] (The legacy leaders might have responded, "Well, duh.") After the general election, Pompeo got a consolation prize when Trump said he would nominate him to head the CIA.

In Arizona, John McCain had often irritated the right wing. Conservative representative Matt Salmon thought about running, but he later told *National Review* that NRSC "reached out to my chief of staff and said, 'You know if Matt runs, we'll be fully supporting McCain.'"[39] Salmon opted out of the race and decided to retire from the House as well. McCain did face a challenge from state legislator Kelli Ward, who got little support from conservative outside organizations. "They were worried she might be a little kooky," said a Republican involved with the groups.[40] A pro-McCain super PAC reinforced these concerns with an online video pointing out her strange positions on chemtrails and vaccines.[41] McCain, who had gotten an early start on fundraising and organization, easily won the primary. In the fall, he beat Representative Ann Kirkpatrick by double digits.

As in 2014, not a single Republican incumbent senator lost a fight for renomination. The successful counterattacks by McConnell and the GOP establishment demoralized conservative outside groups that had scored primary victories in 2010 and 2012.[42] More important, Tea Party PACs had ruined the movement's reputation by spending much of their money on fees and prospecting instead of candidate support.[43] Paul Jossey, a campaign finance lawyer who had done work for such groups, wrote in *Politico*:

> What began as an organic, policy-driven grass-roots movement was drained of its vitality and resources by national political action committees that dunned the movement's true believers endlessly for money to support its candidates and causes. The PACs used that money first to enrich themselves and their vendors and then deployed most of the rest to search for more "prospects." In Tea Party world, that meant mostly older, technologically unsavvy people willing to divulge personal information through "petitions"—which only made them prey to further attempts to lighten their wallets for what they believed was a good cause. While the solicitations continue, the audience has greatly diminished because of a lack of policy results and changing political winds.[44]

The grassroots conservative marks eventually caught on and stopped sending money. The only real Senate primary victory for the Tea Party movement came in Colorado, where Darryl Glenn emerged from a scattered GOP field to take on incumbent Michael Bennet. His campaign never got sufficient momentum, and Bennet won.

In addition to a Senate GOP that had recovered from Tea Party fever, Democrats faced an even greater hurdle to exploiting a favorable map: candidate recruitment. Historically, the House of Representatives has been the main hatchery for Senate contenders. It is easy to see why: House members have political experience, established fundraising networks, familiarity with national issues, and geographical bases of support. During the 114th Congress, in fact, fifty-three senators had served in the House.[45] Before the 1990s, there were plenty of ambitious House Democrats to run for Senate seats. By 2016, however, the party's downballot losses had depopulated the spawning ground. Democrats had a minority of seats, and, to make matters worse, their remaining constituencies were highly concentrated in a few places. Just six states—California, New York, Massachusetts, Illinois, Florida, and Texas—accounted for more than half of the House Democratic Caucus, with California alone contributing one-fifth. Of those six, only Illinois and Florida had GOP seats up for election in 2016. Accordingly, it would be hard to find good Democratic candidates in other states.

Pennsylvania Senator Pat Toomey had won a close 2010 election during a Republican wave year and looked vulnerable. Democrats had retaken the governorship in 2014, so they appeared to be on the upswing. Because of a Republican gerrymander, however, only five of the state's eighteen House members were Democrats, and one of them faced a 2016 felony conviction for corruption. The party settled for Katie McGinty, a former Clinton administration official who had never run for office. She ran a lackluster campaign and, despite spending large sums and leading in many polls, narrowly lost to Toomey.

Like Toomey, Rob Portman of Ohio was another Republican running for reelection in a potentially competitive industrial state. As a former member of George W. Bush's cabinet, he was also open to the charge that he belonged to the old guard of political insiders. Portman turned his status to his advantage, as he built an early fundraising advantage. "The flip side of being a longtime D.C. insider is a mountain of money," a top Democratic strategist said.[46] His political experience also showed in his deft positioning on the issues. His advocacy of Ohio infrastructure projects and his opposition to the Trans-Pacific Partnership (despite his earlier service as U.S. trade representative) earned him the support of several labor unions—unusual for a Republican. With strong support from McConnell, he and New Hampshire's Kelly Ayotte coauthored successful legislation to fight opioid abuse, a growing issue in working-class areas. As in Pennsylvania, a GOP gerrymander had resulted in a small Democratic House delegation (four of sixteen), so the party was hard up for a good challenger. Their final choice was Ted Strickland, a seventy-five-year-old former governor who could hardly run on youth and outsiderism. In the fall, the national Democrats wrote off what was once a potential pickup, and Portman won by more than twenty-one points.

In a couple of Midwestern states, Democrats tried to recycle former senators. To oppose incumbent Ron Johnson in Wisconsin, they chose Russ Feingold, who had served three terms before losing to Johnson in 2010. Johnson had an unremarkable record, and most oddsmakers rated him as the underdog. He fought back by casting Feingold as an insider, making it seem as if the former senator were the incumbent. In one Johnson radio ad, the narrator spoke of "Senator Feingold," while Johnson referred to himself only as a "candidate for Senate."[47] Working in Johnson's favor was the decline in union membership, which had been sharper in Wisconsin than in any other state, meaning that Democrats had less labor money and people-power.[48] Late polls showed a tightening race, and Johnson's 3.4 percent victory margin was a major upset. Meanwhile, a Democratic former colleague of Feingold ran aground in Indiana. Evan Bayh, who had stepped down in 2010, was initially the favorite to replace retiring Republican Dan Coats. Bayh had devoted most of the previous six years to getting rich in the corporate world, spending more time in Washington than Indiana. His Republican opponent, Representative Todd Young, ran ads saying, "After the economy crashed, Indiana families were struggling. We turned to Senator Evan Bayh to protect us from the Washington insiders and Wall Street bankers, who got us into that mess. But instead of going to work for us, Evan Bayh went to work for them."[49] Bayh, like Feingold, could not escape the "insider" label and he lost by nearly ten points.

Two Republican senators had unexpectedly tough races. North Carolina's Richard Burr faced civil liberties lawyer Deborah Ross, and Missouri's Roy Blunt contended with a challenge from secretary of state Jason Kander. In both cases, charges of insiderism plagued the incumbent. Burr had been on Capitol Hill since 1994, first as a House member, then as a two-term senator. Blunt had been in office even longer. His wife and three children were lobbyists, including his son Matt, a former governor of the state. Ross proved to be a strong fundraiser, and Kander made a memorable TV ad rebutting Blunt's attack on his support for gun control. Wearing a blindfold, Kander assembled an AR-15 rifle while discussing his army record and explaining that he wanted background checks "so the terrorists can't get their hands on one of these." With a click of the assembled rifle, he ended, "I approve this message because I'd like to see Senator Blunt do this."[50] Despite their energetic campaigns, both Democrats fell short, and the GOP incumbents won.

In Florida, Democrats thought they had a shot when Marco Rubio announced that he would forgo a second Senate term to focus on his presidential race. After that campaign failed, McConnell persuaded him to change his mind and run for reelection. The good news for Democrats was that they had a couple of House members willing to run for the seat. The bad news was that both were poor candidates. Alan Grayson already had a reputation as the chamber's most obnoxious member—amid abundant competition—and in the summer, allegations of domestic abuse relegated him to also-ran status. On his way out, though, he tried hard to take his primary opponent down with him. Of Representative Patrick Murphy, he said, "He's a 33-year-old nobody who's done nothing in his life. He's never had a serious relationship, never married, no children, never had to support himself, never had a real job, and lived off a trust fund on his daddy's yacht for the first 30 years of his life."[51] The Rubio campaign picked up on the theme, effectively accusing

Murphy of padding his resume. In debates, Rubio displayed the rhetorical skill that had deserted him in the presidential primary campaign, and he won the election by a comfortable margin of more than 800,000 votes.

There were a few bright spots for Democrats. In Illinois, they found a dream candidate: Representative Tammy Duckworth, who had lost her legs as a helicopter pilot in the Iraq War. Republican incumbent Mark Kirk, who had narrowly won in 2010, was always on politically shaky ground in this heavily Democratic state, and most political observers marked him as a sure loser against a war hero. If Kirk ever had an outside chance, he destroyed it during an October debate. After Duckworth called herself a "daughter of the Revolution," Kirk replied, "I forgot that your parents came all the way from Thailand to serve George Washington."[52] Duckworth's mother was born in Thailand, but her father's family did fight under George Washington, and the Illinois Daughters of the American Revolution had honored her with a bronze statue.[53] The racist stupidity of the remark was out of character for Kirk, and some observers speculated that his massive 2012 stroke was to blame.[54] Whatever the reason, he was toast and Duckworth was on her way to the Senate.

Harry Reid's retirement gave the Republicans their best opening to pick up a Democratic seat. Their candidate, Joe Heck, had an impressive background as a physician, brigadier general in the Army Reserve, and three-term House member. He hurt himself by waffling on Trump. He pulled his endorsement after the infamous *Access Hollywood* video, then backtracked, thereby offending both pro-Trump and anti-Trump voters. Democrat Catherine Cortez Masto enjoyed statewide name identification as a former two-term attorney general. Strong Democratic turnout pushed Masto over the finish line and enabled Hillary Clinton to carry the state.

Like Heck, New Hampshire Republican senator Kelly Ayotte flip-flopped on Trump, at first saying that she would vote for him but that she did not endorse him. In a debate, she said that Trump could be a role model for kids but later took it back, explaining that she had misspoken. After *Access Hollywood*, she said that she would not vote for him at all. Democrat Maggie Hassan was the incumbent governor, so she was thoroughly familiar to the electorate. She won by a fraction of a percentage point.

New Hampshire and Nevada worked out the way that Democratic national strategists wanted. During the summer, they figured that the election would be a referendum on Trump. "If there was ever a national election. This is it," said Senator Charles Schumer (D-NY), who was prepared to succeed Reid as party leader. Democrat whip Dick Durbin (D-IL): "History tells us that when you have an extreme candidate, the party of that candidate stays home."[55]

Overall, the Senate results did align perfectly with presidential results. No

Democratic Senate candidate won a state that Trump carried, and no Republican won a state that Clinton carried. The problem for Democrats was that New Hampshire and Nevada were in the minority because Trump carried more states. Despite a gain of two seats, Democrats fell short of control.

Was Trump responsible for the Republican victory? It is possible that he helped the GOP by spurring turnout in key states, but it is unlikely that he deserves the main credit. He lost the aggregated popular tally nationwide, and his share of the vote was generally smaller than that of Republican Senate candidates. Table 5.2 displays the results for the ten states that RealClear-Politics listed as "tossups" or "leans." Only in Indiana and Missouri did Trump get a greater share of the vote than the GOP winner. In Nevada, he won a larger percentage than Heck, but both lost the state.

Most Republican candidates did not reach for Trump's coattails. On the contrary, just as the Democrats were trying to nationalize the election, Republicans were following an "all politics is local" strategy. NRSC executive director Ward Baker made this point explicitly:

[We] have a very clear messaging strategy. Republican Senators are talking to voters like they're running for sheriff. Every message is highly targeted and purposefully local. Our Senators are making sure their voters know they're focused on issues that matter in their states—Rob Portman and Kelly Ayotte are leading the fight against opioid abuse; Roy Blunt is a forceful advocate for mental health funding; John McCain and Ron Johnson are going above and beyond for reform and accountability at Veterans Affairs and VA hospitals. We want to make sure voters are casting votes for Senate candidates based solely on issues related to that Senate race—not up, down, or adjacent on the ticket.[56]

Table 5.2.   **Trump and GOP Senate Candidate Percentages, Selected States**

	Trump	*Senate Candidate*
Arizona	48.1	53.4 (McCain, won)
Colorado	43.3	45.3 (Glenn, lost)
Florida	48.6	52.0 (Rubio, won)
Indiana	57.2	52.1 (Young, won)
Missouri	57.1	49.4 (Blunt, won)
Nevada	45.5	44.7 (Heck, lost)
New Hampshire	46.5	47.9 (Ayotte, lost)
North Carolina	49.9	51.1 (Burr, won)
Pennsylvania	48.2	48.9 (Toomey, won)
Wisconsin	47.2	50.2 (Johnson, won)

Sources: RealClearPolitics, presidential results at http://www.realclearpolitics.com/elections/live_results/2016_general/president/map.html; Senate results at http://www.realclearpolitics.com/elections/live_results/2016_general/senate/.

Republican candidates seldom appeared alongside Trump, with Ron Johnson being a rare exception. They could not count on Trump for much material support. When journalist Robert Draper asked him whether holding the GOP majority meant anything to him, he replied, "Well, I'd like them to do that. But I don't mind being a free agent, either."[57]

In any case, Republicans could fend for themselves. NRSC spent $31 million between August and September, compared with $13 million for its Democratic counterpart. In October, NRSC tapered off, expecting help from outside groups. McConnell and the Senate Republicans could not lawfully coordinate strategy with these groups, but they could "play bridge" by sending signals about what they wanted.[58] Most of the people running such groups had experience in GOP politics, so they were adept at reading these signals. Steven Law, who headed both the Senate Leadership Fund (SLF) super PAC and the 501(c)(4) "dark money" group One Nation, happened to be McConnell's former chief of staff, and he could divine his old boss's wishes. The two groups spent $165 million for Senate Republicans. Of that amount, the SLF spent nearly $38 million on television ads in the final two weeks of the campaign.[59]

HOUSE ELECTIONS

Ever since the 1970s, when Gallup started measuring public approval of Congress, the institution has rarely gotten high ratings. During the 2010s, the bottom fell out, with approval dropping as low as 9 percent and never topping 24 percent.[60] At the same time, the House of Representatives experienced *increasing* reelection rates:

- 2010: 85%
- 2012: 90%
- 2014: 95%
- 2016: 97%[61]

The reasons for this disparity are familiar to those who study Capitol Hill. Lawmakers run for Congress by running against Congress, contrasting their own wisdom and empathy with the foolishness of many of their colleagues. Incumbents take political advantage of the perks of office, keeping up their popularity by providing constituent services and taking credit for federal spending in their districts. Accordingly, there is truth to the cliché that Americans hate Congress but love their own members of Congress. Partisan polarization and geographical clustering have enhanced the effect, leaving most districts uncompetitive under normal conditions. Exit polling in 2016 did not suggest a great deal of ticket splitting, as 92 percent of Democrats voted for their party's congressional candidate, as did 94 percent of Republicans.[62] In this light, it is unsurprising that Democrats scored a net gain of only 6 seats, for a total of 194, well short of the 218 they needed to control the chamber. Republicans ended with 241 seats, a slight comedown from 2014 but still their third-greatest post-election sum since 1928.

The GOP victory seems preordained in hindsight, but for much of the election cycle, Speaker Paul Ryan (R-WI) had his worries. For starters, he came to the speakership under difficult circumstances. Facing pressure from the House Freedom Caucus, a faction of Tea Party conservatives, House Speaker John Boehner announced on September 25, 2015, that he would soon resign from Congress. Ryan, chair of the Ways and Means Committee and the party's 2012 vice presidential nominee, was the one potential replacement who was broadly acceptable both to mainstream conservatives and the Freedom Caucus. Seeing the political pain that Boehner had endured, Ryan balked at taking the job, but he finally agreed. His reluctance proved to be well justified, as Freedom Caucus members soon started sniping at him. Ryan would spend the next year trying to mollify them without letting the House take actions that would jeopardize Republican seats. Above all, he worked to avoid another government shutdown.

At times during the campaign, Trump's unpopularity loomed as a potential threat to House Republicans. Ryan kept his distance from Trump without repudiating him, and Trump was unhappy about it. During a speech in Florida, Trump said, "Wouldn't you think that Paul Ryan would call and say, 'Good going?' . . . No, he doesn't do that. There's a whole deal going on over there. I mean, you know, there's a whole deal going on [and] we're going to figure it out. I always figure things out. But there's a whole sinister deal going on."[63] Calling Ryan "nasty," Trump suggested in an interview that he might not be able to remain as speaker: "I would think that Ryan maybe wouldn't be there, maybe he'll be in a different position."[64] In the end, though, Trump proved not to be ballot-box poison to the House Republicans. After the election, he and Ryan made a public show of unity.

All along, Democrats were not in a strong position to take advantage of any opportunities that Trump might have given them. A weak bench hampered recruiting. Just as diminished numbers in the House made it hard to find good Senate candidates, Democratic weakness in the state legislatures had thinned the ranks of potential House candidates. What is more, minority status made service in the House less politically attractive to Democrats than it was in the 1980s. Freshman Democrats quickly learned that their bills would go nowhere and that they might never chair a committee or subcommittee. In the minority, the only real chance for prominence is a party leadership post. The top three spots belonged to minority leader Nancy Pelosi of California (age seventy-six), party whip Steny Hoyer of Maryland (age seventy-seven), and assistant leader James Clyburn of South Carolina (age seventy-six), who were holding on to their positions. This gerontocracy thwarted the upward mobility of younger Democrats and sent a message to prospective candidates: you must wait a very, very long time to make your mark on Capitol Hill. "I was on the recruitment committee, and a lot of candidates decided to take a pass," Representative Karen Bass told the *New York Times*. "There are people who are new to Congress and have a difficult situation because they are not going to be there for 20 years."[65]

Democrats found it tough to hold onto the talent that they already had, as some well-regarded members hit the exits. Chris Van Hollen (D-MD), former chair of the Democratic Congressional Campaign Committee (DCCC), ran for the Senate. Another former DCCC chair, Steve Israel (D-NY), did not seek reelection in 2016. Xavier Becerra (D-CA), chair of the House Democratic Conference, left Congress after the election to accept appointment as California's attorney general, replacing Kamala Harris, who had won a Senate seat. Janice Hahn, also of California, ran for the Los Angeles County Board of Supervisors. "The circumstances are that gerrymandering and the tamping down the votes causes members to not think we are going to win the majority any time soon," said Alcee Hastings (D-FL). "That then causes people to say, what the hell, and go about their business elsewhere."[66]

Some of the Democrats' problems were self-inflicted. Thomas Mills, a political consultant who ran for a House seat in North Carolina, wrote that DCCC gave his campaign a rude brushoff.

> I've spent 20 years working on political campaigns, and the political organization I encountered in 2016 was an utter disappointment. Back in the '90s when I started out, the DCCC was tasked with contesting as many races as possible and providing staff, training and direction to the campaigns in the field. Today, they're narrowly focused on a small number of highly targeted races. Other campaigns get little attention or support.
>
> Despite their 60-seat deficit heading into 2016, the Democrats didn't appear to do much candidate recruiting except in the most competitive districts. In Texas, Hillary Clinton won in a congressional district where *Democrats didn't even field a challenger*. Numbers, not potential, guided the DCCC efforts. Instead of looking for possibilities, or trying to create them, the committee only paid attention to the districts that looked viable on spreadsheets.[67]

Mills was referring to the 32nd district of Texas, where Democrats failed to see that the Dallas-area constituency was becoming more Democratic, and thus missed a chance to challenge incumbent Republican Pete Sessions.[68]

Although nearly all incumbents who sought reelection were successful, a few did go down. California's 17th district, encompassing much of Silicon Valley, was so deeply blue that both finalists were Democrats. In a rematch of their 2014 fight, incumbent Mike Honda squared off against law lecturer Ro Khanna. Thirty-five years younger than Honda, and with close ties to the area's high-tech industry, Khanna was a better fit for the district. Though Honda won the first time, Khanna never really stopped campaigning. His efforts paid off in victory.

Court-ordered redistricting brought down several members. In Virginia, Republican Randy Forbes switched districts rather than stay in a redrawn constituency that had become much more Democratic. Running in new territory, Forbes lost to Scott Taylor, who had represented part of the district in the state legislature. New lines in North Carolina placed Renee Ellmers (R-NC) into the same district as fellow incumbent Republican George Holding, who came out on top. Corinne Brown (D-FL) probably would have won the Democratic primary in her new district—except for her recent federal indictment for fraud. In the general election, Florida Republicans John Mica and David Jolly lost redrawn districts to Democratic challengers. Jolly had forfeited national GOP support earlier in the year when he went on *60 Minutes* and criticized the fundraising practices of the National Republican Congressional Committee. The winner over Jolly was Charles Crist. A onetime Republican governor of Florida, Crist ran as an independent Senate candidate against Marco Rubio in 2010, then switched parties.

Pennsylvania Democrat Chaka Fattah lost his primary after his felony indictment on federal corruption charges, and he resigned after his conviction. In two of the few remaining marginal districts, Republicans Frank Guinta of New Hampshire and Robert Dold of Illinois fell in rematches with former members that they had previously defeated. In Nebraska, Democrat Brad Ashford lost a closely divided district that voted for Romney in 2012 and Trump in 2016. Conversely, Nevada's Crescent Hardy lost a district that voted for Obama and Clinton.

Two members of the Freedom Caucus went down. In a GOP primary in Kansas, physician Roger Marshall defeated Tim Huelskamp, who had lost his seat on the House Agriculture Committee after fighting with the party leadership. Marshall said that he would put local interests ahead of ideology, and he got a boost when mainstream Republican super PACs poured money into the district. "The establishment's position was always . . . [focused] in competitive seats, in situations where we believed [a different] candidate gave us a strategic advantage. It was never ideological. But now you're seeing more and more activity in these safe seats," GOP operative Brian O. Walsh told *Politico*. "It's like when you have a health problem. First, you try to ignore it, see if it gets better. Then you try to treat it with meds. Now you just have to radiate it."[69] In New Jersey, Scott Garrett lost the general election. He had refused to pay dues to the National Republican Congressional Committee (NRCC) because it had supported gay candidates. When this position got him into trouble at home, NRCC declined to bail him out.

Unlike in 2012, when Democrats could complain that they had lost the House despite winning more combined votes in House races than Republicans, the GOP's 2016 candidates outpolled Democrats by more than a million votes in total.[70] In the Senate races, Democrats held the edge in total votes, but only because the nation's largest state had two Democratic candidates for Senate and no Republicans owing to its peculiar "top-two" primary. Without that anomaly, Republican Senate candidates also outpolled their Democratic rivals nationwide.[71]

STATE GOVERNMENTS

A dozen governorships were up for election in 2016. Among these contests, Republicans extended their winning streak by making a net gain of two. Republicans would now hold thirty-three governorships, their greatest number since 1922. The story of 2016 was a bit more complicated than a simple Republican sweep, however.

Governors handle practical service-delivery issues that often do not always fall into neat partisan or ideological categories. Working under the constraints of the bond market, or state constitutional balanced-budget requirements, Republican governors have acceded to tax increases that would be anathema to their co-partisans in Congress. Similarly, competition among states can make Democratic governors as business-friendly as any Republican. So whereas congressional elections have featured increasing levels of party polarization, red states have elected Democratic governors and blue states have elected Republicans. Though serving overwhelmingly Democratic states, GOP governors Charlie Baker of Massachusetts and Larry Hogan of Maryland both had 2016 approval ratings of more than 70 percent.[72] Louisiana, which has become ruby-red in the past decade, chose a Democratic governor in 2015.

In 2016, Republican gubernatorial candidates took Democratic-held seats in three states. Eric Greitens, a former Navy SEAL who had never held elected office, won the open seat of Missouri's term-limited Democratic governor Jay Nixon. Greitens ran as a political outsider who decried lobbyist influence and promised ethics reform.[73] In New Hampshire, Chris Sununu benefited from name recognition: his father had been governor and his brother had served as a U.S. senator. In Vermont, lieutenant governor Phil Scott ran as a pro-choice, pro-gay moderate who would work across party lines.

Democrats picked up a red-state governorship in North Carolina, but this party turnover had a radically different tone from Vermont's. Republican Governor Pat McCrory signed a "bathroom bill" requiring transgender people to use public restrooms corresponding to the sex on their birth certificates. Various national organizations boycotted the state, and businesses pulled back on expansion plans: by one estimate, the bathroom bill cost the state up to $395 million.[74] The economic repercussions hurt McCrory, and Democratic attorney general Roy Cooper defeated him by a very narrow margin. Complaining that there may have been fraud, McCrory did not concede the bitter race until December. To hobble Cooper, the state's GOP-controlled legislature then passed a measure to strip the governorship of much of its power.

Two other red states voted to keep their governorships in Democratic hands. In West Virginia, incumbent Earl Ray Tomblin was term-limited. Jim Justice, a billionaire businessman who had never held office, ran as a conservative who would promote the state's coal industry. Justice, who had recently been a Republican, emphasized that he was an outsider with no ties to the national Democrats. In Montana, Steve Bullock narrowly won a second term. As the 2020 election approaches, Democrats will probably give Bullock some consideration for the national ticket. The 2016 election showed that the party needs to appeal to rural voters, and Bullock has won three successive elections in this very rural state (once for attorney general, twice for governor). He is relatively young (born in 1966) and well credentialed (Columbia Law), and he has potential ideological appeal as a longtime advocate of campaign finance reform.

In state legislative elections, Democrats largely failed to repopulate their depleted farm club. In 2016, eighty-six of the nation's ninety-nine state legislative chambers held elections, and Republicans made a small net gain, ending up with 57 percent of the nation's 7,383 legislative seats. They concluded with a "trifecta"—control of the governorship and both chambers—in twenty-five states. Democrats had trifectas in just six. This continued Republican dominance in state government has implications far beyond the parties' respective ability to field strong candidates for federal office. Though largely out of the national media spotlight, a great deal of American public policy is decided at the state level.

THE SPECIAL CASE OF CALIFORNIA

California was an outlier in the elections of 2016. Clinton won the state by 4.3 million votes while Trump was winning the rest of the country by 1.4 million. California Democrats gained legislative seats to win two-thirds supermajorities in the state Senate and Assembly, even as Republicans maintained their dominance of state legislatures nationwide. In House races, the state GOP did hold onto several House seats that Democrats had targeted, but the U.S. Senate race was an embarrassment for the party. In a year when the U.S. Senate Republicans defied the odds to keep their majority, California Republicans failed to get a Senate candidate on the general election ballot. Because of its immense size (10.4 percent of the total national vote) and divergent political path, California is worth a closer look.

Contrary to myth, California was not a thoroughly Republican state in the late twentieth century. In nearly every year after 1958, with some brief exceptions, Democrats controlled the state legislature and most of the state's U.S. House seats. During this period, Democrats almost always held at least one of the state's U.S. Senate seats. (The exception came between the elections of 1964 and 1968, when Republicans Thomas Kuchel and George Murphy were both serving.) Two Democratic Browns bracketed the Reagan governorship: Pat Brown won in 1958 and lost to Reagan in 1966, and then his son Jerry succeeded Reagan in 1974. Nevertheless, Republicans were competitive. They carried the state in every presidential election between 1968 and 1988, albeit with California-rooted candidates in four of the six races (Nixon in 1968 and 1972, Reagan in 1980 and 1984). Reagan twice won the governorship by substantial margins, and Pete Wilson won four statewide races: for the U.S. Senate in 1982 and 1988, and for governor in 1990 and 1994.

By the late 1990s, Republican fortunes were slipping. In 1992, Democrat Barbara Boxer succeeded Democrat Alan Cranston, and, in a special election at the same time, Dianne Feinstein easily dispatched the Republican appointed by Pete Wilson to fill his vacant seat. Feinstein won a full term in 1994. Bill Clinton carried the state in 1992 and 1996, and, in the latter election, Republicans lost a short-lived majority in the state assembly. In the 1998 midterm, Democrats took the governorship and most other statewide offices. Arnold Schwarzenegger's victory in a 2003 gubernatorial recall election temporarily revived GOP hopes, but he did little good for Republicans down the ballot. By the time he departed in 2010, the state's flagging economy and his legislative alliances with Democrats had made him a pariah within the party. That year's election brought Jerry Brown back to the governorship and left Republicans without a single statewide office. Meanwhile,

California had become such a reliable state in presidential elections that Republicans dropped any serious effort to contest it. In his losing 1992 race, President George H. W. Bush got 41.4 percent of California's two-party vote. In his winning 2016 race, Trump got only 33.9 percent.

Party registration figures tell a similar story. In 1992, 39.6 percent of the state's voters registered as Republicans.[75] In 2016, that figure was down to 26.8 percent.[76]

The Hispanic vote is the most common explanation for the state party's problems. In 1994, Governor Wilson and many other leading Republicans supported Proposition 187, a ballot measure to deny many public services to undocumented immigrants. Hispanic voters strongly disapproved of this position, but it would be an exaggeration to say that the issue suddenly tipped a large voting bloc against the GOP, since the state's Hispanic voters *already* favored the Democrats.[77] Far more important was that the Hispanic population simply became much bigger and that non-Hispanic whites diminished as a proportion of the state's population. In 1990, 57 percent of Californians identified as non-Hispanic "white alone."[78] By 2015, this group had shrunk to 38 percent, compared with 39 percent identifying as Hispanic.[79] Though non-Hispanic whites had become a minority overall, they still made up the largest group in the electorate because many Hispanics were not yet citizens or under age eighteen, and because turnout was relatively lower among Hispanics eligible to vote.[80] Still, the Hispanic share of the California electorate grew from about 8 percent in 1992 to 31 percent in 2016.[81]

The "Asian alone" population was also growing, from 4 to 12 percent of the electorate. Like Hispanics, they have leaned Democratic. The Vietnamese American population used to be an exception, because of the GOP's anticommunism. But as that issue fades into memory and other issues came to the fore, younger Vietnamese Americans have abandoned the GOP. Republican state legislator Janet Nguyen explained that many of them arrived the United States in poverty and relied on the social services that the GOP disparages: "Going back to the 90s, if you came to me and said those on welfare milk the system, that's offensive to me. That's what you might see a lot for the younger generation, knowing their family came here extremely poor."[82]

There were other reasons for the California GOP's decline. From the 1950s through the 1980s, hawkishness was good politics, and the party could count on the support of white-collar engineers and blue-collar factory workers in the state's vast aerospace industry.[83] The end of the Cold War wiped out this voter base, as the state lost two-thirds of its aerospace jobs between 1990 and 2011.[84] The state's economy shifted toward more Democratic-friendly sectors such as health services and high technology. Santa Clara County, encompassing such technology hubs as San Jose and Cupertino, was once politically competitive. Reagan carried the county in 1984, and Bush ran just four points behind Dukakis in 1988. It also sent Republicans to the U.S. House, including Ed Zschau and Tom Campbell. By 2016, those outcomes were a distant memory. The county gave 73 percent of its vote to Hillary Clinton, and in the race for the 17th congressional district, no Republican even made the general election ballot.

In June 2010, state voters approved the "top-two" primary. Under this system, all candidates for partisan office appear on the same primary ballot. The top two finishers, regardless of party, move on to the general election. Schwarzenegger pushed the proposal on the assumption that it would serve as a moderating force. If candidates could win a primary by appealing to independents and members of the other party, the thinking went, they would have a strong incentive to move to the center. Some Republicans hoped that it would foster the nomination of GOP candidates with wider voter appeal. Evidence for the moderating effect is mixed at best.[85] As for helping the GOP, top two failed. The party simply abandoned swatches of the state, where there were no Republican candidates on the November ballot.[86]

The 2016 election was the first time since the direct election of senators in 1914 that no Republican candidate for Senate made the general election ballot in California. A few competed in the primary, but none got more than 8 percent. The top two finishers were Attorney General Kamala Harris, a liberal from San Francisco, and Representative Loretta Sanchez, a moderate liberal from Orange County. Harris had party support and statewide name identification from her two successful races for state office. Sanchez had less money and visibility, but she might have been a real contender if she had rallied Republicans by clearly running to Harris's right. She did not do so, and more than a third of Republican voters said that they were skipping the Senate race altogether.[87] By the fall, Harris's victory was a virtual certainty, and the public tuned out. The sole moment of interest came at the end of the candidates' only televised debate, when Sanchez finished her closing statement with a dance move known as "dabbing."

THE FUTURE

As they licked their wounds in the aftermath of the 2016 election, Democrats consoled themselves that California was a preview of the nation's political future. With the growth of the Hispanic and Asian populations, they reasoned, the electorate will inexorably turn more liberal and Democratic. Within a few election cycles, they hoped, some red states will start turning purple, then blue. Texas, for instance, already has a large Hispanic population and a growing Asian American presence in certain urban areas. "I think members in the Democratic party do not see us winning the majority until the mid-2020s, when places like Texas turn blue, and it will," said Representative Alcee Hastings.[88]

Maybe, maybe not. For one thing, population projections involve uncertainty. In 2014, the Census Bureau cut its Hispanic population projection for 2050 by 30 million.[89] Reduction in birth rates could slow down the trend, as could slower immigration rates stemming from either economic growth in Latin America or restrictive immigration policies in the United States. In addition, it is risky to assume that the current voting patterns of ethnic groups will persist into the indefinite future. It is possible that Hispanics may become more Republican as they become more affluent. Of course, Republicans cannot bank on such a shift any more than Democrats can take continued Hispanic support for granted: Jewish voters, for instance, have stuck with the Democrats through decades of economic and social ascent.

"It depends" is the only honest answer to questions about future partisan balance in Congress and the statehouses. "Unknown unknowns" such as wars and economic crashes can disrupt social and political life in ways that are impossible to anticipate. Even natural disasters can play a part. Hurricane Katrina hurt Democrats in Louisiana by forcing thousands of African Americans to leave the state, with many never coming back. During the transition from Obama to Trump, the policies of the new administration were a "known unknown." Trump's statements and promises have never been a reliable guide to his behavior, so no one could be confident about what was in store for the next four years. Decisions that trigger intense political opposition and mobilization by Hispanics and Asian Americans could accelerate the "Californization" of states such as Texas. Conversely, economic prosperity and the return of jobs to the Rust Belt could nudge some Midwestern industrial states in the opposite direction.

In the shorter run, it seemed more likely than not that the Republicans would hold onto their gains in Congress. In 2018, the map and the calendar will not help Senate Democrats. Because of the party's good showing in 2012, they must defend twenty-five seats, compared with just eight for the Republicans. Six of the eight are in very strong GOP states, with only Arizona and Nevada looming as potential turnovers. Of the twenty-five Democratic seats, ten are in states that Trump won. In the House, Democrats need to gain twenty-four GOP seats to take the majority, which is about the same number of House Republicans who will represent Clinton districts. But only 15 of 241 Republicans won by a margin of less than 10 percent, and Democrats must defend about a dozen Trump districts.[90]

But before writing off Democratic chances, remember the history with which this chapter started. At the start of 1993, it was the Republicans who looked doomed and the Democrats who seemed indomitable. Two years later, House Democratic Leader Richard Gephardt opened the 104th Congress by saying, "With resignation but with resolve I hereby end 40 years of Democratic rule of this House."[91]

NOTES

1. John T. Pothier, "The Partisan Bias in Senate Elections," *American Politics Quarterly* 12 (January 1984): 89–100.

2. Gary C. Jacobson, *The Electoral Origins of Divided Government* (Boulder, CO: Westview Press, 1990), 112–20.

3. Ibid., 3.

4. Alan Ehrenhalt, *The United States of Ambition* (New York: Times Books, 1991), 126.

5. William F. Connelly Jr. and John J. Pitney Jr., *Congress' Permanent Minority? Republicans in the US House* (Lanham, MD: Rowman & Littlefield, 1994), 156.

6. James W. Ceaser and Andrew E. Busch, *Losing to Win: The 1996 Elections and American Politics* (Lanham, MD: Rowman & Littlefield, 1997).

7. Adam Clymer, "G.O.P. Seems to Gear Ads to Dole Loss," *New York Times*, October 28, 1996, http://www.nytimes.com/1996/10/28/us/gop-seems-to-gear-ads-to-dole-loss.html.

8. Eric Cantor, Paul Ryan, and Kevin McCarthy, *Young Guns: A New Generation of Conservative Leaders* (New York: Simon and Schuster, 2010), 5.

9. Toby Eckert, "Former Comrades Angered by 'Bribe Menu,'" *San Diego Union-Tribune*, February 22, 2006, http://legacy.sandiegouniontribune.com/news/politics/cunningham/20060222-9999-1n22duke.html.

10. Andy Barr, "Dems Talk of 'Permanent Progressive Majority,'" *Politico*, November 7, 2008, http://www.politico.com/story/2008/11/dems-talk-of-permanent-progressive-majority-015407.

11. Leslie Marshall, "Why Democrats Will Win the House in 2014," *US News and World Report*, October 13, 2013, http://www.usnews.com/opinion/blogs/leslie-marshall/2013/03/13/why-democrats-will-win-the-house-in-2014.

12. Paul Steinhauser, "CNN Poll: 75% Say Most Republicans in Congress Don't Deserve Re-Election," CNN, October 22, 2013, http://www.cnn.com/2013/10/21/politics/cnn-poll-shutdown-re-election.

13. John B. Judis, "The Last Days of the GOP," *The New Republic*, October 10, 2013, https://newrepublic.com/article/115134/gop-death-watch-final-days-republican-party.

14. The previous post-Reconstruction low for Democrats was twelve legislatures, which they reached after the elections of 1894, 1896, and 1920. Michael J. Dubin, *Party Affiliations in the State Legislatures: A Year by Year Summary, 1796–2006* (Jefferson, NC: McFarland, 2007), 9–11.

15. Harry Enten, "It's Much Harder to Protect Southern Black Voters' Influence Than It Was 10 Years Ago," FiveThirtyEight, December 5, 2016, http://fivethirtyeight.com/fea-

tures/its-much-harder-to-protect-southern-black-voters-influence-than-it-was-10-years-ago.

16. Kathryn Chakmak, "How the Natural State Turned Red: Political Realignment in Arkansas," undergraduate thesis, Claremont McKenna College, 2015.

17. David Hawkings, "The House's Ideology, in Seven Circles," *Roll Call*, January 19, 2016, http://www.rollcall.com/news/home/houses-ideology-seven-circles.

18. Peter Urban, "Harry Reid Grows More Democratic," *Las Vegas Review-Journal*, October 24, 2010, http://www.reviewjournal.com/news/elections/harry-reid-grows-more -democratic.

19. Justin McCarthy, "Quarter of U.S. Voters Say Candidate Must Share View on Guns," Gallup, October 19, 2015, http://www.gallup.com/poll/186248/quarter-voters-say -candidate-share-view-guns.aspx.

20. Rich Morin, "The Demographics and Politics of Gun-Owning Households," Pew Research Center, July 15, 2014, http://www.pewresearch.org/fact-tank/2014/07/15/the -demographics-and-politics-of-gun-owning-households.

21. Michael Dimock, "Widening Regional Divide over Abortion Laws," Pew Research Center, July 29, 2013, http://www.people-press.org/2013/07/29/widening -regional-divide-over-abortion-laws.

22. Emma Green, "Democrats Have a Religion Problem," *The Atlantic*, December 29, 2016, https://www.theatlantic.com/politics/archive/2016/12/democrats-have-a-religion -problem/510761.

23. Jowei Chen and Jonathan Rodden, "Unintentional Gerrymandering: Political Geography and Electoral Bias in Legislatures," *Quarterly Journal of Political Science* 8 (2013): 239–69, http://www-personal.umich.edu/~jowei/florida.pdf.

24. Alec MacGillis, "Go Midwest, Young Hipster," *New York Times Magazine*, October 22, 2016, http://www.nytimes.com/2016/10/23/opinion/campaign-stops/go-midwest -young-hipster.html.

25. Lisa Lerer, "As Obama Accomplished Policy Goals, His Party Floundered," Associated Press, December 24, 2016, http://abcnews.go.com/Politics/wireStory/obama -accomplished-policy-goals-party-floundered-44383430.

26. Edward-Isaac Dovere, "DNC Insiders Detail Months of Escalating Dysfunction," *Politico*, July 28, 2016, http://www.politico.com/story/2016/07/dnc-debbie-wasserman -schultz-226352.

27. Lerer, "As Obama Accomplished."

28. Barack Obama, "The President's News Conference," December 16, 2016, http:// www.presidency.ucsb.edu/ws/?pid=119865.

29. Emily Badger and Quoctrung Bui, "Why Republicans Don't Even Try to Win Cities Anymore," *New York Times*, November 2, 2016, http://www.nytimes.com/2016/11/ 03/upshot/why-republicans-dont-even-try-to-win-cities-anymore.html.

30. U.S. Bureau of Labor Statistics, "Union Affiliation Data from the Current Population Survey," January 28, 2016, https://www.bls.gov/webapps/legacy/cpslutab1.htm.

31. Kyle Peterson, "The Spoils of the Republican State Conquest," *Wall Street Journal*, December 9, 2016, http://www.wsj.com/articles/the-spoils-of-the-republican-state -conquest-1481326770.

32. Chris Cillizza and Aaron Blake, "Democrats See Map and Math Working to Their Advantage in 2016 Senate Races," *Washington Post*, January 18, 2016, https://www

.washingtonpost.com/politics/democrats-see-map-and-math-working-to-their-advantage
-in-2016-senate-races/2015/01/18/b85657d6-9eb6-11e4-bcfb-059ec7a93ddc_story.html.

33. Jeremy W. Peters and Jonathan Martin, "G.O.P. Weighs Limiting Clout of Right
Wing," *New York Times*, November 6, 2013, http://www.nytimes.com/2013/11/07/us/
politics/gop-weighs-limiting-clout-of-right-wing.html.

34. Carl Hulse, "Leading Republicans Move to Stamp Out Challenges from Right,"
New York Times, March 8, 2014, https://www.nytimes.com/2014/03/09/us/politics/
leading-republicans-move-to-stamp-out-challenges-from-right.html.

35. James Hohmann, " 'The Guerrilla': Mitch McConnell's Long-Shot Challenger,"
Politico, January 22, 2014, http://www.politico.com/story/2014/01/matt-bevin-kentucky
-senate-2014-on-the-ground-mitch-mcconnell-102498.html.

36. Donna Cassata, "Tea Party Ready for Fight with GOP Establishment," RealClear-
Politics, March 1, 2014, http://www.realclearpolitics.com/articles/2014/03/01/tea_party_
ready_for_fight_with_gop_establishment_121771.html.

37. Reid Wilson, "The Untold Stories of the 2016 Battle for the Senate," *The Hill*,
November 15, 2016, http://origin-nyi.thehill.com/homenews/senate/306002-2016s-battle
-for-senate-crushing-the-tea-party.

38. Alex Roarty, "In Kansas, Pompeo Won't Challenge Sen. Moran," *Roll Call*, April
25, 2016, http://www.rollcall.com/news/politics/kansas-pompeo.

39. Alexis Levinson, "How McCain Survived," *National Review*, August 31, 2016,
http://www.nationalreview.com/article/439543/john-mccain-primary-victory-was-won
-old-fashioned-way.

40. Ibid.

41. Arizona Grassroots Action, "Skywriting—Kelli Ward for U.S. Senate," YouTube,
July 14, 2015, https://youtu.be/mpTfbwIpkbk.

42. Paul Kane, "Why Mitch McConnell's Strategy to Quash the Tea Party Is Working," *Washington Post*, September 1, 2016, https://www.washingtonpost.com/news/
powerpost/wp/2016/09/01/why-mitch-mcconnells-strategy-to-quash-the-tea-party-is
-working.

43. Will Tucker, "Scam PACs Keep Money Churning, But Not to Candidates,"
OpenSecrets, July 29, 2015, http://www.opensecrets.org/news/2015/07/scam-pacs-keep
-money-churning-but-not-to-candidates.

44. Paul H. Jossey, "How We Killed the Tea Party," *Politico*, August 14, 2016, http://
www.politico.com/magazine/story/2016/08/tea-party-pacs-ideas-death-214164.

45. Jennifer E. Manning, "Membership of the 114th Congress: A Profile," Congressional Research Service, September 7, 2016, http://www.senate.gov/CRSpubs/c527ba93
-dd4a-4ad6-b79d-b1c9865ca076.pdf.

46. Reid Wilson, "2016's Battle for the Senate: A Shifting Map," *The Hill*, November 16, 2016, http://origin-nyi.thehill.com/homenews/senate/306220-2016s-battle-for-the
-senate-a-shifting-map.

47. Theodoric Meyer, "Johnson Upsets Feingold to Keep Wisconsin Senate Seat,"
Politico, November 9, 2016, http://www.politico.com/story/2016/11/johnson-feingold
-wisconsin-senate-race-2016-election-results-231027.

48. Rich Kremer, "Wisconsin Leads Nation in Declining Union Membership," Wisconsin Public Radio, January 28, 2016, http://www.wpr.org/wisconsin-leads-nation
-declining-union-membership.

49. Todd Young for Indiana, "Evan Bayh: Bayh Left Us," YouTube, September 12, 2016, https://youtu.be/1mQ1RLaWdtI.

50. Missourians for Kander, "Background Checks," YouTube, September 15, 2016, https://youtu.be/-wqOApBLPio.

51. Jason Zengerle, "The Second-Strangest Campaign of the Season," *New York Magazine*, July 26, 2016, http://nymag.com/daily/intelligencer/2016/07/alan-grayson-florida-senate-race.html.

52. Rebecca Sinderbrand, "This Mark Kirk Debate Gaffe Is Stunningly Bad," *Washington Post*, October 27, 2016, https://www.washingtonpost.com/news/the-fix/wp/2016/10/27/yes-it-was-the-most-cringe-worthy-debate-moment-of-the-week.

53. Rorye O'Connor, "DAR Dedicates Women Veterans Memorial," *The Register-News*, Mount Vernon, Illinois, June 20, 2011, http://www.register-news.com/news/dar-dedicates-women-veterans-memorial/article_77ce87be-3ab6-59b7-9896-c487b8f4204e.html.

54. Alex Roarty, "Kirk's Latest Controversy Follows Other Questionable Comments," *Roll Call*, October 28, 2016, http://www.rollcall.com/news/politics/kirks-latest-controversy-begs-question-stroke-blame.

55. Burgess Everett, "Democrats' Surprising Strategy to Win the Senate: Be Boring," *Politico*, June 13, 2016, http://www.politico.com/story/2016/06/democrats-senate-boring-trump-224194.

56. Ward Baker, "Senate Republicans Are Going to Win in November," Medium, May 23, 2016, https://medium.com/@nrsc/republicans-are-going-to-win-in-november-heres-why-62f17fc8cd59.

57. Robert Draper, "Can the G.O.P. Senate Majority Survive Donald Trump?" *New York Times Magazine*, July 12, 2016, http://www.nytimes.com/2016/07/17/magazine/can-the-gop-senate-majority-survive-donald-trump.html.

58. Phil Mattingly, "The Super PAC Workaround: How Candidates Quietly, Legally Communicate," *Bloomberg Business Week*, August 28, 2014, https://www.bloomberg.com/news/articles/2014-08-28/how-candidates-communicate-legally-with-super-pacs.

59. Reid Wilson, "Battle for the Senate: Top of Ticket Dominates," *The Hill*, November 17, 2016, http://thehill.com/business-a-lobbying/306487-battle-for-the-senate-top-of-ticket-dominates.

60. Art Swift, "U.S. Congressional Approval Averages Weak 17% for 2016," Gallup, December 15, 2016, http://www.gallup.com/poll/199445/congressional-approval-averages-weak-2016.aspx.

61. "Reelection Rates Over the Years," Center for Responsive Politics, https://www.opensecrets.org/overview/reelect.php.

62. CNN, "Exit Polls: National House," November 23, 2016, http://www.cnn.com/election/results/exit-polls/national/house.

63. Gabby Morrongiello, "Trump Hammers Ryan: 'There's a Whole Sinister Deal Going On,'" *Washington Examiner*, October 12, 2016, http://www.washingtonexaminer.com/trump-hammers-ryan-theres-a-whole-sinister-deal-going-on/article/2604375.

64. Reid Epstein, "Donald Trump Hints If He's Elected, Paul Ryan Will Be Out of a Job," *Wall Street Journal*, October 11, 2016, http://blogs.wsj.com/washwire/2016/10/11/donald-trump-hints-if-hes-elected-paul-ryan-will-be-out-of-a-job.

65. Jennifer Steinhauer, "Democrats' Weak Bench Undermines Hope of Taking Back

Senate," *New York Times*, August 25, 2016, http://www.nytimes.com/2016/08/26/us/poli tics/democrats-weak-bench-undermines-hope-of-taking-back-senate.html.

66. Billy House, "For Ambitious House Democrats There's Nowhere to Go but Out," *Bloomberg*, January 7, 2016, https://www.bloomberg.com/politics/articles/2016-01-07/ for-ambitious-u-s-house-democrats-there-s-nowhere-to-go-but-out.

67. Thomas Mills, "How the Democratic Party Lost Its Way," *Politico*, December 10, 2016, http://www.politico.com/magazine/story/2016/12/how-the-democratic-party-lost-its -way-214514.

68. Katie Leslie, "Is Dallas Rep. Pete Sessions Vulnerable After Clinton Won His District?" *Dallas Morning News*, December 12, 2016, http://www.dallasnews.com/news/ local-politics/2016/12/12/sessions-culberson-see-districts-turn-blue-presidential-race-age -trump-signal-long-term-trouble/.

69. Elena Schneider, "The GOP Establishment Strikes Back," *Politico*, August 15, 2016, http://www.politico.com/story/2016/08/gop-establishment-strikes-back-house-free dom-caucus-226997.

70. "2016 National House Popular Vote Tracker," https://docs.google.com/spread sheets/d/1oArjXSYeg40u4qQRR93qveN2N1UELQ6v04_mamrKg9g/edit#gid = 0.

71. Aaron Blake, "3 Election Stats Liberals Love That Don't Mean As Much as They Seem," *Washington Post*, December 13, 2016, https://www.washingtonpost.com/news /the-fix/wp/2016/12/13/3-election-stats-liberals-love-that-dont-mean-as-much-as-they -seem/.

72. "America's Most (and Least) Popular Governors," Morning Consult, September 20, 2016, https://morningconsult.com/state-governor-rankings.

73. Summer Ballentine, "Missouri GOP Governor Candidate Greitens Touts Outsider Role," Associated Press, July 27, 2016, http://www.columbiamissourian.com/news/elec tions/missouri-gop-governor-candidate-greitens-touts-outsider-role/article_22d57f6e -1819-5071-879c-e3597dc522c0.html.

74. Emma Grey Ellis, "Guess How Much That Anti-LGBTQ Law Is Costing North Carolina," *Wired*, September 18, 2016, https://www.wired.com/2016/09/guess-much-anti -lgbtq-law-costing-north-carolina.

75. California Secretary of State, "60-Day Report of Registration," September 8, 2000, http://elections.cdn.sos.ca.gov/ror/ror-pages/60day-presgen-00/historical-registra tion-stats-60-day-close.pdf.

76. California Secretary of State, "60-Day Report of Registration," September 9, 2016, http://elections.cdn.sos.ca.gov/ror/ror-pages/60day-gen-16/hist-reg-stats.pdf.

77. Fred Bauer, "Pete Wilson Did Not Make California Turn Blue: Unraveling a Myth," *National Review*, January 21, 2016, http://www.nationalreview.com/article/ 430032/immigration-republicans-hispanic-vote-california-pete-wilson.

78. U.S. Bureau of the Census, "Demographic Trends in the 20th Century," November 2002, https://www.census.gov/prod/2002pubs/censr-4.pdf.

79. U.S. Bureau of the Census, "Quick Facts: California," 2016, http://www.census .gov/quickfacts/table/PST045215/06.

80. Mark Baldassare et al., "Race and Voting in California," Public Policy Institute of California, September 2016, http://www.ppic.org/main/publication_show.asp?i = 264.

81. See exit poll data for 1992 at http://www.cnn.com/ELECTION/1998/states/ CA/polls/CA92PH.html and for 2016 at http://www.cnn.com/election/results/exit-polls/ california/president.

82. Matt Levin, "From Loyal to Lost? Vietnamese Voters and the GOP," CalMatters, November 2, 2016, https://calmatters.org/articles/from-loyal-to-lost-vietnamese-voters -and-the-california-gop.

83. Michael Oden, "When the Movie's Over: The Post–Cold War Restructuring of Los Angeles," in *Local Consequences of the Global Cold War*, ed. Jeffrey A. Engel (Stanford: Stanford University Press, 2007), 135.

84. Robert A. Kleinhenz et al., "The Aerospace Industry in Southern California," Los Angeles County Economic Development Corporation, August 2012, http://www.laedc .org/reports/AerospaceinSoCal_0812.pdf.

85. Betsy Sinclair summarizes the evidence in "Introduction: The California Top Two Primary," *California Journal of Politics and Policy* 7 (2015), http://escholarship.org/uc/ item/4qk24589.

86. Javier Panzar, "GOP Dead Zones: You Won't Find Any Republicans to Vote for in Big Areas of L.A. County," *Los Angeles Times*, October 26, 2016, http://www.latimes .com/politics/la-pol-ca-gop-dead-zone-20161026-snap-story.html.

87. Mark Baldassare et al., "Californians and Their Government," Public Policy Institute of California, October 2016, http://ppic.org/content/pubs/survey/S_1016MBS.pdf.

88. House, "For Ambitious House Democrats."

89. Jens Manuel Krogstad, "With Fewer New Arrivals, Census Lowers Hispanic Population Projections," Pew Research Center, December 16, 2014, http://www.pewresearch .org/fact-tank/2014/12/16/with-fewer-new-arrivals-census-lowers-hispanic-population -projections-2.

90. "56 Interesting Facts About the 2016 Election," *Cook Political Report*, December 16, 2016, http://cookpolitical.com/story/10201.

91. "Excerpts from House Speech by Gephardt on Ceding Control to G.O.P.," *New York Times*, January 5, 1995, http://www.nytimes.com/1995/01/05/us/104th-congress -democratic-leader-excerpts-house-speech-gephardt-ceding-control.html.

Chapter Six

Aftermath and Future

Not since the election of 2000 had the maneuvering and emotion of a presidential contest continued so long after Election Day. In 2000, multiple recounts left the result in Florida—and hence in the nation—in doubt. Legal disputes, including cases before the Supreme Courts of Florida and the United States, angry demonstrations on both sides, and organized efforts to sway electors finally did not end until after December 12, when the U.S. Supreme Court ruled in *Bush v. Gore* that the latest Florida recount had to stop.

In 2016, no sooner had Donald Trump's victory become clear than protestors filled the streets in Los Angeles, Philadelphia, Oakland, Portland, Indianapolis, and elsewhere, venting their rage at the triumph of the Orange. (Upon investigation, it turned out that many of the young protestors had not voted for Hillary Clinton but for Jill Stein, Bernie Sanders as a write-in, or not at all. Some said that they would have been in the streets protesting if Clinton had won, too.[1]) College administrators around the country felt compelled to issue statements soothing their inconsolable students, sometimes offering snacks and therapy.[2] As in 2000, the leader in the nationally aggregated popular vote lost in the Electoral College, leading to a renewed debate over that institution. A losing candidate—this time Green Party nominee Jill Stein—requested recounts in Wisconsin, Michigan, and Pennsylvania. Nearly five million people signed an online petition calling on electors from Trump states to vote for Hillary Clinton instead, in order to "to protect the Constitution from Donald Trump, and to support the national popular vote winner." Trump, the petition asserted, was not fit to serve: "His scapegoating of so many Americans, and his impulsivity, bullying, lying, admitted history of sexual assault, and utter lack of experience make him a danger to the Republic."[3] When it became apparent that this appeal would fall on deaf ears, a new effort was launched. Democratic electors in Colorado and Washington mounted legal challenges to their states' laws requiring electors to vote for the candidate for whom they were pledged.[4] Pointing to Alexander Hamilton's vision for the electors found in *Federalist* no. 68, the so-called Hamilton electors sought to free electors everywhere from their pledges in order to form a bipartisan anti-Trump coalition. Ideally, they would come together behind an alternative Republican candidate; failing that, they would at least try to deprive Trump of thirty-seven of his electors, thus throwing the election into the House of Representatives, where they hoped a more broadly acceptable candidate might emerge. Far from developing suddenly, in the immediate wake of Trump's win, the idea of the electors acting on their own judgment to find a winner other than Trump or Clinton had been floated in an op-ed in the *Wall Street Journal* as early as September 8.[5] From Election Day until they voted at their state capitols on December 19, Republican electors around the country reported lobbying and downright harassment on a level not seen since 2000, and possibly surpassing even that year. The political website *Politico* reported two days before the electors voted:

> The nation's 538 presidential electors have been thrust into the political foreground like never before in American history. In the aftermath of a uniquely polarizing presidential contest, the once-anonymous electors are squarely in the spotlight, targeted by death threats, harassing phone calls and reams of hate mail. One Texas Republican elector said he's been bombarded with more than 200,000 emails.[6]

When the electors actually met, they were greeted by last-ditch demonstrations outside numerous capitols calling on them to "say no to Trump." In Sacramento, hundreds of Californians gathered, although their state's Clinton electors were not key to the strategy; protestors ranged from conservative #NeverTrump remnants to angry Democrats to a sizeable contingent from the Revolutionary Communists. Given that Trump was heavily criticized after the third presidential debate for declining to promise that he would accept the results of the election, it was ironic that it was ultimately his opponents who were unwilling to accept the results.

While this turmoil was playing out—leaving open a theoretically possible but extremely unlikely scenario in which Trump would not actually become president—his transition proceeded apace and confirmed that he would be an unconventional outsider and disrupter. The week after the election, Trump removed Chris Christie as head of the transition effort, replacing him with Vice President–elect Mike Pence and signaling a major role for Pence in the administration. Trump's initial announcement of appointments included immigration hard-liner Senator Jeff Sessions as attorney general as well as three retired generals from the armed forces, several businesspeople, a philanthropist known for her commitment to school vouchers, famed neurosurgeon (and former Republican primary opponent) Ben Carson, and fewer individuals than usual with prior federal administrative experience. Trump also took a courtesy phone call from the president of Taiwan, breaking four decades of U.S. policy aimed at not irritating communist China, and he brokered a deal that kept one thousand jobs at the Carrier air conditioning factory in Indiana after operations had been slated to leave for Mexico.

Though the Carrier deal won Trump mostly positive headlines—the biggest critics were conservatives who decried his abandonment of free-market principles—the Taiwanese call and cabinet choices stirred greater controversy. The president-elect fanned partisan flames by travelling around the country to a series of in-your-face victory rallies and resumed his hard-hitting Twitter habit. Trump's opponents doubled down on accusations that his victory was the result of Russian interference. On December 9, a secret CIA assessment was reported, not only reiterating the conclusion that Russia had been behind the hacks that eventually showed up in WikiLeaks but also concluding that Russia's aim had "clearly" been to help Trump win the election.[7] The FBI counter-intelligence division, however, was not so sure about Russia's intent, and it was later revealed that the Republican National Committee had also been a target of Russian hackers but had warded them off with more effective cybersecurity.[8] A group of computer scientists purported to show that Russia could have hacked voting machines in the crucial Rust Belt states of Pennsylvania, Michigan, and Wisconsin, though election officials and intelligence agencies found no evidence of such interference, and a variety of sources from *Scientific American* to *The Daily Beast* promptly debunked the claims.[9] This campaign reached its peak when Democrats sought (unsuccessfully) to require electors to receive an intelligence briefing on Russian hacking before voting on December 19.

Trump did little to allay concerns, getting into a Twitter snit against U.S. intelligence agencies after they issued their report—fuming that "These are the same people that said Saddam Hussein had weapons of mass destruction"—and then announcing his intent to appoint Exxon CEO Rex Tillerson, who had close business ties to Russia, as secretary of state. In response to the allegations, President Obama announced a set of economic sanctions against Russia.[10] Not until January, after a partially declassified intelligence report was released to the public and the president-elect had received a confidential briefing, did Trump concede that Russia had been involved.[11] Democratic concerns about the Bear, notably absent in 2012 when Obama ridiculed Mitt Romney for citing Russia as America's most dangerous adversary, were undoubtedly a mixture of sincere concern about a troubling act of foreign interference in the U.S. political process and a partisan desire to use what was at hand to delegitimize the incoming Trump administration before it had a chance to take office.

However, the final attempts to block Trump did not come close to succeeding, and they ended with a whimper. Stein's recounts, undertaken either to help Clinton or to raise funds for Stein herself (it was never clear which), failed to uncover irregularities on behalf of Trump or move the results in her or Clinton's favor. In Wisconsin, the recount ended with Trump's lead having expanded by 131 votes;[12] in Michigan, it may have exposed Democratic voter fraud before being halted by courts. Similarly, the attempt to deny Trump in the Electoral College failed to make a dent. Courts ruled against the Colorado and Washington dissidents, while John Kasich, whom the Hamilton electors had fixed on as a possible compromise candidate, declared that he was not interested: "[T]his approach, as well meaning as it is, will only serve to further divide our nation, when unity is what we need. The election is over. Now is the time for all of us to come together as Americans."[13] Although Harvard law professor Lawrence Lessig, who had briefly run for the Democratic presidential nomination, intimated a week before the vote that there might be as many as twenty Republicans prepared to jump ship,[14] in the end only two Texas electors did so. One voted for former Texas congressman and presidential aspirant Ron Paul; the other chose Kasich. Five Democratic electors abandoned Clinton, four in Washington State and one in Hawaii, giving three votes to Colin Powell, one to Bernie Sanders, and one to Native American leader Faith Spotted Eagle. Three other Democratic electors tried to vote for someone other than Clinton—one each for Sanders from Minnesota and Maine and one for Kasich from Colorado—but either changed their votes to Clinton or were replaced by alternates. It was the largest number of defections from electors pledged to a living presidential candidate in U.S. history. There had been a handful of years with a larger number of faithless electors, but only in a vice-presidential contest or when the presidential nominee to whom they had been pledged died before the vote. And it was the first time since 1972 that an elector had defected from the winning side. These were all signs of the unpopularity of both of the major party nominees. In the end, all of the post-election "Stop Trump" efforts resulted in a bigger Trump lead in Wisconsin and a bigger Trump win in the Electoral College, where the final tally was 304 for Trump against 227 for Clinton. Nothing succeeds like success.

Although the results of the election were solidified beyond even the smallest doubt, other big uncertainties remained about the future of American institutions and the future of politics and policy in the United States.

INSTITUTIONS AND POLITICAL REFORM

The debate about the Electoral College was, needless to say, renewed. The standard argument against it was, as always, that it allowed someone with the most nationally aggregated popular votes to lose the presidency anyway. Defenders of the Electoral College were quick to point out that the system forces candidates to reach a broad geographical coalition across the country, which Hillary Clinton did not do. Interestingly, Gallup polls taken in the aftermath of the election showed that Americans were now closely divided on the question of the Electoral College. In the late 1960s, about four in five Americans said they wanted to replace the Electoral College with a direct national popular vote. After the 2000 election, about two in three said the same thing. Following the 2016 vote, the plurality in favor of replacing the Electoral College with a national popular vote was only 49 percent to 47 percent—probably not coincidentally, almost exactly the split between the Clinton vote and the Trump vote on November 8.[15] The second realization of the "plurality-loser" scenario in sixteen years did not move opinion against the Electoral College, but apparently it caused voters to see the issue less abstractly. The 46 percent who voted for Trump undoubtedly concluded they liked the Electoral College very much, thank you. With two-thirds of states under GOP control and only half of Americans favoring a change, the prospects of a constitutional amendment abolishing the Electoral College are virtually nonexistent.

Efforts on behalf of the National Popular Vote Interstate Compact were revived; the compact, originated in 2006, consists of states that have agreed to give their electors to the winner of the national popular vote, and it will go into effect as soon as states with 270 electoral votes have joined. As of late 2016, ten states and the District of Columbia with 165 electoral votes had become part of the compact, but several difficulties stood in the way of the idea. One is that there is no official national popular vote, nor does there exist any mechanism to force a national recount if the national aggregated totals are very close. Another is that the Constitution requires interstate compacts to be approved by Congress; although some Supreme Court cases have suggested that only compacts touching on federal powers need to be approved, there would undoubtedly be a legal dispute on this point. Not least, only heavily Democratic states have joined the compact so far, and Republican states seem unlikely to do so. Like the more ambitious constitutional amendment it was meant to render unnecessary, this project is probably stalled.

However, tensions over the institution may continue, or even grow, especially if Democratic support continues to be highly geographically concentrated and elections remain closely contested. Before 2000, the electoral system had only produced one clear case of the plurality loser and a handful of contestable instances.[16] If it becomes commonplace, consistently favors one party over the other, and appears locked into place, it could become a major source of political discontent.

The election of 2016 also focused attention on questions about voting mechanics. During the campaign season, Donald Trump raised concerns about voter fraud. After Election Day he amplified these concerns, claiming that he would have won the national popular vote if it were not for fraud by millions of illegal voters.[17] These claims were widely ridiculed, and Trump offered no supporting evidence. This did not mean, however, that there were not real concerns around the country related to possible voter fraud. Bladen County, North Carolina, seemed to have been the epicenter of a substantial absentee ballot fraud scheme run by a Democratic-funded Political Action Committee that may have ultimately touched a total of eleven counties in that state.[18] The presidential recount in Michigan revealed that 37 percent of precincts in Wayne County (Detroit) could not be recounted because their voting machines registered more votes than they should have given the number of voters signed in on the rolls, indicative of the possibility of systematic fraud.[19] These episodes will doubtless increase the scrutiny of elections by those interested in more stringent ballot security, though the remedy most often proposed—voter ID requirements—would not have stopped the fraud alleged in either North Carolina or Michigan. At the same time, progressives continued to complain that voter identification laws constituted "voter suppression" aimed at young, poor, and minority voters.[20]

Another voting mechanics issue was raised as a result of the rapid and frequent shifts in the race from Labor Day through Election Day. The issue was the widespread prevalence of early voting throughout the United States. In 2016, thirty-four states allowed voters to vote early with no excuse needed, either by absentee ballot or at early voting polling places. Three additional states conducted their entire election by mail ballots that were delivered to voters weeks early.[21] Some states began voting as early as mid-September. Every time after October 1 that some new twist came in the story of the campaign, the question arose: How many early voters would have voted differently if they had only known the new piece of information? By October 9, when Republican officeholders were busy fleeing Trump's apparently sinking ship, nearly half a million Americans had already voted, and commentators argued that these early votes made it impractical to replace Trump at the top of the Republican ticket.[22] By October 28, when FBI Director Comey announced the reopening of the Clinton email investigation, millions had voted. Between then and November 6, when the investigation was again closed, still more had cast their ballots. Altogether, it was estimated that 40 percent of American voters voted before Election Day. Critics of early voting have long pointed to the danger that early voters forfeit the ability to take into account late-breaking developments. The 2016 election seemed to validate those concerns. Prior to 2016, some states had already moved to shorten their early voting periods. It seems likely that more will do so.

If the Electoral College, ballot security and access, and early voting will be fertile grounds for debate after 2016, one perennial issue having to do with the structural context of elections is likely to subside after 2016: campaign finance. Ever since the *Citizens United v. Federal Elections Commission* and *SpeechNow.com v. Federal Election Commission* court decisions led to the creation of super PACs and coincided with the explosion of "outside money" in federal elections, one school of thought has seen *Citizens United* as an unalloyed evil facilitating the takeover of American politics by "big money." In 2014, Senate Democrats even voted for a constitutional amendment that would have overturned *Citizens United* and given Congress unquestioned power to regulate campaign speech, a controversial move that drew criticism from both conservatives and the American Civil Liberties Union. If the 2016 election showed anything, though, it was the limits of "big money" in elections, even after *Citizens United* and *Speech Now.* In the Democratic primaries, Hillary Clinton outraised Bernie Sanders by a modest amount, but Sanders was still able to raise large amounts through small donors, pose a persistent challenge, and win 44 percent of the total Democratic primary vote.[23] On the Republican side, Donald Trump, who had raised $67 million through mid-June, was vastly outspent by Jeb Bush ($162 million), Ted Cruz ($158 million), Marco Rubio ($125 million), and even Ben Carson ($77 million); yet he won the nomination.[24] Bush raised more money for his campaign, directly or indirectly, than any other candidate in the GOP field, but dropped out after the third contest after finishing sixth in Iowa, fourth in New Hampshire, and fourth in South Carolina. Comparing Clinton and Trump through the general election, Clinton's campaign committee spent $498 million, Trump only $248 million. Outside groups supporting Clinton spent an additional $206 million to $75 million by pro-Trump groups.[25] Altogether, Clinton spent or had spent on her behalf more than twice as much money as Trump. Yet Trump won the presidency. Clinton's champagne budget and shiraz voters fell to Trump's beer budget with voters to match. It seems unlikely that the evils of big money will be a compelling story for (at least) the next few years.

Americans could look to the presidential nominating system with disappointment, asking what went wrong to cause the major parties to offer the public such an unsatisfactory choice. Didn't the parties have an incentive to put forward popular and appealing candidates? It would be a good question, but the answer was not simple. In the past, parties were able to nominate appealing candidates because there was a "party," an organized set of officeholders and long-term party leaders who acted as trustees and managed the

process with electability in mind. Institutionally, perhaps the biggest implica-
tion of the 2016 election, in both the nomination and the general election
phase, was the utter triumph of one might call democratic norms against what
one might call representative norms—the collapse of anything resembling
mediating structures between election results and election outcomes. In the
nominating phase, the biggest controversy on the Democratic side (at least
until the WikiLeaks revelations that forced Debbie Wasserman Schultz out
as Democratic National Committee chair) was the substantial number of
superdelegates and their overwhelming preference for Hillary Clinton, even
in states won soundly by Bernie Sanders. Sanders and his supporters
responded by demanding reduction or elimination of the superdelegates; in
the end, the Democratic National Convention Rules Committee voted to
reduce the number of superdelegates by two-thirds in 2020.[26] There can be
no question that if Clinton's delegate lead had rested entirely on superdelegates, her nomination would have been seen as illegitimate by Sanders supporters and a large proportion of the American people.

In the Republican nomination contest, there was a very real possibility for
an extended period of time that no candidate would enter the national convention with a majority of delegates. A vigorous debate ensued over whether the
delegates should, at that point, simply nominate the candidate with the most
votes in the primaries (Trump) or the candidate they deemed best using their
own judgment (Cruz, or possibly Kasich, Romney, or some undetermined
option). Indeed, in state after state, Ted Cruz's campaign used its superior
organization and grasp of the rules to elect delegates who were pledged to
vote for Trump on the first ballot due to primary results but would support
Cruz on subsequent ballots as well as on platform or rules disputes. Even
after Cruz and Kasich dropped out of the race, leaving Trump as the sole
survivor, #NeverTrump activists argued that delegates should be unbound
and encouraged to find a more suitable standard-bearer for the Republican
Party. Advocates of this position had math and history on their side. Party
rules required an absolute majority of delegates to nominate. Failure by a
candidate to achieve that number meant that a majority of party delegates did
not support that candidate. In the abstract, it also probably meant (and, in
this particular case, did mean) that a majority of party voters supported other
candidates. Calling on the delegates to respond to a deadlocked convention
by finding the most broadly acceptable nominee had a long and storied tradition, as did taking advantage of the rules to maximize one's second or third
ballot strength. Advocates of Trump's position had on their side the entire
democratic, plebiscitary ethos of the nominating system since the McGovern-
Fraser Commission. Exit polls of GOP primary voters consistently showed
that roughly two-thirds believed that if no candidate came to the convention

with a majority of delegates in hand, the convention should pick the candidate with the most primary votes rather than the one they thought best.[27] Most Republican voters were not willing to allow convention delegates to act as trustees even if that was the only way to avert the nomination of a minority candidate with the highest unfavorable ratings of any nominee since polling began.

When action moved to the Electoral College, the same debate played out: Should the electors act as trustees or as delegates? If electors pledged to Trump were to break out of their commitments to vote for a different (and, by their lights, better-qualified) candidate, would they be heroes or traitors? The history of pledged electors was a much longer one, going back to the nation's third presidential election. But even here, the original conception was arguably grounded in a different ethos that saw the electors as respected and knowledgeable members of their communities who would put a damper on demagoguery and other negative byproducts of popular election. As we have seen, in the end, the arguments for trustee electors fell on deaf ears. The laws of twenty-nine states operated to prevent defections, as did the deeply entrenched predominant democratic ethos of that system, enunciated in 1796 by a Federalist voter from Pennsylvania who wrote a letter to the *Gazette of the United States* complaining about an elector pledged to John Adams who voted for Thomas Jefferson instead: "What, do I choose Samuel Miles to determine for me whether John Adams or Thomas Jefferson shall be president? No! I choose him to act, not to think."[28] Once such norms are widely accepted, it is not easy to undo them; the electors of 2016 had a difficult time acting independently of their party pledge in part because not one of them had been elected to serve as respected and knowledgeable members of their communities whose job was to exercise independent judgment and put a damper on demagoguery. On the contrary, every one of them had been elected as part of a party slate, whose individual names did not even appear on the ballot—elected with the understanding that they would loyally support the nominee of their party. Altogether, though scholarly arguments have been heard for forty years about the importance of restoring the parties as intermediary institutions capable of counterbalancing the candidate-centered nature of the current nominating system, voters showed no sign at all of sympathizing with that argument, or even understanding it. The cultural shift that would be required to have allowed Ted Cruz to win on the second ballot of the Republican convention or a spate of faithless electors to hand John Kasich a win in the Electoral College—and to have those results accepted as legitimate—is enormous, and very difficult at this point to imagine. For the foreseeable future, we will be riding the tiger of plebiscitary democracy.

POLITICS AND POLICY

The political conversation that began the day after Election Day was radically different than what most observers had foreseen. They had expected Democratic triumphalism, the confirmation of the "coalition of the ascendant," accompanied by a blizzard of Republican recriminations. (Did Trump lose because the Republican establishment didn't back him? Because Ted Cruz didn't endorse him soon enough? Because his campaign was not technically proficient? Or just because he was singularly unqualified and ill equipped to be president?) Instead, Republicans tried to make sense of an unexpected victory and began grappling with the implications of a mostly conservative party led by a populist outsider who sometimes sounded like a New Dealer. Democrats were the ones forming a circular firing squad.

The first, most obvious political result of the 2016 election was that Barack Obama's legacy was shattered. Both Obama and Clinton had framed the election as test of that legacy, an opportunity for Americans to continue the course of the previous eight years. The election resulted in more than a win for Donald Trump. Given results nationwide, it could reasonably be seen as a broad victory for the Republican Party. Most voters said they wanted change, and there could be little question that they would get it. Obamacare was going to be on the chopping block, though getting agreement among Republicans on how to replace it would be challenging and would expose Republicans to serious political risks. A spate of controversial Obama executive actions would doubtless be reversed in short order. The entire thrust of tax and regulatory policy would change, replacing Obama's emphasis on redistributionism with a new focus on growth. Obama's climate change policy would be altered, probably dramatically, and defense and foreign policy would be put on a new, more nationalist basis, though exactly how would play out gradually. Obama's chance to shape the Supreme Court was lost as well; the Scalia seat would likely go to another conservative. Because Trump was ideologically amorphous, one could not predict a consistently conservative outcome, but one thing was clear: Obama progressivism, which was not ideologically ambiguous and whose standard-bearer had become Hillary Clinton, had been stopped in its tracks, at least for the time being. Republicans would have opportunities for conservative policymaking at least until 2018, if not beyond.

Victory always smooths over a party's internal contradictions for a time. Republican divisions, deep and intense, had been exposed to the world as recently as a few weeks before Election Day, when dozens of GOP leaders abandoned Trump in the wake of the *Access Hollywood* tape. On November 9, those divisions were submerged but hardly resolved. Trump's election night speech promised, before anything else, a one-trillion-dollar infrastructure program, and it was clear that he would be continuing his attack on free trade. At the same time, he moved to appoint not only a cabinet of outsiders but also what David McIntosh of the Club for Growth called "the most conservative [cabinet] since Reagan's"[29] and reiterated his plan to repeal the Affordable Care Act and rescind a number of controversial Obama executive orders, making conservatives happy. When supply-side guru Stephen Moore met with congressional Republicans shortly after Election Day and told them that the conservative party of Ronald Reagan had been replaced by the populist working-class party of Donald Trump, many were shocked, but some accepted that Trump was now the pacesetter.[30] If President Trump pushes for his own version of the stimulus package that every Republican member of the House opposed in 2009 or pushes to remove the United States from free trade agreements (like NAFTA) that more Republicans than Democrats voted to enact, Republicans in Congress will have to decide whether they are members of Reagan's or Trump's party; when Congress moves to limit entitlement programs or send aid to Ukraine, Trump will have his own challenges. Republicans who belatedly embraced Trump in victory will also face a difficult decision if he should bring a less sanguine outcome in the 2018 elections or if he should prove himself not up to the task of governing.

In the summer of 2016, *National Review* contributor Dan McLaughlin posited two tests for whether the Republican Party was becoming Trump's party in substance. One was whether key GOP figures Paul Ryan, Marco Rubio, and John McCain, who embodied an alternative vision of their party, were defeated in their primaries by their openly Trumpist challengers; the other was whether Trump ran ahead of "normal" Republicans in Senate races in November.[31] As it turned out, Ryan, Rubio, and McCain all won their primaries handily, and most GOP Senate candidates ran ahead of Trump in November. McLaughlin assumed that Trump would lose in November; his victory meant that the traditional GOP would have to coexist with Trump, and perhaps even bend to him in unpredicted ways. On the edges of the party remained Evan McMullin, hoping to build a new conservative movement and continuing to duel with Trump by the medium of Twitter. The future of conservatism was not necessarily synonymous with the future of the Republican Party, and conservatives ranging from McMullin to the *Weekly Standard* and the *National Review* were thinking hard about what of Trumpism could be tolerated and what had to be opposed. In other words, what, going forward, would become the core of conservatism, the non-negotiable elements? And would those elements consist only of certain policies or include tests of character or conduct? On these matters, there was no consensus. However, even in the worst case, the Republicans' day of reckoning was put off for a while.

Democrats, however, were thrust at once into unexpected disarray. Like all minority parties, they would have to decide when (if ever) to accommodate the new president and when to obstruct him. More important for the long term, they would have to decide whether to tack further to the left or move toward the center. In the primary season, Democrats' heads were with Hillary, but it was clear their hearts were with Bernie. The leading candidate for chair of the Democratic National Committee was Minnesota congressman Keith Ellison, one of only two members of the House to support Bernie Sanders early in his campaign. However destructive the party's march to the left had become, there was not in late 2016 any organized force within the party either able or willing to divert it. Even if Clinton had won, there was no recognizable remnant of 1990s centrist Clintonism surviving in the Democratic Party—not on welfare, not on the budget, not on crime or abortion. "Safe, legal, and rare" had been replaced with "safe, legal, and taxpayer-funded up until the last second of pregnancy."

There was a debate, nevertheless, about whether this course was advisable. Some in the party argued that 2016 was a fluke, and that no future adjustments were necessary. The coalition of the ascendant would become unstoppable within a few years. House Minority Leader Nancy Pelosi commented, "Well, I don't think that people want a new direction."[32] When House Democrats reelected her as their leader, they seemed to agree. Others on the center-left declared that 2016 showed Democrats that they needed to redirect a stronger appeal to working-class whites, or even that they had become dangerously contemptuous of the great middle of the country and needed to reform their attitude before they could compete effectively. Some analysts suddenly declared that it was Democrats who had an emerging Electoral College problem. Democratic congressman Tim Ryan, who unsuccessfully challenged Pelosi for her leadership position, observed on national television that "we're not even a national party anymore."[33] How Democrats choose to address this debate will be an important question in American politics for at least the next four years. In the further future, without a change of course by Democrats, the prospect looms of the first openly socialist major party in U.S. history.

More generally, the Trump phenomenon had the potential to cut across the traditional party coalitions. Though they did (barely) hold onto this group in 2016, Republicans ran the risk of forfeiting their hold on white college graduates; Democrats' hold on the white working class, already weakened long before 2016, was further endangered. During the campaign, Trump also made a play for black votes that could be redoubled, and might even bear a little fruit. If the Democratic share of the black vote were to fall from 90 percent to 80 percent, a number of blue states could tip into the red column or be made more competitive.

A related question that bears watching is whether party polarization would continue growing or would recede. In 2016, Donald Trump had it both ways: he benefited from near-unity among Republican voters while running as a "post-ideological" outsider disconnected from the official Republican Party. Shortly after his election, there were signs that he would continue to gain from automatic party loyalty divorced from a substantive philosophical understanding of what the party stands for. Polls showed that since July 2016 there had been a dramatic change in the perceptions of Vladimir Putin by Republican voters, and in the opposite direction by many Democrats. Republicans had become much less unfavorable toward Putin and Democrats more unfavorable.[34] The party tribes were sticking together, even if doing so required them to be malleable about what they believed.

However the parties sorted out, politics in 2016 had become more vitriolic and more apocalyptic. The candidates' supporters seemed further apart than ever, with large proportions of each camp holding the opposing candidate to be not only wrong or accountable for unsuccessful performance in office but also fundamentally flawed and unfit. This feature of the election campaign was doubtless strongly connected to the particular characteristics and background of the candidates themselves, which provided many sound reasons for sensible people to reach that conclusion, but that may not have been all that was at work.

After Election Day, there was considerable talk about cocooning, the tendency of people to live in areas with like-minded people, working and befriending like-minded people, and receiving news from sources that are tilted toward their own point of view. Even Facebook algorithms dish up news stories that are compatible with the political tendencies of the reader. They are thus constantly reinforced in their political prejudices and have little interaction with alternative ways of looking at the world. A Trump voter who gets most of his news from the *Sean Hannity Show* on Fox News or the Clinton supporter who is tuned to MSNBC all day will find little to challenge their preconceptions and much to drive them further apart from each other.

Cocooning, of course, was a trend closely related to the re-emergence of the partisan press, wherever it was found: on cable news television, talk radio, political blogs, social media, or even network TV and major newspapers. Altogether, according to a study by the Shorenstain Center on Media, Politics, and Public Policy, Donald Trump was treated negatively in 77 percent of the general election news stories about him, compared to 64 percent negative coverage of Clinton. Of ten major news outlets—ABC, CBS, NBC, CNN, and FOX television and the *New York Times, Washington Post, Los Angeles*

Times, Wall Street Journal, and *USA Today* newspapers—FOX news was the most positive, with 73 percent of its coverage of Trump negative. The other nine outlets had at least 80 percent negative coverage of Trump. Fortunately for Trump, the last two weeks of the campaign were his best media weeks, with only two-thirds of the coverage negative.[35] Conservative commentator Victor Davis Hanson observed, "No wonder the fading establishment media is now distrusted by a majority of the public, according to Gallup—and becoming irrelevant even among progressives."[36] No one could offer a plausible remedy for cocooning, though in the long run it had the potential to threaten national unity, and perhaps even peace. Trump did, however, find a way around the hostility of the media, relying on demotic rhetoric and a straight-to-the-people campaign of tweets and rallies.

At the same time, one of the factors driving social division over the last three decades has been the rise of an aggressive "multiculturalism" that makes identity politics, especially by minorities, the core of political activity. As a frequent critic of "political correctness," it was clear from the beginning that Trump was a threat to this version of identity politics. Although it was clear what Trump was against, it was never quite clear what he was for: the end of identity politics or the creation of a new, counterbalancing identity politics. On the one hand, he emphasized citizenship and the nation. On the other, his obvious appeals to the white working class and his seeming lack of discomfort with the support of white nationalists led many to suspect that he was engaged in a new form of identity politics catering to that identity group. His attack on Judge Gonzalo Curiel as unable to give him a fair trial because he was a "Mexican" was little more than a warmed-over reverse application of Critical Race Theory, long popular in elite law schools, to the case at hand. The expectation nourished by the left that identity politics could remain unidirectional forever, encouraging everyone but whites to obsess about race, was always a risky gambit. While Trump was debating with himself, Democrats began a debate over whether their future lay with a doubling down on their version of identity politics or a move in a different direction.[37] A great deal in American society and politics will depend on which Trump emerges in the White House and which argument prevails among liberals. Among other things, given demographic trends, the long-term viability of the Republican Party may depend on which approach Republicans choose; liberal identity politics aimed at minorities showed its shortcomings in 2016, but a new version aimed at whites will likely have a short shelf-life in a country becoming less white by the year.[38]

Of course, the importance of which President Trump emerges is true across a wide range of policy areas where candidate Trump gave conflicting guidance. On immigration, he began by promising to deport all 11 million illegal immigrants and ended by promising to deport the criminal element among them, an estimated 2 million. On terrorism, he began by threatening to cut off entry to the United States by all Muslims and ended promising to cut off entry by people coming from countries with a serious terror problem where "extreme vetting" could not be accomplished. On foreign policy, Trump seemed at once belligerent and isolationist; his trade and security proposals, if taken literally, had the potential to unravel seven decades of U.S. strategy forged in the aftermath of the Depression and World War II, strategy bred by lessons that had been learned at a terrible price. Smoot-Hawley and "America First" isolationism had not worked well in the 1930s. Yet Trump had made his name as a negotiator and might have been doing nothing more in the campaign than laying down markers, starting points for better deals. That Trump shifted during the campaign on some of his bedrock positions without losing the loyalty of his most enthusiastic supporters, and that his advisers saw him as "post-ideological," demonstrated the limits of issue voting, even in the primaries where it is often thought to be crucial.

Trump's own inconsistency on policy, and certain apparent features of his character and temperament, will also be put to the test by events. It is statistically likely that the nation will experience a recession by 2020, regardless of the wisdom of Trump's economic policy. Abroad, a number of potential time bombs are ticking, alongside the need—certainly from Trump's point of view—to restore American credibility after the "red line" retreats of the Obama era. Although his favorability ratings climbed to the mid-40s after Election Day, Trump will have to face whatever crises emerge without the benefit of anything resembling a deep reservoir of affection and support from the American public. On the contrary, he entered office with historically weak ratings. Hillary Clinton, had she been elected, would have borne the same difficulty.

The biggest question mark of politics in the Trump presidency will be whether Trump will lead a constitutional revival or a further (perhaps final) descent into post-constitutionalism. On the one hand, Trump promised to roll back the most egregious of President Obama's executive power grabs and to appoint constitutionalist judges with the imprimatur of the Federalist Society and the Heritage Foundation. His early cabinet appointments indicated an intention to restore some respect to federalism in education and environmental policy.

On the other hand, it was far from clear that Trump had any deep knowledge of or interest in the Constitution beyond what was necessary to win over conservatives in the campaign. At a talk for House Republicans shortly after wrapping up the nomination, Trump reportedly promised to defend Article I of the Constitution, Article II, and all the way through Article XII.[39] (There are only seven articles in the Constitution.) It was one thing to promise to roll back Obama's edicts but quite another to promise not to do anything similar when his own priorities were stymied; this he did not do. To the contrary, his campaign was filled with outsized promises to exert personal leadership to get things done. At a speech in Bismarck, North Dakota, Trump told the crowd, "Politicians have used you and stolen your votes. They have given you nothing. I will give you everything . . . I'm the only one."[40] "I will give you everything . . . I'm the only one" is not a sentiment consistent with limited, constitutional government.

None of this is to imply that the country was at a constitutional crossroads in November 2016 and that it was Trump's victory alone that posed a danger to the Constitution. Arguably, it was much worse than that. If Trump offered one particular version of demagogic anti-constitutionalism, Hillary Clinton offered a different style of anti-constitutionalism, less passionate and more technocratic, but no less of a danger to constitutional norms. Clinton, after all, endorsed all of Obama's overreach and proposed some of her own. She was the one who answered two debate questions about the Supreme Court with no substantive reference to the Constitution, who embraced in full the progressive dogma that the federal government can permissibly do anything the progressive imagination can concoct. Both exhibited authoritarian tendencies in their own ways: Trump proposed tightening libel laws to crack down on a critical media; Clinton endorsed forcing nuns to pay for abortifacients. One could be excused for fearing that the nation was headed for a post-constitutional future no matter who won. During the campaign, social commentator Joel Kotkin expressed the fear that "Rather than a choice, we face a contest between two different kinds of imperial pretenders."[41]

What had made possible such a choice? And what, specifically, had made Trump possible?

As commentators frequently note, politics is downstream from culture. In many ways, American culture, including political culture, was fit for a Donald Trump in 2016 in a way it would not have been thirty or forty years earlier. Trump was a billionaire businessman, a consummate showman, and a rising political figure with (it turned out) strong political instincts. But he was also a celebrity cult figure, a reality TV star, a narcissist of the first order, a notorious playboy and strip-club owner, a serial fantasist, and a figure with no political experience and no obvious interest in or knowledge of key public policy issues. In an earlier era—but well within living memory—anyone with that profile would have been disqualified as a contender for the presidency long before the Iowa caucuses. Things had changed in American society.

Donald Trump's victory, as surprising as it was, could be seen as the logical conclusion of a number of political and social trends going back one, two, or even four decades. Trump was the most extreme version of the outsider type to actually advance to the presidency, but glorification of the outsider, and elevation of the prospects of the outsider, has been a feature of American politics since the McGovern-Fraser Commission and the candidacies of George McGovern and Jimmy Carter; Barack Obama himself had served less than three years in the U.S. Senate before beginning his campaign for president. A number of other outsider analogues had paved the way for Trump, including George Wallace, Pat Buchanan, and Ross Perot, who had each trumpeted, so to speak, many of the same themes.

Barack Obama had also cleared the way for a celebrity cult of personality with the Greek temple that framed his nomination acceptance speech, while his supporters contributed cult-like songs and online encomiums to his glory. (Who can forget Obama Girl and the children's choir singing his praises?[42]) Bill Clinton and his defenders had already normalized a postmodern conception of truth in politics—a conception embraced in 2016 by both Hillary and the Donald, who was estimated by *Politico* to tell an untruth once every three and a half minutes in speeches[43]—as well as the notion that a pattern of sexual misconduct did not establish unfitness for high office. Mass narcissism, which made its triumphant entry in the 1960s and 1970s with the New Left, the counterculture, and the "Me Decade," was already a confirmed staple of American life that allowed a person to become wealthy by inventing a mechanism to make it easier to take pictures of oneself. The coarsening and vulgarization of society, under way for several decades with the full cooperation of crucial elements of popular culture, made it possible for Trump to talk and act in a certain coarse and vulgar way without politically fatal consequences. Did he really say anything about women that wasn't repeated a dozen times a day on the run-of-the-mill hip-hop radio station? The contemporary decline of old-fashioned courtesy, seen in social settings on a daily basis, was simply carried by Trump into the political arena, perhaps altering the norms of campaigning forever. Indeed, Trump's whole take-no-prisoners style of communication—140 characters or less, sometimes funny, often insulting or harsh, almost always self-promoting—had already become quite familiar to both social commentators and American teenagers, The old virtues of sobriety, of modesty, of mature self-control seemed to belong to a different country than the one Trump sought to lead. That fact said as much about the country as it did about him.

The stage was set, but Trump still had to perform. Defying the odds more than any victorious candidate for president since Harry Truman, Donald J. Trump was, in many respects, a one of a kind in American politics. No one— not Jimmy Carter, not Andrew Jackson—had been more of an outsider. No one had disrupted his own party and the conventions of politics more. No one had, in a single election, laid low the reigning dynasties of both his own party (the Bushes) and the other party (the Clintons). But that was looking in the rearview mirror. Looking to the future, Trump may be only the first of a new type. The most powerful institutional trend (the triumph of unmediated democracy) combines with the most powerful social/political trend (a social free-for-all with collapsing rules) to establish conditions favorable not just to Trump but also to candidates like Trump. He has established a new model for political success: celebrity outsiderism plus personal wealth plus a demotic rhetoric of memorable everyday language. And if anything in politics is certain, it is that victory breeds imitation.

NOTES

1. Abigail Hauslohner and Mark Berman, "Anti-Trump demonstrators say nationwide protests are 'just a taste of things to come,'" *Washington Post*, November 16, 2016, https://www.washingtonpost.com/news/post-nation/wp/2016/11/16/anti-trump-demonstrators-say-nationwide-protests-are-just-a-taste-of-things-to-co me/.

2. Pardes Seleh, "NC State Provides Students with Post-Election Comfort Food, Therapy," *The Daily Wire*, November 11, 2016, http://www.dailywire.com/news/10707/nc-state-provides-grieving-students-post-election-pardes-seleh.

3. "Electoral College: Make Hillary Clinton President," https://www.change.org/p/electoral-college-make-hillary-clinton-president-on-december-19-4a78160a-023c-4ff0-9069-53cee2a095a8.

4. Rachel Riley, "Colorado electors plan to challenge state law in bid to derail Donald Trump's victory," *The Gazette*, December 3, 2016, http://gazette.com/colorado-electors-plan-to-challenge-state-law-in-bid-to-derail-donald-trumps-victory/article/1591550.

5. David B. Rivkin Jr. and Andrew M. Grossman, "Let the Electoral College Do Its Duty," *Wall Street Journal*, September 8, 2016, A13.

6. Kyle Cheney, "Electors Under Seige," *Politico*, December 17, 2016, http://www.politico.com/story/2016/12/electors-under-siege-232774.

7. Adam Entous, Ellen Nakashima and Greg Miller, "Secret CIA assessment says Russia was trying to help Trump win White House," *Washington Post*, December 9, 2016, https://www.washingtonpost.com/world/national-security/obama-orders-review-of-russian-hacking-during-presidential-campaign/2016/12/09/31d6b300-be2a-11e6-94ac-3d324840106c_story.html.

8. Ellen Nakashima and Adam Enthouse, "FBI and CIA give differing accounts to lawmakers on Russia's motives in 2016 hacks," *Washington Post*, December 10, 2016, https://www.washingtonpost.com/world/national-security/fbi-and-cia-give-differing-accounts-to-lawmakers-on-russias-motives-in-2016-hacks/2016/12/10/c6dfadfa-bef0-11e6-94ac-3d324840106c_story.html?utm_term=.8d9686e5a3bf; Shane Harris, Devlin Barrett, and Julian E. Barnes, "Republican National Committee Security Foiled Russian Hackers," *Wall Street Journal*, December 16, 2016, http://www.wsj.com/articles/republican-national-committee-security-foiled-russian-hackers-1481850043.

9. Rachael Revesz, "Computer Scientrists Say they have strong evidence election was rigged against Clinton in three key states," Independent, November 22, 2016, http://www.independent.co.uk/news/world/americas/wisconsin-michigan-pennsylvania-elec tion-hillary-clinton-hacked-manipulated-donald-trump-swing-a7433091.html; Carl Bialik and Rob Arthur, "Demographics, Not Hacking, Explain the Election Results," FiveThirty-Eight, November 23, 2016, http://fivethirtyeight.com/features/demographics-not-hacking -explain-the-election-results/; Ryan F. Mandelbaum, "Closer Look Punches Holes in Swing-State Election Hacking Report," *Scientific American*, November 23, 2016, https://www.scientificamerican.com/article/closer-look-punches-holes-in-swing-state-election-hacking-report/; Shane Harris, "Sorry, Hillary Clinton Fans. There's 'Zero Evidence' of Election Hacking," *The Daily Beast*, November 23, 2016, http://www.thedailybeast.com/articles/2016/11/23/sorry-hillary-there-s-zero-evidence-of-election-hacking.html.

10. David Jackson, "Obama sanctions Russian officials over election hacking," *USA Today*, December 29, 2016, http://www.usatoday.com/story/news/politics/2016/12/29/barack-obama-russia-sanctions-vladimir-putin/95958472/.

11. Julie Hirschfeld Davis and Maggie Haberman, "Donald Trump Concedes Russia's Interference in Election," *New York Times*, January 11, 2017, https://www.nytimes.com/2017/01/11/us/politics/trumps-press-conference-highlights-russia.html.

12. Matthew DeFour, "Completed Wisconsin recount widens Donald Trump's lead by 131 votes," *Wisconsin State Journal*, December 13, 2016, http://host.madison.com/wsj/news/local/govt-and-politics/completed-wisconsin-recount-widens-donald-trump-s-lead -by-votes/article_3f61c6ac-5b18-5c27-bf38-e537146bbcdd.html.

13. Steve Peoples and Andrew Welsh-Huggins, "John Kasich's blow to Hamilton Electors: Ohio governor says he doesn't want to be written in," *Salon*, December 7, 2016, http://www.salon.com/2016/12/07/ohio-governor-tells-electors-not-to-vote-for-him-over -trump/.

14. Kyle Cheney, "Lessig: 20 Trump electors could flip," *Politico*, December 13, 2016, http://www.politico.com/story/2016/12/donald-trump-electors-lessig-232598.

15. Art Swift, "Americans' Support for Electoral College Rises Sharply," Gallup, December 2, 2016, http://www.gallup.com/poll/198917/americans-support-electoral-col lege-rises-sharply.aspx.

16. The clear case was 1888, when Benjamin Harrison defeated Grover Cleveland despite trailing in the nationally aggregated popular vote. Contested cases include 1824, when only three-fourths of states chose their electors by popular vote; 1876, when there was massive fraud and a controversial electoral commission to assign contested electoral votes; and 1960, when Alabama's split electoral vote complicates efforts to tabulate the national popular vote winner.

17. Michael D. Shear and Maggie Haberman, "Trump claims, with no evidence, that 'millions of people' voted illegally," *Boston Globe*, November 27, 2016, https://www.bos tonglobe.com/news/politics/2016/11/27/donald-trump-says-without-illegal-votes-won -popular-vote-too/B6KClZcV7x2whk4Jjn6aZP/story.html.

18. "Protests filed in Bladen and 11 other counties over alleged fraudulent absentee ballots," http://www.wbtv.com/story/33718588/protests-filed-in-bladen-and-11-other -counties-over-alleged-fraudulent-absentee-ballots.

19. Joel Kurth and Jonathan Oosting, "Records: Too many votes in 37% of Detroit's precincts," *Detroit News*, December 13, 2016, http://www.detroitnews.com/story/news/politics/2016/12/12/records-many-votes-detroits-precincts/95363314/.

20. Liz Kennedy, "Voter Suppression Laws Cost Americans Their Voices at the Polls," Center for American Progress, November 11, 2016, https://www.americanprogress.org/issues/democracy/reports/2016/11/11/292322/voter-suppression-laws-cost-americans-their-voices-at-the-polls/.

21. "Early Voting," Ballotpedia, https://ballotpedia.org/Early_voting.

22. John Fund, "Early Voting Has Made It Impossible to Replace Trump," *National Review*, October 9, 2016, http://www.nationalreview.com/node/440896.

23. Josh Stewart, "Following the Money Behind the nearly $500 million Democratic primary," Sunlight Foundation, June 21, 2016, http://sunlightfoundation.com/2016/06/21/following-the-money-behind-the-nearly-500-million-2016-democratic-primary/.

24. "Which Presidential Candidates Are Winning the Money Race," *New York Times*, June 22, 2016, http://www.nytimes.com/interactive/2016/us/elections/election-2016-campaign-money-race.html.

25. "2016 Presidential Race," Center for Responsive Politics, http://www.opensecrets.org/pres16.

26. Tina Sfondeles, "Democrats changing superdelegate rules; a Sanders win," *Chicago Sun Times*, July 24, 2016, http://chicago.suntimes.com/news/democrats-changing-superdelegate-rules-a-sanders-win/.

27. "Republican Exit Polls," CNN, http://www.cnn.com/election/primaries/polls.

28. "Faithless Electors," FairVote, http://www.fairvote.org/faithless_electors.

29. Andrew Restuccia, Nancy Cook, and Lorraine Woellert, "Trump's Conservative Dream Team," *Politico*, November 30, 2016, http://www.politico.com/story/2016/11/trump-conservative-dream-team-231972.

30. Jonathan Swan, "Trump adviser tells House Republicans: You're no longer Reagan's party," *The Hill*, November 23, 2016, http://thehill.com/homenews/campaign/307462-trump-adviser-tells-house-republicans-youre-no-longer-reagans-party.

31. Dan McLaughlin, "How to Tell If the GOP Has Become Trump's Party," *National Review*, August 5, 2016, http://www.nationalreview.com/corner/438740/heres-how-you-can-tell-if-gop-has-become-trump-party.

32. JulieGrace Brufke, "Pelosi Says Democratic Party Doesn't Want New Direction," *The Daily Caller*, December 4, 2016, http://dailycaller.com/2016/12/04/pelosi-says-democratic-party-doesnt-want-new-direction/.

33. Tim Hains, "Pelosi Challenger Rep. Tim Ryan: Democrats 'Are Not a National Party' Anymore," RealClearPolitics, November 231, 2016, http://www.realclearpolitics.com/video/2016/11/21/pelosi_challenger_rep_tim_ryan_democrats_are_not_a_national_party_anymo re.html.

34. Matthew Nussbaum and Benjamin Oreskes, "More Republicans Viewing Putin Favorably," *Politico*, December 16, 2016, http://www.politico.com/story/2016/12/gop-russia-putin-support-232714.

35. Chris Cizzilla, "Donald Trump was right. He got incredibly negative press coverage," *Washington Post*, December 7, 2016, https://www.washingtonpost.com/news/the-fix/wp/2016/12/07/donald-trump-was-right-he-got-incredibly-negative-press-coverage/.

36. Victor Davis Hanson, "The Trump Nail in the Media Coffin," *National Review*, December 22, 2016, http://www.nationalreview.com/article/443263/mainstream-media-trump-opposition-exposed-their-bias-irrelevance.

37. See, for example, "Columbia Professor Says Democrats Need to Move Beyond

Identity Politics," National Public Radio, November 25, 2016, http://www.npr.org/2016/
11/25/503316461/columbia-professor-says-democrats-need-to-move-beyond-identity-po
litics; Froma Harrop, "Democrats must drop identity politics," *Denver Post*, November
15, 2016, http://www.denverpost.com/2016/11/15/democrats-must-drop-identity-politics/;
Craig Mills, "Here's Why Democrats Must Not Abandon Identity Politics," *The Daily
Beast*, December 20, 2016, http://www.thedailybeast.com/articles/2016/12/21/here-s
-why-democrats-must-not-abandon-identity-politics.html; Matthew Yglesias, "Democrats
neither can nor should ditch 'identity politics,'" *Vox*, November 23, 2016, http://www
.vox.com/policy-and-politics/2016/11/23/13685988/democrats-identity-politics.

38. See Wendell Cox and Joel Kotkin, "The Future of Racial Politics," RealClear-
Politics, December 9, 2016, http://www.realclearpolitics.com/articles/2016/12/09/repub
licans_and_the_future_of_racial_politics_132523.html.

39. Cristina Marcos, "Trump slips on Constitution particulars at House GOP meeting," *The Hill*, July 7, 2016, http://thehill.com/blogs/ballot-box/presidential-races/286879
-trump-slips-on-fact-about-constitution-during-meeting.

40. Eli Stokels, "Unapologetic, Trump promises to make America rich," *Politico*, May
26, 2016, http://www.politico.com/story/2016/05/unapologetic-trump-promises-to-make
-america-rich-223632.

41. Joel Kotkin, "Battle of Imperial Pretenders—Trump vs. Clinton," *Los Angeles
Daily News*, May 15, 2016, http://www.dailynews.com/opinion/20160515/battle-of-impe
rial-pretenders-x2014-trump-vs-clinton-joel-kotkin.

42. See "Crush on Obama," YouTube, https://www.youtube.com/watch?v = wKso
XHYICqU; "Sing for Change Obama," YouTube, https://www.youtube.com/watch
?v = TW9b0xr06qA.

43. Patrick Reis, "16 falsehoods spewed by Trump and Clinton," *Politico*, November
6, 2016, http://www.politico.com/story/2016/11/2016-election-fact-checking-230814.

Index

About the Authors

James W. Ceaser is Harry F. Byrd Professor of Politics at the University of Virginia and a senior fellow at the Hoover Institution, Stanford University. He is the author of several books on American politics and American political thought, including *Reconstructing America* (1997), *Nature and History in American Political Development* (2006), *Designing a Polity* (2010), *Epic Journey: The 2008 Elections and American Politics* (revised 2011), and *After Hope and Change: The 2012 Elections and American Politics* (revised 2015).

Andrew E. Busch is Crown Professor of Government and George R. Roberts Fellow at Claremont McKenna College, where he teaches courses on American government and politics and serves as director of the Rose Institute of State and Local Government. Busch has authored or coauthored several books on American politics, including, most recently, *After Hope and Change: The 2012 Elections and American Politics* (revised 2015), along with more than thirty articles and chapters in edited volumes.

John J. Pitney Jr. is professor of government at Claremont McKenna College. He is the author of *The Art of Political Warfare* (2001) and coauthor of *Congress' Permanent Minority? Republicans in the U.S. House* (1994), *Epic Journey: The 2008 Elections and American Politics* (revised 2011), and *The Politics of Autism* (2015). Professor Pitney is a frequent contributor to the popular press and hosts the widely read blog *Epic Journey*.